Dup

THE TREATY OF MEDICINE LODGE

The Story of the Great Treaty Council as Told by Eyewitnesses

The Treaty of

Medicine Lodge

THE STORY
OF THE GREAT
TREATY COUNCIL
AS TOLD BY
EYEWITNESSES

Douglas C. Jones

University of Oklahoma Press
Norman

LIBRARY OF CONGRESS CATALOG CARD NUMBER: 66–22709

Copyright 1966 by the University of Oklahoma Press, Publishing Division of the University. Composed and printed at Norman, Oklahoma, U.S.A., by the University of Oklahoma Press. First edition.

Dedicated to the memory of my maternal grandmother Callie Agnes Stockburger, who lived out her life in the valley of the West Fork of White River in the state of Arkansas, but who perhaps had a grandparent of her own at the great treaty meeting.

PREFACE

After a long hot summer of unsuccessful negotiations with Northern Plains Indians, representatives of the United States in the fall of 1867 concluded the Treaty of Medicine Lodge with leaders of the Southern Plains tribes. The treaty represented the last effort of the United States to reach a diplomatic settlement of disputes with all the hostile tribes south of the Platte River. Clearly outlined was the beginning of a system that would eventually confine the Indians to specific reservations, by force if necessary, and included for the first time in an Indian treaty were provisions for civilizing the tribes.[1]

The site of the great treaty meeting was near present Medicine Lodge, Kansas, in Barber County, seventy miles west-southwest of Wichita. The agreements reached there were a departure from all previous negotiations, for set forth in clear and definite language was the decision of the white man to absorb the Plains Indian culture. The intention was not simply to remove the Indian from the area whites would eventually desire to settle, but to change him, to make him fit the pattern of white civilization, to put a plow in his hands and a wooden roof over his head.[2]

The Treaty of Medicine Lodge did not stop frontier war. It did

[1] General E. E. Lindquist, "Indian Treaty Making," *Chronicles of Oklahoma*, Vol. XXIV (Winter, 1948–49), 427–30.

[2] Charles Kappler, *Laws and Treaties*, 977–89.

mark the beginning of a new period in the Plains conflict. The treaty is like a highway roadsign—pointing out what is ahead without really influencing the course of the road. From Medicine Lodge onward, little doubt existed in anyone's mind concerning the purpose of the United States. The war would no longer be intended to clear red hostiles from along the routes of travel or from areas populated by white men. There would no longer be attempts to place the tribes in far corners and allow them to live as they pleased. Instead of being pushed aside, the Indian was now to be swallowed.[3] On the one hand, a people would be fighting to dominate the Great Plains and everything on it. On the other, a people would be struggling, not for land alone but for survival.

Negotiations were conducted in essentially three sessions, and the result of each was an agreement between the Peace Commission and the tribes represented at that particular session. But because the terms were so nearly identical, and because the three documents taken in total are the result of a single thrust for peace on the Southern Plains, the treaty is referred to here in the singular.

Although the Treaty of Medicine Lodge is somewhat obscured in a frontier history dotted with the fiery moments at Adobe Walls, the Battle of the Washita, the disaster of Little Big Horn, and the thousands of smaller, violent spasms between white men and red, the importance of negotiations was not overlooked by the nation's press. For even though field correspondents were relatively new to the growing journalism fraternity, newspaper representation at the councils was unusually large, and the correspondents' accounts exceptionally detailed. The narrative presented here is taken from those accounts. It does not come from the records of United States officials who were charged with the conduct of negotiations but from the pages of newspapers one century old, newspapers that had the enterprise, vision, and money to send special correspondents to Kansas to report at first hand what was happening on the banks of the Medicine Lodge.

Thanks to the Ned Buntline—Frank Triplett variety of journal-

[3] For changing Indian policy, see Ray A. Billington, *Westward Expansion*, 210, 472; John D. Hicks, *The American Nation*, 127.

ism—and equal thanks to the many exaggerated, distorted, and often false reports that had a way of appearing and reappearing in what was frequently a sensational press—mid-nineteenth-century newspapers have never enjoyed a particularly solid reputation for truth.[4] The result has generally been a not too skillfully disguised contempt on the part of many historians for newspapers and newspaper reporters of that period. With good cause, press accounts of hair-raising escapades have often been viewed with skepticism, coming as they did from excited, biased, untrained, and often emotionally distraught sources.[5] With this idea of nineteenth-century news reporting current, a study of the newspaper reports of Medicine Lodge was expected to reveal a vast difference between official records and newspaper accounts. Surprisingly, there was no such revelation.

The newspapermen who went to Medicine Lodge, all of whom were professionals, told essentially the same story as that found in the official reports. As a matter of fact, they told it better. For their media were personal, human documents in no way comparable to either the impersonal prose of journals, minutes, or accounts of officialdom or the objective, extensively edited, and bloodless modern news story. The Medicine Lodge news reporter was no more biased than were the officials duly appointed to negotiate the treaty, and in most instances he was less emotionally involved. He had a distinct advantage over his modern counterpart: There was a passion and spice about his work impossible in today's "factual" straight news story. More importantly, because he was not expected to write "objectively," his readers could take him for what he was—a human being with human feelings telling a story about other human beings.

Yet, these newsmen were not holdovers of early American journalism—instead they were forerunners of twentieth-century reporting. Set down in the press camps of World War II, in Korea, or in South Viet Nam, they would be recognized immediately for what they were—reporters of the news.

[4] J. Cecil Alter, *Jim Bridger*, 295.

[5] Elmo Scott Watson, "The Indian Wars and the Press," *Journalism Quarterly*, Vol. XVII (December, 1940), 301–10.

Research for this study revealed that little previous work had been done on the Medicine Lodge negotiations as covered in the nation's press. Elmo Scott Watson listed the newsmen he thought present at the councils but made no effort to evaluate their work.[6] Oliver Knight's study of reporters who covered the Indian fights has been the only major effort at evaluating the newspapermen's accounts of the Great Plains, but Knight's reporters are covering combat rather than diplomacy.[7]

Attention in this work has been focused on the men of the press corps sent to Medicine Lodge specifically to cover the councils, and the published product of their efforts. Two questions guided our investigation: First, how did the correspondents' accounts compare with official records? Second, to what extent did the reporters agree with one another in their stories? Throughout the narrative, these comparisons are made, and parallels are sometimes drawn between the Medicine Lodge reporter and the modern newsman. This volume, in other words, is a news story, told by newsmen. But what really emerges is not a study of the correspondents: It is the story of the great Medicine Lodge peace councils.

Being newspapermen—and good ones—the correspondents at Medicine Lodge would have agreed that the important thing was the event itself, and that their own part in it was secondary. The real story was not that a field press corps was maturing, beginning to develop the techniques which would eventually lead to the extensive system of news reporting which is the foundation of the modern press. The real story was the confrontation of white man and Indian across the peace table. The men of the Medicine Lodge press party would surely have been pleased that their accounts of what happened would someday form the backbone of a treaty story.

Therefore, in appreciation, first and foremost acknowledgment must go to those newsmen of one hundred years ago. For the support and services so generously given, grateful acknowledgment is ex-

[6] Elmo Scott Watson, "A Checklist of Indian War Correspondents," *Journalism Quarterly*, Vol. XVII (December, 1940), 310–12.

[7] Oliver Knight, *Following the Indian Wars*.

tended the state historical societies of Missouri, Kansas, and Wisconsin; the National Archives; Office of the Chief of Military History, Department of the Army; and the journalism and history faculties at the University of Wisconsin. A special note of gratitude goes to Professors Oliver Knight and Scott Cutlip, both of the University of Wisconsin, for their encouragement and advice; and to my wife, Mary, I am deeply indebted for her inspection of this manuscript, which she accomplished with the mind of a critic and the heart of a poet.

DOUGLAS C. JONES

June 8, 1966
Alexandria, Virginia

CONTENTS

ILLUSTRATIONS

THE TREATY OF MEDICINE LODGE
The Story of the Great Treaty Council as Told by Eyewitnesses

ONE

"YOU SHOWED US THE ROAD
AND WE TRAVELED IT"

—Comanche

Following the tragedy of the Civil War came more full, exciting years. There was rebuilding, change, and expectation. The nation's energy showed in the pages of its newspapers, where stories appeared of events that would shape America. In the north was a money boom, a new bridge was going up between Brooklyn and Manhattan, and a cable being laid across the Atlantic would soon link Europe and the United States. Oil recently had been discovered in Pennsylvania; out of Chicago they were running railroad cars in which a person could sleep as he traveled—the car was called a Pullman. President Andrew Johnson was being threatened with impeachment. The streets of southern cities were filled with federal soldiers and the backwash of war's human rubble, political opportunists, and the victims of an overwhelming poverty.

The industrial pulse of the nation was quickening. There were new lumber industries, and plans were being made to raise and harvest large and profitable rice and cotton crops. Along the Mississippi Valley, towns were astir with travelers and railroad men. Cattle were being driven overland from Texas to markets in Missouri and Kansas. Denver was already a metropolis, and the Latter Day Saints had begun building their great Mormon Temple in Salt Lake City. Mineral strikes were being made everywhere, and the West Coast was filling with people, many pushing east into the mountains and beyond. In frontier posts on the Great Plains, from the Canadian border to the Río Grande, troopers of the Regular Army

3

were stationed once more—although at no point were they in sufficient strength to protect against raids and attacks.

Of all the occurrences of that eventful time, the most significant trend was that of western expansion—an old story by 1867, yet one made new once more by the conclusion of the war and the coming of the railroad.[1] During the war, Congress had encouraged westward movement with passage of the Homestead Act and various railroad legislation, both of which dispensed large portions of the public domain.[2] Before the guns had ceased shrouding the valleys of Tennessee and Virginia with bitter gray smoke, immigrants began pushing beyond the settled edges of Kansas and Nebraska. With war's end, the tempo and the volume increased.

Immigrants moved westward for many reasons, from many places. Boatloads of European immigrants were arriving, and not all of them were trapped in the shops and factories of the northeast. Some of the westward moving tide were those who had lost everything at Appomatox, and they went because they were displaced, dispossessed, and disenchanted. Others went because they were tired of crowded, growing cities and wanted a new country in which to grow. Many had sensed the breadth of the nation as they marched across it—or parts of it—during the war, and they wanted to see more. The destruction of slavery freed thousands of Negroes, and many of them, too, joined the movement. And although the immigrant of 1867 was not usually the gold-crazed visionary that many earlier travelers west had been, many of them made the journey hoping to make their fortunes in cows, timber, minerals, or railroads.

The Dakotas, Nebraska, Kansas, Texas, and New Mexico had been crossed many times before by wagons, headed for California gold, Oregon farms, or the Mormon promised land, the Denver and Nevada diggings. The great central plains and prairie had served as a highway to places farther along. But when the railroads started building beyond the settled western borders of Iowa, Missouri, and Ar-

[1] Albert Britt, *Toward the Western Ocean*, 190, 322; Frank P. Morse, *Cavalcade of the Rails*.

[2] Henry Steele Commager (ed.), *Documents of American History*, 411.

kansas, there was a vast difference. People no longer passed through; they came as settlers, claiming the land as their own.[3]

Something about a railroad is starkly permanent. Passing wagons left deep ruts in the Great Plains—some are still there—but these were only marks on the soil, soon to be blown, washed, and filled with grass, becoming a symbol of something past. Steel rails are more than a symbol. They mean more than passing. They are particularly permanent when the mere fact of their presence draws people along them to stop off at scattered intervals where there is water and timber —or promise of it—to build sod shanties, clapboard shacks, or frame houses with real glass in the windows.

The native North American who sat his scrawny pony and watched his land filling with white people was not particularly clean, cultured, or righteous by Anglo-American standards. But whatever else he may have been, the Plains Indian, by any standards, was not stupid. In the old days he had watched and laughed as greenhorn rushees and immigrants scrambled across his hunting grounds. As the buffalo ranges became speckled with sod and wooden lodges and were spanned by the railroad, the Indian knew the time for laughing was past.

Of course, the Plains tribes did not contest the coming of the whites simply because of houses and railroads. These things were only the latest hot points of friction in a relationship that had matured from mutual curiosity to bitter hostility between two peoples with extremely divergent values, aspirations, and ambitions.[4] The Anglo-American settler was endowed with courage, stubbornness, and the unwavering conviction that he was superior in every important way to the Indian. The presence of another—to him pagan—people on the land he desired was no obstacle. The Indian way of war did nothing to help the situation. For despite the recent carnage of the Civil War, most whites felt a fight should be conducted as a respectable, standup shooting match between plainly seen and easily identifiable

---

[3] James C. Olson, *A History of Nebraska*, 107; Robert E. Riegel, *America Moves West*, 45–68.

[4] Roy H. Pearce, *The Savages of America*; Loring Benson Priest, *Uncle Sam's Stepchildren*, 57.

opponents. In 1867, as today, the white man had not become fully reconciled to the shocking techniques of guerrilla war—a vicious game of terror, stealth, treachery, ambush, night raid, and the abduction and slaughter of women and children.[5]

To the frontiersman, nothing could excuse the horror of Indian warfare. But instead of drawing back from the conflict, the white man pitched in and became as brutal as the red. For there were no common interests to bring the two together, and there was a complete disregard for one another's feelings and rights. The results of their continued association were predictable.[6] They would not long exist side by side.

The Indian obstacle to Plains settlement in 1867 was divided roughly into three areas, identified geographically and by the major wild tribes' ranging habits.[7] In the north were the Sioux and Cheyenne, between the Platte River and Canada from Minnesota to the Rockies. From the Platte River to the Arkansas was the country of the Arapahoes and Southern Cheyennes. Their hunting grounds began about where the Kansas River forks and becomes the Saline and Smoky Hill, extending as far west as Denver. In the south, beyond the Arkansas, was Comanche and Kiowa land.

Comanche wars with the whites were a century and a half old by 1867. Early Comanche raids against Spanish settlements were recorded as early as the first quarter of the eighteenth century.[8] The Great Comanche War Trail, running from the Texas Panhandle to the Río Grande and far beyond, was the route of countless war parties which struck Spaniards, Mexicans, and Texans with haughty impartiality. Early Spanish and Mexican punitive expeditions against the Comanches were unsuccessful.[9] Texans had better success in later years when they organized their own raiding parties composed vari-

[5] H. D. Fey and D'Arcy McNickle, *Indians and Other Americans*, 25–26, 31.

[6] Helen Hunt Jackson, *A Century of Dishonor.*

[7] Commissioner of Indian Affairs, *Annual Report, 1867*, 309ff.; John Joseph Mathews, *The Osages: Children of the Middle Waters*, 663; Mari Sandoz, *The Buffalo Hunters.*

[8] Rupert N. Richardson, *The Comanche Barrier to South Plains Settlement;* Ernest Wallace and E. Adamson Hoebel, *The Comanches: Lords of the South Plains.*

ously of Rangers, militia, Regular Army troops and vengeful citizens armed with shotguns and Colt revolvers.

The war in Texas was particularly vicious, though not generally as barbarous as it sometimes became farther north. It was a war against base camps, with the Texans striking hard at Indian villages when they could be found, and the Indians attacking isolated ranches and farms. The casualties among the women and children of both sides did not serve to dampen the hot tempers and unbending hatred that made Indian war in the Southwest such a bitter affair. The continuing movement of settlement westward in high plains Indian country was only one point of irritation. The Santa Fe Trail, originally established as a trade route, became a highway for settlers. The traders were generally a tough, well-armed lot able to take care of themselves, but the immigrants were mostly ill equipped to handle a marauding, night-raiding band of Comanches or Kiowas.[10]

Attempts to negotiate with the wild tribes of the south always seemed to fail because of treachery and deceit on one or both sides, following a pattern established in other areas where Indians and white men had come together. There were a few major battles in the south, but for the most part the Indian problem in Texas was one of long, slow agony—the blood letting on a drop by drop magnitude which seldom brought a full military response. Bitterness towards the Indians in Texas was nurtured by the sight of the destroyed and mutilated families who had been attacked while trying to scratch a living from the land of the high plains. Exactly how many died will never be known. Comanches kept no records.[11]

At the northern end of the Great plains, trouble with the Sioux was comparatively recent. In the 1840's and 50's, when immigrants and gold seekers made the Platte and other northern streams their roads

[9] Edward H. Spicer, *Cycles of Conquest; Lesley Byrd Simpson* (ed.) *The San Saba Papers*, 153–55; J. Evetts Haley, "The Great Comanche War Trail," *Panhandle and Plains Historical Review*, Vol. XXIII (1950), 11 ff.

[10] James Mooney, "Calendar History of the Kiowa," 177; George E. Hyde, *Indians on the High Plains*, 64–66; Mildred Mayhall, *The Kiowas*, 74.

[11] Commissioner of Indian Affairs, *Special Report*, 1867, 315; John Graves, Wirth, *Soldier and Brave*, 6–12, 15–20.

to the west, trouble quickly developed.[12] Before the Civil War, army troops had been sent to subdue the Sioux and Northern Cheyennes. During the war, there was the terrible massacre of whites along the Minnesota River by the Santee Sioux, an ugly incident that brought a furious response from local militia and which gave rise all across the frontier to fears of general Indian uprisings.[13]

Efforts following the Civil War to make treaties with the northern tribes were fruitless. Important chiefs stayed away from treaty councils, and white settlers and travelers ignored government promises to the Indians intended to protect their lands.[14] On one occasion, even as peace commissioners were making promises to guarantee the Indians' territorial demands, troops were pushing into the Powder River country to protect travelers headed for mining country farther west. This—the Bozeman Trail—was the focus of Sioux trouble in 1867. Less irritating to the northern tribes was the main-line Union Pacific construction along Platte River, southern edge of the Sioux buffalo range. Even so, war parties provided a few moments of wild excitement for railroad work gangs as the tracks neared the present site of Cheyenne, Wyoming.

Although the northern and southern extremes of the Great Plains did not provide exceptional examples of Indian-white co-operation, the worse situation existed in the Central Plains—that rolling country between the Platte and the Arkansas cut from east to west by the Kansas–Smoky Hill river system. Two factors made this area the major source of concern. First, it was the buffalo range and traditional hunting ground of the Southern Cheyennes and Arapahoes, and second, it was being bisected by a railroad. The Union Pacific, Eastern Division—later the Kansas Pacific—was pushing west with heavy government support. Anything that stood in the way was bound to attract attention at the highest levels of government. The Cheyenne Indians were a barrier, opposing as a fundamental of sur-

[12] Gen. W. T. Sherman, Ltr., *Annual Report, Secretary of War, 1867*, 65–67; Conrad L. Wirth, *Soldier and Brave*, 6–12, 15–20.

[13] 40 Cong., 2 sess., *H.R. Exec. Doc. No. 13, Special Report, Secretary of the Interior*, 3–36.

[14] *Ibid.*, George Bird Grinnell, *The Fighting Cheyennes*, 184–239.

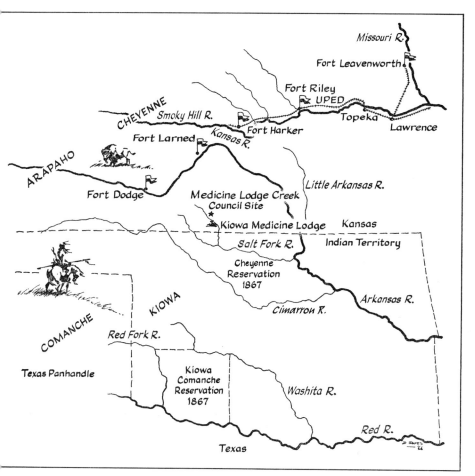

THE TROUBLED AREA OF 1867

The four major tribes who came to Medicine Lodge cannot be so easily associated with specific segments of the land, as indicated here. However, some idea is presented of the general ranging areas of the four tribes in relationship to the council site at Medicine Lodge.

vival any venture that would destroy their herds or eliminate the hunt.[15]

A decade of bad feeling between the Cheyennes and whites made peaceful settlement of the Smoky Hill issue extremely doubtful in 1867. As had been the case in the north, initial Cheyenne trouble was with immigrants. At first, misunderstandings had seemed of little importance—a stolen cow here, a few wild shots fired there. But as the Cheyennes and Arapahoes saw their land being pinched between advancing farmers from the east and the established settlements around Denver in the west, they became less and less willing to accept gracefully even the smallest irritation. There continued to be strong sentiment in both tribes for peaceful settlement, however.[16] Too frequently, though, the voice of the peacemaker was lost in the sound of gun fire.

The 1861 Treaty of Fort Wise relegated the Cheyennes and Arapahoes to the plains of eastern Colorado, south of the Arkansas, a territory wholly unsatisfactory to most leaders of both tribes. Later, at the Treaty of the Little Arkansas, the Indians were given hunting rights north of the Arkansas in Kansas, a provision completely unsatisfactory to Kansas settlers.[17] The good intentions of the Little Arkansas peace commissioners went for naught because so many of the Indian leaders stayed away from the councils. Most authorities agree that the main reason for this boycott was the Sand Creek Massacre, which occurred the year before the treaty meetings were held.[18]

In November, 1864, a band of Cheyennes under Black Kettle—reputed to be a peace seeker among the Cheyennes—moved into camp near Fort Lyon, Colorado. After a summer of Indian depredations, the governor of Colorado was in no mood to listen to Black Kettle's suggestions for peace talk. What followed is still hotly debated among frontier historians and Indian buffs. One side is of

[15] Samuel Bowles, *Our New West: Records of Travel*, 45–68; Britt, *Ocean*, 322.

[16] LeRoy Hafen and Ann W. Hafen (eds.), *Reports From Colorado: The Wildman Letters*, 210.

[17] Kappler, *Treaties*, 892–99. [18] Stanley Hoig, *The Sand Creek Massacre*.

the opinion that Black Kettle wanted peace for the snow months and that with the coming of spring he would be back on the war trail. The other side contends that Black Kettle was seriously concerned about the war and that he was tricked into camping within striking distance of the Colorado militia. In any event, strike the Colorado militia did. Claims were made by the soldiers that fresh prizes of war were discovered in the Cheyenne lodges along Sand Creek; there were counter-claims by the Indians that the brutal militiamen returned to Denver to celebrate their victory, displaying trophies of the fight—scalps and the severed hands and fingers of their victims, many of them women and children.

Indian reaction to Sand Creek was predictable. Violence spilled over into the northern and southern areas. It was difficult to tell which tribes were hostile and which were not—a chronic problem during Indian wars. Kiowas were seen in Kansas, Southern Cheyennes were riding with the Sioux, mail routes were blocked, small settlements beseiged, lonely travelers butchered without knowing why.

With the bitter gall of Sand Creek still fresh, and a useless treaty signed by only a handful of their leaders, the Cheyennes in 1867 found a new portend of disaster—the railroad inching into buffalo country. Had it all been deliberately planned, conditions for continued hostility could not have been improved.

In the spring of 1867, Major General Winfield Scott Hancock, commander of the Department of the Missouri, aroused by reports of Cheyenne and Kiowa depredations, goaded by Kansas Governor Samuel Crawford, and apparently convinced that he could restore order on the Smoky Hill with a show of force, rode out of his Fort Leavenworth headquarters at the head of a strong column of infantry and cavalry. His purpose, as he stated it, was to talk peace with the hostiles.[19] If the Indians wanted a fight, however, the General was prepared to give it to them. Riding as a war correspondent with the expedition was Henry M. Stanley of the *Missouri Democrat*.[20]

[19] Maj. Gen. W. S. Hancock, *Reports of Gen. W. S. Hancock upon Indian Affairs with Accompanying Exhibits.*
[20] Henry M. Stanley, *My Early Travels and Adventures in America and Asia.*

Hancock's soldiers marched back and forth across Kansas, the General did indeed talk with a few tribesmen, and by his order a Cheyenne village on the Pawnee Fork of the Arkansas was burned. This action—although there were no Indian casualties—caused a great deal of bitterness, and the Kansas situation was aggravated rather than helped. Among those most bitter were the Indian agents of the Department of the Interior who were with Hancock, and who claimed that the General was ill informed about the hostility of the band of Cheyennes whose lodges he burned.[21] Hancock returned to his base in a foul temper, for not only was he set upon by the Indian agents, but the Seventh Cavalry under Lt. Col. George Armstrong Custer had chased about the plains without catching any Indians, leaving the men and horses of the Regiment near exhaustion. Following this, Custer made an unauthorized trip to visit his wife, leaving the Regiment at the far western end of the state—for which Hancock arrested the golden-haired horseman. What had been worse, a small party of men trying to reach Custer during his gallop had been caught by hostiles and massacred.

Henry Stanley, eyewitness to much of this, gave an account of the Central Plains problem, one of the first that had been done by a professional journalist from the East. What Stanley saw was the muddled relationship that existed between the army and the Department of the Interior, compounding the confusion of a guerrilla war with an organization itself divided.

There was considerable unrest among the tribes of the Great Plains in 1867, an unrest only indirectly connected with the white men. The uneasy situation resulted in part from the constant Indian migrations that had been going on since the first English settlements were established on the East Coast.[22] In the Southwest, the Spanish had never been inclined—or able—to populate New Mexico and West Texas to such an extent that native populations were pushed into new

<hr />

[21] George Armstrong Custer, *My Life on the Plains*, xi; Charles J. Brill, *Conquest of the Southern Plains*, 14, 74–79.

[22] W. Eugene Hollon, *The Southwest Old and New*, 273–94; Mathews, *Osages*, 650–51.

lands. But as Anglo-American pioneers moved westward, they brought with them a kind of permanent settlement that meant the end of local Indian culture. The Indians were physically moved—as in the case of the Five Civilized Tribes—were driven west by war, or simply felt the pressure of white settlement and moved on their own initiative.[23] As more tribes drifted onto the edge of the Great Plains, space to roam freely dwindled. Traditional enemies found themselves next door to one another, and the proximity of tribes unused to each other created new enmities. Cherokees pushed Osages, Osages pushed Kiowas, Kiowas pushed Cheyennes, Cheyennes pushed Pawnees. The Great Plains had become a dumping ground for all the tribes of the east, a condition which the old inhabitants resented, and fought. War parties riding against other Indians became a menace, for once set in motion, such a well-armed and painted group could be expected to strike anyone in its path, Indian or white.

On the white man's side, where the Department of the Interior was charged with Indian affairs, there was bickering and backbiting. The army found itself reluctantly involved, for not only did the military logistical system handle a great deal of the supply load for the Indian agencies, where there was shooting trouble only the army had the authority necessary to be effective—authority in the form of sabers and Gatling guns.[24] Thus, when there was friction, both government agencies were caught up in it, neither understanding— or even caring—where the other department's authority began or ended. Neither was satisfied with the way the other conducted Indian operations.[25] Both were convinced that the other was biased and bullheaded. There were accusations and counteraccusations of graft, ineptitude, brutality, ignorance, and almost anything else slanderous one side could think of to say about the other. Too often, the accusations were well founded. There were few men on the fron-

---

[23] Mathews, *ibid.*, 653–55.

[24] Martha Buntin, "Difficulties Encountered in Issuing Cheyenne and Arapaho Subsistence," *Chronicles of Oklahoma*, Vol. XIV (March, 1936), 37–45; Fairfax Downey, "Frontier Army," *Army*, Vol. XIII (February, 1963), 48–52.

[25] Commissioner of Indian Affairs, *Annual Report, 1868*, 2–22; Maj. Joel H. Elliot (MS), Official Report, Nov. 2, 1867.

tier who had not been touched by this dismal quarrel and taken sides in it.

Henry Stanley saw only dimly the three-sided nature of the conflict—army, Interior, and Indian. By the close of the Hancock campaign he understood but little of the Indians' side and that of the Interior Department, and it was only natural that his dispatches would reflect the army's prejudices. His loyalties at that time were solidly with the companions with whom he had shared the march. But before the end of 1867, Stanley would know much more about the Great Plains problem, for he was one of the newspaper correspondents sent to cover the peace councils in October on the Medicine Lodge.

TWO

"COME TO US AS FRIENDS"

—Kiowa

End the Indian Menace on the Great Plains! That was the cry during the summer of 1867. It was also the subject of discussion in Congress, of editorials in newspapers. It was an injunction that found little opposition among the articulate of the nation. The problem was—*How?* War or negotiation?

The literature that has grown out of those turbulent times often indicates that eastern newspapers stood for a policy of leniency—of appeasement, of soft, missionary treatment of the red man—while farther west, nearer the Indian problem, editors were demanding tough treatment, military action. This is an easy generalization to make, but painting newspaper reaction to the problem in such stark hues of black and white is suspect. On closer examination, the thesis insofar as 1867 is concerned falls flat.

For example, James Gordon Bennett's *New York Herald* commented: "To attempt to exterminate the Indian race would be a work of years and an expense of hundreds of millions of dollars, as was well demonstrated in Florida."

The *Herald*'s correspondent hardly exhibited a molly-coddling attitude. His comment, rather, was a hard, economically oriented one on the Indian problem.

But from the *Cincinnati Gazette* there was this editorial: "The facts are obvious and men are either idiots or knaves who do not see that nothing short of the strong arm of the government will subdue these demons of the Plains."

This was the hard line, and the paper was nearer the Indian frontier than was Bennett's *Herald*. But farther west still, from a July issue of the *Chicago Times:* "If reservations are not selected which are remote, there will be no guard against contacts with demoralizing whites and rascally traders. . . . [We hope there will be an end] to our costly, inhuman and seemingly endless Indian problem."

Was this the plea for a furious, violent charge to crush the Indian? Was it an accusation that all the trouble was caused by the heathen red man? Hardly. And still closer to the Indian problem, from the *Missouri Democrat* in St. Louis: "We can hardly blame them for being savages, for our government and our people have certainly taken very little pains to make them anything else."

And closer still, a newspaperman wrote of the chief executive of Kansas: "It is a little remarkable that Governor Crawford admits that our Indian trouble arises from the mismanagement of the government."

A man most serious in his appeals for justice and nonviolent action, the author of this line was Milton Reynolds. He was editor and sometimes field correspondent of a newspaper located in the middle of the Indian trouble. From his desk at the Lawrence, Kansas, *State Journal*, he could look through his window and see blanket-clad figures moving on the street outside.

Actually, newspapers, regardless of where located, with rare exception leaned toward negotiation rather than war. To keep the record straight, most of those rare exceptions were on the frontier, it was true. However, there is little evidence that they chose the hard line because of their extensive or intimate knowledge of the Indian situation; there is some evidence that the war criers wanted action because it meant troops in town along with the lucrative army contracts for local traders.

At any rate, it was difficult to find an established, large-circulation newspaper that hewed strictly to the tough policy line. All agreed that if negotiations failed, the army should be prepared to punish the Indians severely. All agreed, too, that something had to be done, and fast. Negotiate first, shoot if necessary, but do it at once. There were many interests involved and many reasons and pressures for a rapid settlement. On other major problems of the day, Congress might bicker. But there was little argument on the Indian question; it had to be settled.[1]

The *American Cyclopedia and Register of Important Events* for 1867 summed up the Plains problem in one statement: There were frontier disturbances caused by ". . . intrusions on Indian reservation lands, laying of railroads through Indian hunting grounds, and inefficiency in handling Indian affairs."

And so, on July 14, Senator John B. Henderson, of Missouri, presented a bill in Congress "To treat with certain hostile Indians . . . now warring with the United States or committing depredations . . ." on the Great Plains. The bill created a Peace Commission to negotiate an agreement with the Plains Indians to ". . . remove the causes of war; secure the frontier settlements and railroad construction; and establish a system for civilizing the tribes."[2]

"Establishing a system for civilizing . . ."—this was the unique phrase that set the 1867 Peace Commission apart from the ones before it. It was a definite commitment to something new. No longer was the Indian to be pushed away into some remote corner in the hope that he would behave himself and stay clear of white men. Now he would be remodeled into a red counterpart of the white man—he would learn to appreciate the values of personal property, the satisfaction of pushing a plow, and the beauty of settling down forever in a wooden house enclosed by fences and cavalry patrols.

With only minor changes in wording, the Henderson bill—40 Cong., 1 sess., S.B. No. 136—was passed and forwarded to President Andrew Johnson. It was returned to Congress with the President's signature on July 30.[3]

Members of the Peace Commission named in the bill were Senator

[1] *Congressional Globe,* Vol. 38, 460–62, 673; U.S. Congress (HR), *Report of the Indian Peace Commission, Exec. Doc., No. 97,* 15 (hereinafter cited as *Peace Commission*); "The Indian Wars," *The American Cyclopedia and Register of Important Events,* 1867, Vol. VII, 399–400.

[2] *Cong. Globe,* 667; *Peace Commission,* 1 f.

[3] *Cong. Globe,* 755.

17

Henderson, chairman of the Senate Indian Affairs Committee; N. G. Taylor, Commissioner of Indian Affairs, Department of the Interior; Samuel F. Tappan, former officer of the Colorado militia who had headed a military investigation of the Sand Creek Massacre in 1864; and John B. Sanborn, who had served for the Department of the Interior at the Treaty of the Little Arkansas. Military members appointed by the President were Lieutenant General William Tecumseh Sherman, commander of the Division of the Missouri—he controlled all military troops and installations west of the Mississippi, from Canada to Mexico; Major General William S. Harney, retired Indian fighter; and Major General Alfred H. Terry, commander of the Department of Dakota, one of Sherman's most important subordinate commands.[4]

Among the civilian members, Taylor was probably best known, and certainly he was most interesting to the press. He was variously described in the newspapers as a huge man who wore gold-rimmed eye glasses and a wig, would go to any lengths to pamper the Indians or curry favor with the President, and enjoyed poetry reading. Taylor was the natural target of sharp and scalding words by many of the nation's editors, but a few papers, including the *Chicago Times*, expressed confidence in him.

Of the military members, Sherman was undoubtedly the most widely known, and he was mentioned often in the press accounts of the negotiations. He was held up by the newspapers as the strong, silent man of the frontier. Reporters who came in close contact with him did not like Sherman personally—in fact, most of them despised him—but they showed a marked respect for him.

After the members of the Commission were named and the army representation had been announced, the story was played prominently by much of the press—most newspapers printed the entire Henderson bill. Along with this, there were a great many stories comparing Sherman and Taylor. One paper reported that Sherman had called the Commission a "humbug," and items of similar stripe

[4] *Ibid.*; J. P. Dunn, *Massacres of the Mountains*, 357; *Chicago Times*, July 23, 1867.

18

painted the General as a vicious Indian hater intent on wiping out the tribes.[5]

The press did Sherman a great disservice in this regard. Not all major newspapers saw him as bloodthirsty, but apparently enough of them did to create a lasting impression. Many scholarly works even today claim that Sherman favored war and extermination of the Indian. There can be little doubt that General Sherman was a tough, fighting soldier; he was not afraid of Indians or anyone else. But he was a realist, too, and he knew that a war with the Indians would be a long and unhappy affair for the army. He said as much in his letters and official reports.[6]

Sherman did not go to Medicine Lodge. In the first meetings of the Commission with the northern tribes, Sherman spoke to the Indians as he had always spoken to everyone—bluntly. Shortly thereafter, he was recalled to Washington. Conclusive proof has never been found that Sherman's brusque manner with the red men was cause for his recall. In his place President Johnson appointed Major General C. C. Augur, commander of the Department of the Platte, another of Sherman's subordinate commands. Harney was left as the ranking military man in the field with the Commission. Harney, though less renowned, was cut from the same ramrod pattern as Sherman. In spite of his temporary withdrawal from the field operations, Sherman remained the senior soldier on the Peace Commission, and he was one of the principals in preparing the final report to Congress.[7]

A few days after the President's announcement of the military membership of the Commission, Senator Henderson was off to the frontier.[8] Perhaps he took this opportunity for some political fence mending in his home state; more likely his nervous energy would not allow him to sit in Washington when he could be in St. Louis at Sherman's headquarters discussing the coming trip to the Great Plains.

[5] *Harper's Weekly*, Sept. 7, 1867.

[6] *Sec. of War*, Sherman Report, 1867, 34–36.

[7] *Dictionary of American Biography*, I, 427–28; VIII, 280–81; XVIII, 378–79; *New York Herald*, Oct. 9, 1867; *New York World*, Sept. 27, Oct. 7, 1867.

[8] *New York Herald*, July 27, 1867.

Taylor, moving more slowly, met with the President on July 22 to discuss the Indian negotiations.[9] The newspapers reported Taylor's trips in and out of the White House, but nothing was written about the conversations between Taylor and the President.

With the exception of Henderson, all the civilian members of the Peace Commission were in Washington at the time of Taylor's meeting with the President. The Indian Commissioner collected his staff—including Sanborn and Tappan—and started for St. Louis by train. One member of the party was A. S. H. White, a Department of the Interior employee sent on the trip to assist Taylor. White also served as the Secretary of the Interior's man-on-the-scene.

Waiting for the group to assemble, General Sherman sent specific instructions to his subordinates throughout the Division of Missouri. To General Winfield Scott Hancock, commanding the district where the Medicine Lodge meetings would occur, Sherman wired, "I want the deliberations of this Commission to be as little disturbed by the acts of our troops as possible."[10] For the time being, Sherman's instructions served to confine the majority of the frontier army to their posts. In the early days of August, the hostile tribes appeared to be slackening their activities as well. There were fewer reports from the upper Platte and the Smoky Hill of war parties loose on the Plains. It seemed as if the hostilities on the frontier had ceased temporarily in anticipation of what the Peace Commission would do.

Early meetings between Harney, Henderson, and Sherman were not reported by the press. It was not yet time for the newsmen to converge on the Commission. St. Louis newspapers treated the gathering officials with the same detachment shown by the presses of New York and Chicago. If there were few detailed accounts of the Commission's activities, more than enough editorial advice was given. Editors used many column inches of space to tell the Commission how it should do its job. The *Chicago Times* commented, " . . . secure the Indians a government that will insure order and guard against

---

[9] Edwin C. McReynolds, *Missouri: A History of the Crossroads State*, 281–83; *New York World*, July 23, 1867.

[10] *Indian Peace Commission*, *"Journal of Proceedings"* (MS), Aug. 7, 1867.

the machinations of rascally whites." *Harper's Weekly* viewed the problem as somewhat akin to establishing a zoo, where Indians could be cared for and watched closely. Most optimistic observer of all was the *New York World*, which suggested that formation of the Peace Commission would ". . . certainly lead to a peaceable solution to the Indian troubles."[11]

With the press generally expressing high hopes for the Peace Commission's success on the Plains, the Commission assembled and conducted their first meeting. The date was August 7, and the place was the Southern Hotel in St. Louis.[12]

They decided to deal first with the Sioux, and plans were made to travel up the Platte, returning later to Kansas where councils would be held with the Southern Plains tribes. As Sherman dispatched orders to his departmental commanders alerting them to the movement of the Peace Commission, Taylor sent instructions to his Indian agents for collecting the tribes at the designated points.[13] The commission would talk with the Sioux near Fort Laramie and with the Southern tribes on the Plains near Fort Larned, Kansas.

St. Louis papers reported the proceedings during the Southern Hotel meetings in which the Commission discussed plans for travel, feeding the Indians who would come to talk peace, and other administrative details. On August 9, correspondents were not allowed to attend the meetings, but according to its minutes, the Commission continued to discuss the same subjects they had introduced earlier when reporters were present.[14] Among other things, the Commission set their meeting with the Southern tribes for the first full moon of October.

Preliminary arrangements made, the Peace Commission moved to Fort Leavenworth, Kansas, crossing the state of Missouri by train.

[11] *Chicago Times*, July 23, 1867; *Missouri Democrat*, July 26, 1867; *New York Herald*, July 22, 1867; *New York World*, July 22, 1867; *Harper's Weekly*, August 17, 1867.

[12] "Journal," Aug. 6, 1867; *New York Herald*, July 28, 1867; *New York World*, July 22, 1867.

[13] *Sec. of War*, 67, 35–37, 65; *Atchison Daily Champion*, Sept. 17, 1867.

[14] "Journal," Aug. 9, 1867.

On high bluffs above a big bend of the Missouri River, Fort Leavenworth and the adjacent city of Leavenworth was a sizable settlement of more than 20,000 people. Jumping-off point for both the Oregon and Santa Fe trails, it was also the headquarters of General Hancock's Department of the Missouri. Leavenworth had stood on the western edge of white settlement for many years, but when the Peace Commission went there in 1867, the Indian frontier lay many miles west. It still stood as a reserve strong point, with roads leading out from it into central Kansas. Just to the south of the town, the Kansas River flowed into the Missouri from the disputed Smoky Hill Range two hundred miles away, and up the Missouri to the north were Omaha and Council Bluffs, eastern end of the main-line Union Pacific.

In Hancock's headquarters, the Commission took a great deal of testimony on the Plains situation—from soldiers, traders, and Indian agents. Commission members heard accounts of the Hancock campaign, of Kiowa raiding in Kansas, and of crooked Indian agents and inept army officers. Some of the stories they heard conflicted. Some would be retold again, later, during the discussion at Medicine Lodge. All served to alert the commissioners to the complexities of the frontier problem.

As though Indians on the war trail did not provide sufficient trouble, reports came of cholera raging at Fort Harker—a post through which the commissioners would pass during their southern journey. One newspaper reported seventeen summer deaths from cholera in the Harker area alone, and other frontier posts also were hard hit.

The Commission first took official notice of the press corps during the Leavenworth meetings. There had been little need to be concerned with the press before reaching Leavenworth because the Commission had only traveled across Missouri. But once they left Hancock's territory, there would be little pause until hostile country was reached. The Commission decided that the same rules should apply that were generally followed when correspondents traveled with military expeditions. In such cases, the reporter submitted an application for permission to accompany the party, with approval dependent on the senior military commander in whose department the newsman intended to operate. Before leaving St. Louis, the Commission had approved two such applications—one for the *Chicago Times* and one for the *Cincinnati Commercial*.[15]

By the time the Commission reached Leavenworth, no one had joined from the *Times*, but George C. Brown was there representing the *Commercial*. Brown, who had been on the frontier for a number of months, had reported the Hancock expedition, but unlike Stanley, who rode with the troops, Brown filed his campaign stories from the relative comfort of an Omaha hotel room. In the official minutes of the Commission meetings, the *Chicago Times* and the *Cincinnati Commercial* had the distinction of being the only newspapers mentioned.

Tappan brought up the subject of correspondents during a Commission meeting, and after a short discussion the members agreed to limit the press corps to six reporters. This rule was never enforced, however—there were more than six recognized newspaper correspondents at Medicine Lodge. One was an official member of the Commission. He was John Howland, *Harper's Weekly* artist, who had signed on with the group in St. Louis as a shorthand stenographer.

Before the Commission started the trip north, Taylor had an opportunity to talk with Thomas Murphy, head of the Central Indian Superintendency. This subdivision of the Department of the Interior Bureau of Indian Affairs was roughly equivalent to the area under military control of General Hancock—the Department of Missouri. Murphy was in charge of all the Indian agents operating in Kansas and the Indian territory. While the Commission was in Leavenworth, he drove in from his Atchison office to confer with his chief on the problem of assembling the Southern tribes. Murphy was a very respected figure in Atchison, and his movements were reported in minute detail by the *Atchison Daily Champion*, one of the many fiery little newspapers that flourished on the frontier.[16]

---

[15] *Ibid.*, Aug. 13, 17, 1867.
[16] *Atchison Daily Champion*, Aug. and Sept., 1867.

Up the Missouri to Omaha, then on toward Fort Laramie along the Platte—the northern leg was made in sweltering heat. The only happy note was the river steamer the Commission used—they at least had bunks to sleep in, and there was no dust. The last days of August and most of September were spent with representatives of the Northern Plains wild tribes, in an unsuccessful attempt to come to terms. The only thing gained was a promise from the Indians that they would assemble and talk again. The *Missouri Democrat*, an ardent Commission booster, complained that the northern trip was a dismal failure, and there was hope expressed that the journey into Kansas would prove more useful.

There were many disappointments. Commissioner Taylor received word of serious illness in his family, and he hurried back to Washington. Sherman had been recalled to the capital by Commanding General U. S. Grant. President Johnson had begun his fight with the Congress that would end in bitterness and impeachment before another summer passed. When the Commission—what was left of it —arrived in Leavenworth, it quickly dispersed, except for three men, with each member going his way on his own business. A. S. H. White and Howland worked over the notes they had taken on the northern trip.[17] White had hoped to have a report off to his Interior Department superiors as soon as the talks with the Northern tribes were complete, but the report was not finished on schedule. The delay, White explained, was because of the difficulty in transcribing Howland's shorthand. The other member of the Commission who stayed on the frontier was Sanborn. He was busy buying gifts to be given the Indians in Kansas, putting down his transactions, dollar by dollar, in black ink on the pages of a long ledger.[18] He wrote with a round, full penmanship, the flourish and delicacy looking oddly out of place in the records of dried beans and plug tobacco.

Meanwhile, Superintendent Murphy and his subordinates were busy in Kansas and Indian Territory spreading the word of coming

[17] A. S. H. White, Ltr. to Sherman, Nov. 2, 1867.
[18] "Journal," Aug. 13, 17, 1867; Stanley, *Travels*, 192–200; *Frank Leslie's Illustrated Newspaper*, Oct. 26, 1867; *Missouri Democrat*, Aug. 7, 8, 1867.

peace talks. Although some of the Commission members had antici-
pated the meeting's being held near Fort Larned, Murphy selected
the area where Medicine Lodge and Elm creeks converged on the
southern edge of Kansas.[19] He sent a letter to Fort Leavenworth
suggesting the site, and the next time the Commission met, it agreed
to hold the councils of peace at Medicine Lodge, near the site of
Kiowa sun dances of previous years.

In the first week of October, the Commission reassembled. From
Leavenworth, they boarded the cars of the Union Pacific, and with
the Commission was the same group of reporters who had traveled
on the abortive trip up the Platte. When the train passed through
Lawrence, Milton Reynolds, Lawrence *State Journal* editor, joined
the group. He was a small, slender man with a closely cropped mustache and a short goatee. At one of the many stops made by the train
west of Lawrence, the press party was increased once more—S. F.
Hall, the *Chicago Tribune*. Hall had been in southern Kansas, traveling between the military posts and frontier settlements where the
Arkansas River flowed south into country of the Five Civilized Tribes
—through what is now the eastern end of Oklahoma.[20]

George Brown, of the *Commercial*, had been joined for the southern trip by another Cincinnatian, H. J. Budd of the *Semi-Weekly
Gazette*. Rounding out the press corps—and each of these had been
up the Platte with the Commission—were Solomon T. Bulkley, *New
York Herald*, William Fayel, *Missouri Republican* of St. Louis,
James E. Taylor, artist for *Frank Leslie's Illustrated Newspaper*,
Stanley and Howland. Altogether, there were nine newspapermen
with the Peace Commission as it moved along the Union Pacific road
to Fort Harker.[21]

[19] "Journal," Aug. 13, 1867; *Chicago Times*, Sept. 14, 1867.

[20] Stanley, *Travels*, 217; *Chicago Times*, Sept. 25, 1867; *Missouri Democrat*,
Sept. 26, 1867; *Frank Leslie's Illustrated Newspaper*, Oct. 26, Nov. 16, 1867.

[21] "Journal," Sept. 18, 1867; Kappler, *Treaties*, 982, 989; A. A. Taylor,
"The Medicine Lodge Peace Council," *Chronicles of Oklahoma*, Vol. II, (June,
1924), 98; T. A. McNeal, "The Indians Agree to Abandon Kansas," *Kansas Historical Collections*, Vol. VI (1897–1900), 344–46; *Chicago Times*, Oct. 12, 1867;
Cincinnati Commercial, Sept. 27, 1867; *Missouri Democrat*, Oct. 19, 1867.

Perhaps the size of the press party was a reflection of press interest in the Central Plains route to the Pacific, where construction gangs for the railroad had been so consistently harassed. On the main-line Union Pacific, there had been forays against road gangs, but the railroad had continued to march up the Platte, and by October, 1867, it had reached Cheyenne, Wyoming. It had, indeed, progressed so far that the Bozeman Trail problem had practically disappeared before the Peace Commission set foot on the Plains. Miners who had once used the Bozeman Trail could travel to the end of the tracks on the Union Pacific, thence take horse or mule north into the Montana diggings, avoiding the hostile Powder River country. In Kansas, a showdown was obvious—the railroad was headed directly into the heart of the great Smoky Hill buffalo range.[22]

As for the correspondents, their interest in the situation was surely aroused on that smoky, rattling trip to Harker. In addition to hearing members of the Commission talk about the Indian difficulties, some of the news correspondents themselves were well acquainted with specific trouble spots. Reynolds and Hall, particularly the former, were not greenhorns. One of the irritations discussed time after time was the Treaty of the Little Arkansas.

The Southern Cheyennes and Arapahoes thought the treaty made on the Little Arkansas gave them hunting rights all along the Smoky Hill. Sanborn knew the clause that gave some weight to the Indian contentions; Article II said the Cheyennes and Arapahoes were:

> ... expressly permitted to reside upon and range at pleasure throughout the unsettled portions of that part of the country they claim as originally theirs, which lies between the Arkansas and the Platte Rivers.

The Smoky Hill would be included in this description. The crux of the problem, however, was that Indians expected the "unsettled" portions of their country to stay that way—the whites did not. As those who rode the cars with the Peace Commission could see for

[22] U.S. Congress (HR), *Report of the Secretary of War, 1868–69, Exec. Doc. No. 1, 3*; *Sec. of War 67,* 65–66; Grinnell, *Cheyennes,* 207–49.

themselves, the Central Plains route through Kansas—the one headed directly for the Smoky Hill—was ideal for railroad construction. Most of the railroad survey teams had long before agreed that this route was superior to the Union Pacific road along the Platte—there was more potable water and timber along the Kansas and Smoky Hill rivers. But the main-line Union Pacific enjoyed one advantage: It did not pass directly through a well-defined buffalo range. The Platte had always seemed a boundary of sorts between northern grazing lands and those on the Central Plains—just as important, it was also a boundary between tribes along much of its course, if Indians could be said to have boundaries.[23]

The Union Pacific Eastern Division was placed in particular jeopardy by the Hancock expedition, after which raids increased sharply. According to some railroad officials, only heavy army formations could make further work possible. Governor Crawford, of Kansas, said civilization in his state was on the verge of destruction. To give the situation proper perspective, General Sherman said later that although Indians caused a little trouble here and there, they were incapable of stopping the railroad.[24] Counterclaims notwithstanding, early summer of 1867 had been a time of considerable bloodshed in Kansas, and although it had abated, the causes and the contending factions were still there in October.

Undoubtedly the correspondents' interest—and that of their editors—centered on the Cheyenne and Arapaho trouble in Kansas; there was yet another factor to whet the appetite of sensation hunters. South of the Arkansas, watching the Kansas war with hungry eyes,

[23] Commissioner *Report 67*, 309f.; Kappler, *Treaties*, 888; O. P. Byers, "Railroading in the Wild West," *Kansas Historical Collections*, Vol. XVII (Winter, 1926–27), 341f.; Mrs. Frank C. Montgomery, "Fort Wallace and Its Relationship to the Frontier," *Kansas Historical Collections*, Vol. XVII (1926–27), 193; *Chicago Times*, Aug. 15, 20, 1867; *Missouri Democrat*, Aug. 10, 14, 1867.

[24] *Peace Commission*, 12f.; *Sec. of War 67*, 36f.; Donald J. Berthrong *The Southern Cheyennes*, 240–75; Elizabeth B. Custer, *Tenting on the Plains*, 560f.; Marguerite Merrington (ed.), *The Custer Story*, 208; Samuel J. Crawford, *Kansas in the Sixties*, 252; Marvin H. Garfield, "Defense of the Kansas Frontier," *Kansas Historical Quarterly*, Vol. I (February, 1932), 330; *Chicago Times*, Aug. 22, 26, 29, 1867; *New York Herald*, Aug. 3, 5, 6, 1867.

one might imagine, were the Comanches and Kiowas. Many observers of the scene in 1867 claimed that these tribes had not broken treaty obligations and promises—or perhaps these same observers simply chose to ignore what had been happening south of Red River. Comanches had moved into the high plains country of the Panhandle and the Staked Plains, and they had driven out the Apaches—at least most historians think this is what happened. When the Kiowas migrated into the same country and became close and continuing friends of the Comanches, the Southwest knew little peace. The western edge of Texas had been scourged by their war parties—right through the Civil War and afterward. The Comanche-Kiowa combination—which meant murder, kidnapping, and rape to Texans—was capable of war on a vicious scale in Kansas. There were uneasy reports that the young men of both tribes were in a constant state of excitement over Cheyenne exploits on the Smoky Hill.[25]

When the Peace Commission arrived at Fort Harker, the answer to the Kansas problem lay one hundred miles away in the lodges of the tribes who were already waiting along the Medicine Lodge—so painfully assembled by Murphy and his people. To the members of the press party, perhaps wild Indians seemed remote. Ellsworth—where the Commission party left the train—was only a tiny village of something like five hundred persons. The settlement was mostly tentage, like other end-of-the-tracks mushroom towns. But when army wagons carried the group into Fort Harker, there was every sign of safety. As was the case with most plains forts, there were no walls surrounding the buildings, but there was a great deal of military activity and show of strength. Infantry, artillery, and cavalry troops were there—four companies of the Seventh Cavalry had only recently arrived at Harker for temporary duty. There were units of the Kansas militia, but most of the soldiers at the garrison at Harker were regulars.[26] As the Commission arrived, it was greeted

[25] Wallace and Hoebel, *Comanches*; Richardson, *Comanche Barrier*; Col. W. S. Nye, *Carbine and Lance*, 55; William C. Nunn, *Texas under the Carpetbaggers*, 177; William E. Dunn, "Spanish Reaction against French Advances toward New Mexico," *Mississippi Valley Historical Review*, Vol. XI (December, 1915), 350.

[26] *Sec. of War 67*, 40–45.

with music by the Thirty-eighth Infantry regimental band. Refreshments were served by the ladies of the garrison, and the Commission members were relieved to find cholera no longer a threat.

On October 8, the day after their arrival at Harker, the representatives of the United States moved two miles closer to their meeting with the hostile tribes, crossing the Smoky Hill River and camping for the first time on the open plains. Stanley wrote that as the members of the press corps sat looking back across the river—watching the flag over Fort Harker—they became aware for the first time of the constant Kansas wind that would be their companion for the next three weeks.[27] On the Medicine Lodge, the hostiles were waiting.

[27] "Journal," Oct. 10, 1867; *Chicago Times*, Oct. 13, 1867; *Missouri Democrat*, Oct. 19, 1867.

THREE

"I WANT TO ROAM THE PRAIRIE"

—Kiowa

After dark on October 8, the campfires glimmered along the Smoky Hill, and a pattern of Commission organization was developed that would continue throughout the Medicine Lodge trip. There was the official party with the commissioners and the Kansas delegation which had joined the expedition at Leavenworth—it included Governor Samuel Crawford and Senator E. G. Ross. In this group also were the secretaries, aides, ambulance drivers, Commission cooks, interpreters, and newspaper reporters. Nearby was the wagon park, the fires of the teamsters lighting the long lines of picketed mules and the wagons loaded with Indian gifts and Commission supplies. Finally, its fires only dimly seen on the open prairie to the southwest, was the military escort. William Fayel wrote in the *Missouri Republican* that the Commission contingent looked like a little army.[1] It was, indeed, a little army with command functions centered in the official party, supply with the wagon train, and combat elements in the escort.

On that first night no sentries were posted. There was obviously little thought of any danger from hostiles so close to Fort Harker. The correspondents spent the evening telling stories, making jokes, and enjoying each others' fellowship about the open fire. John Howland awed the other reporters with tales of his travels in the southwest and his command of the Spanish language. Henry Stanley, impressed with the entire press party, praised them as a good-hearted,

[1] *Chicago Times*, Oct. 12, 1867; *Missouri Democrat*, Oct. 19, 1867.

30

brave, and skillful group. His opinion was not shared by all. S. F. Hall found it highly distasteful that one of the newsmen—whom Hall was kind enough not to mention—managed to get very drunk even though the group went to bed shortly after dark in anticipation of an early-morning start on the trail.[2]

It was a varied company, with a wide range of temperament and talent. In the group were representatives of nine metropolitan papers, and some of the newspapers represented were the largest and most respected news gatherers in the country. The copy these reporters would prepare during the Medicine Lodge venture would appear in many places over a period of weeks and months, through distribution by regional press associations, exchange agreements between newspapers, and outright theft of material. For the collection and dispatch of this material, the newsmen would receive small return in most cases. The *Missouri Democrat*—Stanley's paper—paid a correspondent $15.00 a week in 1867. Some eastern papers paid more, but others paid only by the amount of copy published.[3] To earn their money, the reporters would write many pages in longhand, sometimes under the most trying of conditions: "As I close, a sand storm is prevailing . . . which renders letter writing almost impossible." They would deliver opinions on the Indian problem, local politics, Plains civilization, and the effectiveness of the government's Indian policy. They would tell of the fears, aspirations, avarice, and nobility of almost everyone they met. They would describe the treaty meetings, the country, the Indians, the commissioners, and themselves.[4]

It was often difficult in the mid-nineteenth century to know who had written a particular news story. The identity of the material submitted by the Medicine Lodge press party began to emerge only after an extended study of the various news stories published about Medicine Lodge and the Peace Commission. Fayel's, Howland's and

[2] *Ibid.; Chicago Times*, Oct. 19, 1867.

[3] Charles S. Diehl, *The Staff Correspondent*, 18 ff.; Don Seitz, *The James Gordon Bennetts*, 134, 275f.; Elmo Scott Watson, *A History of Newspaper Syndicates*, 4–21; *The Army Navy-Journal*, Dec. 7, 1867.

[4] *New York Herald*, Oct. 30, 1867.

Stanley's writing is easily recognized—their editors always gave them by-lines. Only initials were used with Budd's copy in the *Cincinnati Gazette* and with Hall's in the *Chicago Tribune*. George Brown signed his stories "Center," which was his middle name, and he identified himself by name in the body of much of his copy. James E. Taylor's drawings in *Leslie's Illustrated Newspaper* were always credited to him in accompanying captions or stories.

Reynolds—who had been asked by William Story, editor of the *Chicago Times,* to cover the treaty meetings as a stringer for the *Times*—signed his work "Otoe" or "Seminole," for the Chicago paper. How Reynolds identified himself in his own paper is not known. Numerous fires over the years have destroyed the files of the Lawrence *State Journal,* and thus far, none of the issues for the fall of 1867 have been found. The *Times* copy was unquestionably Reynolds. He became famous in journalism circles throughout Kansas and Oklahoma for his use of Indian pseudonyms. Eventually, he used the pen name "Kicking Bird" almost exclusively. He took the name from a Kiowa chief whom he admired.[5]

Only the *New York Herald* failed to provide any clue to the authorship of its stories on the treaty councils. However, Brown, Fayel, and Stanley reported that Solomon T. Bulkley represented the *Herald*. Bulkley had been with the James Gordon Bennett organization for a number of years. He had reported the Civil War for the *Herald,* and at the battle of Brandy Station, Virginia, 1863, he had been captured by Confederates and imprisoned at Castle Thunder in Richmond. After an unsuccessful attempt to escape, he had been exchanged in 1864—having been a prisoner of war for seven months—and he continued to cover the Virginia campaigns for the Bennett paper. He came to Medicine Lodge with a well-established journalism reputation.[6]

[5] Kansas Historical Society, "Indian Treaties and Councils Affecting Kansas," *Kansas Historical Collections,* Vol. XVI (1923–25), 786; *Chicago Times,* Oct. 19, 1867; *Chicago Tribune,* Oct. 19, 1867; *Cincinnati Commercial,* Oct. 10, 1867; *Cincinnati Gazette,* Oct. 22, 1867; *Missouri Democrat,* Oct. 19, 1867; *Missouri Republican,* Oct. 19, 1867; *New York Herald,* Oct. 30, 1867.

[6] Emmet Crozier, *Yankee Reporters,* 375f.; J. Cutler Andrews, *The North Re-*

Milton H. Reynolds, known for his work with the Lawrence *State Journal*, dispatched stories for the *Chicago Times* under the signatures "Otoe" and "Seminole." Reynolds became a well-known journalist throughout Kansas and Oklahoma, where he used the pseudonym "Kicking Bird" almost exclusively.

Chronicles of Oklahoma

Little Robe, who had violent words with his agent while arrangements were being made for the Cheyenne council. On his return to the Medicine Lodge later, the newspaper correspondents saw him as one of the leaders of the Cheyenne band. The chief was a good example of the men of his tribe, handsome, strong, dignified, and self-reliant.

Bureau of American Ethnology Collection Smithsonian Office of Anthropology

Little Bear, one of the Cheyenne chiefs who most impressed the newsmen. This photograph was made about eight years after the treaty meetings.

Bureau of American Ethnology Collection Smithsonian Office of Anthropology

General William Tecumseh Sherman, not present at the councils, but whose presence was felt if not welcomed by the news correspondents.

Brady Collection, U.S. Signal Corps
National Archives

General Winfield Scott Hancock, shown during the Civil War when he gained justifiable reputation as a soldier. Campaigning against the Plains Indians was an assignment he found not so well suited for a display of his talents. The newsmen treated him kindly, however.

Brady Collection, U.S. Signal Corps
National Archives

General C. C. Augur was not a great favorite with the press corps at Medicine Lodge, but neither did he suffer their abuse. That he replaced General Sherman for the Kansas portion of the treaty trip made him acceptable to most of them.

Brady Collection, U.S. Signal Corps
National Archives

Governor Samuel Crawford, of Kansas, shown here in the uniform of a United States lieutenant colonel, reported to the Peace Commission that a general Indian war was imminent. He made his point so strongly that many of the reporters suspected his motives.

Senator John B. Henderson, of Missouri, the Peace Commission spokesman during the treaty meetings and major source of information for the newspaper correspondents. His driving energy irritated at least one other member of the Commission, but more than any other individual he guided the course of the peace talks.

Satanta, the Kiowa chief who entertained and perhaps frightened the news reporters. He loved whisky, the buffalo, and his bugle, but no one was ever sure how much he loved the white man, even when he said he did.

The correspondents did not come to know old Satank, the mustached Kiowa, until moments before he departed the treaty camp. Then, for a few moments they were thrilled at his depth and power of expression.

In a letter written in 1888, Milton Reynolds claimed that Thomas Knox covered the treaty for the *New York Herald*. But none of the correspondents mentioned Knox at the time. Perhaps Knox was not known personally by any of the reporters in the press group, but certainly they must have known him by reputation. During the Civil War, Knox had come into direct conflict with General Sherman. Accused of violating censorship regulations, he had been arrested, court-martialed, and expelled from Sherman's area of operation. It would seem unlikely that such a man would have been ignored by other newspapermen. During the Medicine Lodge trip, the *Herald* published only one "Special Correspondence" column. The rest of the story was told in short wire dispatches. There was no indication from any of this material that there were two reporters on the scene from the *Herald*.[7]

It seems that Reynolds must be charged at the outset with an error in fact—but it must be remembered that the error was not a part of Reynolds' material written at the time; it was written twenty-one years later.

Reynolds, despite his notoriously bad memory, at the time of Medicine Lodge was more intimately acquainted with the Indian situation than any other correspondent in the press party. Others had traveled on the Plains; others had covered certain aspects of the problem; but Reynolds lived with it every day. Educated at the University of Michigan, he had moved to the Kansas frontier in 1862. Three years later he established the *State Journal* as a daily newspaper. Both Fayel and Stanley had probably heard of the little Kansas editor—working out of St. Louis as they did—and both regarded him with respect. Fayel always wrote "Mister" in front of Reynolds'

ports the Civil War, 105; Louis M. Starr, *Bohemian Brigade*, 189; Stanley, *Travels*, 217; *Cincinnati Commercial*, Sept.. 27, 1867; *Missouri Democrat*, Oct. 21, 1867:; *Missouri Republican*, Oct. 24, 1867.

[7] Edwin Emery, *The Press and America*, 297; Bernard A. Weisberger, *Reporters for the Union*, 283f.; McNeal, "The Indians Agree to Abandon Kansas, *Kansas Historical Collections*, Vol. VI (1897–1900), 344; Thomas H. Guback, "General Sherman's War on the Press," *Journalism Quarterly*, Vol. XXXVI, (Spring, 1959), 173; *New York Herald*, Oct. 9, 21, 30, Nov. 1, 1897.

name, an honor the *Missouri Republican* correspondent afforded few men short of the President of the United States. In addition to providing story copy to the *Chicago Times*, Reynolds also dispatched stories to the *New York Herald*.[8]

At that time, Reynolds took little notice of his fellow journalists— he never mentioned them in his stories. However, in his 1888 letter he said that Stanley was the biggest liar he had ever seen, going on to say that Stanley represented the *Cincinnati Commercial*. Once more, Reynolds' memory served him badly. He took little part in the correspondents' campfire and other social activities, and after more than twenty years he may have remembered Brown—who was *Commercial* correspondent—and put Stanley's name on the Cincinnati man. It is interesting to speculate that Reynolds remembered the paper but forgot the man, because in the matter of lying, their copy indicates strongly that Brown far outshone Stanley.[9]

Stanley was the only man in the press party who would one day be world famous. Born John Rowlands, he had come to the United States and taken the name of his adopted mentor in New Orleans. During the Civil War, he had been at one time or another on both sides, and it was during this period that he decided to become a newspaperman. After Medicine Lodge, he would join what many journalists consider the greatest paper of the mid-nineteenth-century—the *New York Herald*. Perhaps he owed a great deal to his Medicine Lodge experience. He was providing copy for Horace Greeley's *New York Tribune*, and on his first meeting with James Gordon Bennett, of the *Herald*, Bennett said that he had been impressed with Stanley's stories from the frontier—even though they were printed in Bennett's great competition paper. A. A. Taylor, son of the Indian Commissioner who went to Medicine Lodge a teen-aged boy

[8] Berlin B. Chapman, "The Pottawatomie and Absentee Shawnee Reservations," *Chronicles of Oklahoma*, Vol. XXIV (July, 1949), 253ff.; Dan W. Perry, "The Honorable Milton W. Reynolds," *Chronicle of Oklahoma*, Vol. XXIV (March, 1936), 46–62; Dan W. Perry, "Oklahoma, A Foreordained Commonwealth," *Chronicles of Oklahoma*, Vol. XXIV (March, 1936), 37ff.

[9] McNeal, "The Indians Agree to Abandon Kansas", *Kansas Historical Collections*, Vol. VI (1897–1900), 344.

acting as a Commission secretary, described Stanley as a great man and a respected news corresponndent, but these comments came only years later when "Doctor Livingston, I presume" had made Stanley a world renowned figure.[10] Whether this was Taylor's opinion at the time he knew Stanley on the Plains is anybody's guess.

If Stanley was well thought of by the other members of the Medicine Lodge press gang, they neglected to say so. None of them mentioned his name, although Brown and Fayel recognized the fact—Fayel somewhat reluctantly—that the *Missouri Democrat* had a correspondent in the party. Brown called Stanley "Spooner" and said the Welshman wrote nothing but wild theories about Indian policy. Fayel indicated that Stanley was always at the wrong place at the wrong time, having to rush up at the last moment in order to see what was happening. Fayel's description of Stanley's charging into the Commission camp on a mule, trying to hold his hat in place, his legs flying out at the sides, was not calculated to develop increased respect for the *Democrat* reporter among St. Louis readers.

For his own part, Stanley was favorably inclined toward his fellow reporters. On one occasion he wrote that one of the correspondents in the party had extreme difficulty keeping his facts straight—and there is a strong suspicion that he was talking about Brown—but by and large he spoke of his fellow journalists with respect.[11] His particular favorite was John Howland. Stanley admired the *Harper's Weekly* artist for his quick wit and his fluency in Spanish. Stanley and the artist had at least one thing in common—both took notes of the council meetings in shorthand.

It was Howland and S. F. Hall of the *Chicago Tribune* who provided most of the stories and jokes around the reporters' evening campfires. Everyone liked Howland. George Brown said the *Harper's* artist was a lively and likable character who wore various items of frontier gear that he had picked up in his travels—among them

[10] Oliver Carlson, *The Man Who Made News: James Gordon Bennett*, 384; Taylor, "The Medicine Lodge Council," *Chronicles of Oklahoma*, Vol. II (June, 1924), 99; *New York Tribune*, Oct. 23, 1867.

[11] *Cincinnati Commercial*, Sept. 27, 1867; *Missouri Democrat*, Oct. 20, 1867; *Missouri Republican*, Oct. 24, 1867.

fringed buckskin leggings and a Navy Colt revolver. Brown was apparently an old friend of the other Cincinnati correspondent, H. J. Budd. Each wrote of the other in glowing terms. Brown said that Budd was an "Indian authority," but after a close study of Budd's work the reasons for such an evaluation are a complete mystery.[12]

There was little more than the occasional comment of a fellow newsman to distinguish the individual members of the Medicine Lodge press group. Time would bring some measure of fame to a few of them. Bulkley, Reynolds, and Stanley have become a part of journalism's history. The names Fayel, Howland, Stanley, and Taylor remain in the official documents produced by the Peace Commission—each of them signed as witnesses the treaties made at Medicine Lodge.[13] But for most of them, and for the others—Brown, Budd, and Hall—no clues have been found of their record as journalists or of their later accomplishments. If any of them were well known in 1867, their contemporaries made no note of it, and their fame, if any, has been obscured for almost a century. As so often happens in the study of history, we find them as players in the drama for only a short time, and then they are gone—even though they were as effective at their jobs as the others whose names we remember. They leave nothing but a few lines of fading black copy in the yellowed pages of aged newspapers which are seldom read or seen. But they were there; they went to Medicine Lodge with all the others.

As the Peace Commission broke camp on the morning of October 9, the newsmen in the party stood in the buffalo grass watching the column form as they ate their breakfast of cold ham, hardtack, fried potatoes, and sardines. George Brown apparently relished every bite —beginning with that first meal, he seldom failed to describe in great detail everything that was consumed, either food or drink.

Perhaps many of them looked back wistfully at Fort Harker on the north bank of the Smoky Hill. During their short stay, clean blankets in army barracks, the gracious ladies of the garrison, and the busy

[12] *Cincinnati Commercial*, Sept. 27, 1867.
[13] Kappler, *Treaties*, 982, 986, 989.

confusion of the troops made hostile country seem a long way off. Now they faced the open prairie and a hard week's ride in army ambulances. Stanley counted ten of the light horse-drawn vehicles in the column.[14]

In the wagon park, teamsters were pulling mules into harness, tightening canvas over Indian treaty gifts, and raising a cloud of dust. The correspondents could hear the loud bellow of the drivers above the din of braying mules pressed into the traces with deafening vocal protests. Breaking camp was a colorful routine—and loud. Certainly the mules could have been heard for miles downwind by any Indian who might be listening. In the official party camp, soldier teamsters tucked carbines under the driver's seats and hitched their two-horse teams. Negro orderlies cleared away the last tin cups and plates, storing them in compact wooden boxes, and loaded the rolled tents into wagons—along with folding tables, field desks, camp stools, weapons, and suitcases.

Already, the reporters found the shoulders of their coats dusted with a fine powder. Most of them were dressed as they had been on the train—waist coats and business suits. Howland, however, wore a bush hat, a buckskin jacket, and his large revolver. The column formed, and the reporters scrambled into their assigned ambulances.

The Commission vehicles led the way out of the campsite with the correspondents following close behind. When the ambulances cleared the wagon park, the teamsters whipped their mules and brought the heavy wagons into line. Ahead, on the open prairie, waited the escort, formed in columns of two, ready to lead the party to the Arkansas. Fayel and Reynolds—riding in the same ambulance —saw armed troopers far out on either flank.[15] There could have been no better reminder that they were close to unfriendly country.

Until then, they had not needed a military escort. Commission business had never taken them far from an established military installation. But in Kansas they would be days away from any fort

[14] *Chicago Times*, Oct. 13, 1867; *Cincinnati Commercial*, Oct. 13, 1867; *New York Herald*, Oct. 23, 1867.
[15] *Chicago Times*, Oct. 21, 1867; *Missouri Republican*, Oct. 19, 1867.

37

and traveling in slow vehicles across Arapaho and Cheyenne hunting country, and not too far from Kiowas and Comanches. If the present truce suddenly ceased, the loaded wagons and the many animals in the column would become the irresistible plum of any war party.

To provide for the Commission's safety, a Presidential order had been issued in August, placing all army officers on the frontier under the command of the Peace Commission.[16] An agency outside the army, in effect, in this rare instance, exercised operational control over military combat units. General Sherman's presence on the Commission, however, stifled any protests from the army because the General commanded the entire military establishment in Kansas anyway. In Sherman's absence, General Harney assumed the duties of senior military member of the Peace Commission, and in this capacity he controlled directly troops placed at the disposal of the Commission.

Prior to the arrival of the Peace Commission, General Hancock had ordered four companies of the Seventh Cavalry to Fort Harker for escort duty. Only two of them—"G" and "M" companies[17]—rode out of Fort Harker with the Commission. The horse soldiers were supported by the Gatling guns of "B" Battery, Fourth Artillery.[18] Fort Harker was home station for this Gatling unit, which was carried on army lists in 1867 as artillery even though its weapons were not artillery pieces at all but the very effective machine guns. Stanley described the escort in his first dispatches from the Plains, mistakenly identifying the mounted artillerymen as a third company of cavalry. Before the trip was finished, and he had had the opportunity to see the escort more closely and at greater length, he undoubtedly recognized the rapid-fire horse-drawn weapons—they had been along on the Hancock expedition which Stanley covered. But the *Missouri Democrat* reporter never bothered to correct his mistake.

At this point, one difference in modern reporting and in methods

---

[16] Maj. Gen. C. C. Augur, Letter to the Peace Commission, Oct. 12, 1867.

[17] "Company" is the correct term; the term "troop" was not used for cavalry units until a later time.

[18] *Sec. of War 67*, Troop Lists, 40–42.

38

used by the Medicine Lodge press group becomes apparent. In describing the escort, the reporters disagreed on their facts in a great many areas. Yet any of the details could easily have been checked with the escort commander—a procedure the modern correspondent would follow as a matter of course. But minor details of a story never seemed terribly important to these nineteenth-century reporters. They seemed purposely to avoid spending their effort digging out such trivia. They had none of the modern reporter's adoration of minutia. Perhaps it bored them.

Reynolds said there were 200 mounted men in the escort, Brown gave the figure as 150. For the record, Army reports for 1867 indicate that two companies of the Seventh Cavalry would have totaled about 160 men. If the artillery are counted as mounted troops the total comes to about 200.[19] Present-for-duty strengths fluctuated so much from day to day because of sickness, detached service, and desertion that had the escort commander been asked on the spot for his strength he likely would have stopped to count.

None of the reporters named the escort commander properly, if they named him at all. He was identified as Major Allen by some of the reporters. No such major may be found on the rolls of the Seventh Cavalry during this period. He was actually Major Joel H. Elliot, second in command of the regiment. The *Army Register* for 1867 lists Lieutenant Colonel George Armstrong Custer as the commander, but he was not actually present.[20] Custer was still under arrest for absenting himself without proper authority during the Hancock campaign.

Custer's dynamic personality was already leaving its mark on the regiment. There had been internal bickerings and grumblings among many of the officers of the command as a result of Custer's deploy-

[19] *Ibid.*, Adjutant General Report, 475; *Army Lineage Book*, 21–26; *Department of the Army Troop Returns*, 7th Cavalry, 1867; *Cincinnati Commercial*, Oct. 21, 1867.

[20] *Official Army Register*, 34; *Troop Returns*; Richardson, *Comanche Barrier*, 270–74; William E. Connelley, "The Treaty Held at Medicine Lodge," *Kansas Historical Collections*, Vol. XVII (Winter, 1926–27), 602; *Missouri Democrat*, Oct. 21, 1867; *Missouri Republican*, Oct. 19, 1867.

ment of the regiment during the Hancock expedition. None of the Medicine Lodge correspondents took any note of a problem in the two escort companies. However, that something was lacking in morale is illustrated by this fact: For the year ending in September, the Seventh Cavalry reported 512 cases of desertion, for the highest desertion rate in the U.S. Army during 1867—and it is doubtful that the record has been broken since.

The young escort commander whom the reporters identified incorrectly was riding toward a meeting with Indians who would kill him the following year. On the Washita River in 1868, Elliot and a small band of enlisted men would be cut off from the rest of the regiment and slaughtered—by Indians probably correctly identified as Cheyennes, with possible assistance from Comanches and Kiowas. An incident which occurred at the Washita was to be the beginning of a split in the regiment that would plague its officers all the way into the valley of the Little Big Horn. Many subordinates accused Custer of running out on Elliot at the engagement at Washita, claiming that he ordered the regiment away too quickly when the battle turned nasty—leaving Elliot to die.

But in October of 1867, the Big Horn was ahead, and the Washita. The men of the Seventh Cavalry rode as guard for the Peace Commission without the fame and tradition that would later be theirs. The red-and-white guidons fluttering at the head of each company march unit did not yet have the luster of great fighting campaigns. For the Medicine Lodge trip, the "Garry Owen" regiment was simply another unit of the frontier army.

George Brown was first to notice the civilian scouts with the army escorts. He watched them riding ahead of the main body of troops, and out of sight across the rolling plains. Throughout the day they would return, talk with officers of the escort, then ride ahead once more. After the party drew away from the river—the Smoky Hill—Fayel watched the country for game, but saw none. Trees were becoming scarce. During the first day, a few ranches and farms were scattered along the small streams, but the farther south the escorted party traveled, the fewer signs of habitation they could see.[21] The march covered about thirty miles the first day, and camp was made that night on Cow Creek near Fort Zarah. On October 10, they continued toward Fort Larned, swinging west and following the Big Bend of the Arkansas.

At noon each day there was a break in the monotonous ride when the column stopped for lunch. During these halts, outriders were changed. Small parties of troopers rode out to relieve the flank guards. When the wagons were parked, there seemed to be a constant movement of cavalry around them on all sides.

The correspondents would dismount and stretch their legs in the scant shade cast by the ambulances while orderlies unpacked chests of tin eating gear. Soldiers and civilians alike generally lunched on cold meat, cooked that same morning, and hard army crackers. Generals Harney or Sanborn usually brightened the noontime meal by producing a bottle and passing it around. Most of the newsmen used telescoping metal cups, which when not in use could be tucked away in their pockets. George Brown was particularly appreciative of the mid-day bracer, and for his readers back in Cincinnati he explained the merits of warm hospitality and strong liquor. The records show that Sanborn had purchased nine gallons of brandy for the Commission. Whether the noon nips came from this official supply or Harney's and Sanborn's private stock was never fully explained. At any rate, before the trip was over, Sanborn discovered that he had not purchased nearly enough—the supply was exhausted before the thirsty travelers got back to civilization.[22]

While the column was in motion, the reporters were usually segregated from the official party—only Reynolds occasionally rode with the commissioners. The noon stops were a good time for the newsmen to talk with the members of the Peace Commission and size them up. General Harney seems to have made a favorable impression

[21] *Chicago Times*, Oct. 13, 1867; *Cincinnati Commercial*, Oct. 21, 1867; *Missouri Democrat*, October 19, 1867.
[22] Peace Commission, "Accounts Current," *(MS)*, John Sanborn.

on all the newsmen. If Commissioner Taylor was remarkable in breadth, Harney was equally so in height. He had snow-white hair and beard, pale blue eyes, and a sharp hawk nose. He carried himself as though he was on parade—even when sitting down. "He towers above all," wrote Stanley, "like Saul, the chosen of Israel, a goodly man, a tried soldier and gentleman."[23]

Harney took advantage of lunch stops to confer with Major Elliot on the disposition of the escort for the afternoon journey. Sanborn checked his charges, too—the wagon drivers. At an early St. Louis meeting, the Commission had elected Taylor president, Henderson spokesman, and Sanborn purchasing agent in charge of supplies and gifts. Harney had been elected to nothing, but with Sherman gone, he was automatically in charge of all arrangements for movement and defense. The reporters thought him well suited to the task.

Opinion was not so solidly in favor of Sanborn, even though he did share his brandy as frequently as did Harney. Obviously enthusiastic about his work, he was usually last to take his place in one of the lead ambulances after the column stopped. He would run up and down the line of wagons shouting to his drivers, warning them to stay closed up during the march. Sanborn always had a red face, and, according to Stanley and Brown, he was jovial, well mannered, and intimately acquainted with the Indian problem. But Budd wrote in the *Cincinnati Gazette* that Sanborn was "after the almighty dollar." He gave no reason for his opinion nor evidence of its validity.

Early in the trip, Budd had displayed his chronic bad temper in his dispatches. All the correspondents at one time or another said harsh, bitter things about the people around them, but they said many good things as well. Budd found little that he could admire. Out of this large group, the only other reporter in Budd's class for verbal viciousness was Brown—also from Cincinnati. The two men generally held similar opinions concerning people they met. Perhaps Brown took the lead from Budd in some instances—he admitted to a great admiration for Budd. They disagreed about Sanborn, how-

23 "Journal," Aug. 6, 1867; Wirth, *Soldier and Brave*, 35.

ever. Brown believed the small logistical manager for the Commission to be a good man.[24]

By the end of the second day, the appearance of the country had changed. They were in buffalo grazing land, and the grass was thick and high. Fayel—always with an eye out for the farmers among his prospective readers—said the land along the Big Bend of the Arkansas would be profitable for stock raising but that it would never do for grain crops—an interesting observation for central Kansas. Fayel's comment is not absurd when one recalls that only a few years earlier everything west of Missouri was known as the Great American Desert.

As they moved along the Arkansas, the correspondents noticed the rise of flat country to the west that led to the high plains of western Kansas and eastern Colorado, and as far as they could see there were no trees. In the afternoon they met a small party of horsemen traveling east—toward Fort Zarah—and Reynolds heard them mention to the commissioners that Indians from the hostile tribes had set fire to the prairie up ahead. Once the party of travelers had passed out of sight to their rear, the reporters searched the horizon but they could see no horsemen except their own outguards. But before night they saw the fires, burning far out on the barren plains. Dense, black smoke was visible, but the wind quickly carried it away. Brown thought the fires were set by Cheyennes, and he told his readers that those tall warriors had set the torch to the prairie in protest of the Peace Commission's approach. He did not explain how he knew this. None of the others made any such assumptions: They watched and made note of the uneasy conversation among the Peace Commissioners.[25]

As the column closed up for the night's camp, the reporters replaced the dusty coats they had taken off earlier in the day. A chill was in the air, and when the sun went down everyone moved close around their fires. In the darkness beyond the firelight, the cavalrymen could be heard riding back and forth slowly. They were near

[24] *Cincinnati Commercial*, Oct. 22, 1867.
[25] *Chicago Times*, Oct. 13, 1867; *Missouri Republican*, Oct. 21, 1867.

Mule Creek, a small tributary of the Arkansas, about thirty miles from Fort Larned. Waiting for the orderlies to cook their meal, the correspondents stood near the ambulance and watched the fires burning on the prairie. Although it had been a dusty day's ride, there is no record of anyone's leaving the camp to bathe in nearby Mule Creek.

Sometime after dark, a mounted messenger rode into camp from Fort Larned. Reynolds apparently had been visiting the official party and was still in their camp when the rider arrived—he was the only correspondent who mentioned the mounted courier. Soon after the rider dismounted, Commissioner Taylor called a meeting in his tent, one of the few spur-of-the-moment meetings held by the Peace Commission which was recorded in the official minutes.[26] The newsmen were not invited to attend, and from all indications Reynolds was the only reporter who knew the meeting took place.

The emergency meeting resulted from a breakdown in the tribal feeding plan established by the Commission in St. Louis. Here is an excellent example of how confusion seemed to attend the efforts by two separate agencies to administer to the Indians, even when the procedures involved were relatively simple. Indeed, it seemed in dealing with the Indian tribes, there was really no such thing as a simple procedure—any plan went wrong, not because of Indian activity but because of misunderstandings or intentional efforts by one department to abuse or thwart the other.

The Commission had realized that collecting the tribes would take time—all of the Indians could not suddenly appear at the treaty grounds overnight. One thing that might keep the early arrivals in place was food. Therefore, it was planned that once the tribes began arriving at Medicine Lodge, they would be fed by the government.

Indian feeding had always seemed to be an army responsibility. When the Department of the Interior had been created in 1849, the Army Quartermaster was retained as the agency for rationing the tribes. It made a great deal of sense considering that the army already had an established system working and the Department of the Interior did not. In each army department there was an Indian super-

[26] "Journal," Oct. 10, 1867.

intendent whose duties included purchase and distribution of food to the Indian agencies, where army subsistence officers supervised issue. Sherman made use of this system for the Peace Commission when he ordered the Department of the Missouri to make 50,000 rations available for the Indians who would gather at Medicine Lodge. In addition to this army-purchased food, a great deal of subsistence was bought by Sanborn directly from Commission funds.[27]

All of this food—no matter who bought it—was collected at Fort Harker, the end of the tracks. From there it was hauled by the army wagons or by rigs hired by the Peace Commission—through their agent, Thomas Murphy—to Fort Larned. There is was stored for issue to the Department of the Interior people who would provide for its shipment to Medicine Lodge. After his talks with Taylor at Fort Leavenworth, Thomas Murphy had hired a group of men to handle this detail.[28]

As Indians began to arrive on Medicine Lodge Creek, Murphy's task force started to feed them. This group of men was headed by D. A. Butterfield, a well-known trader, freighter, and stage-line operator on the Kansas frontier who was intimately acquainted with the many tribes to be assembled for treaty talks. As Murphy dispatched rations from Fort Larned, Butterfield received them at Medicine Lodge. Wagons had been going back and forth between Larned and the treaty site for a number of days before the Commission moved out of Harker.[29]

Then General Sherman—from Washington—wired his commander at Fort Larned that no further issue of rations would be made until arrival of the Peace Commission. Murphy's supply was suddenly cut off, and his subordinates were seventy miles from the nearest army troops, among 5,000 Indians—some undoubtedly with traces of paint still on their faces—and there was no food. Murphy was afraid the lives of his advance party were in jeopardy, and hoping to break

[27] Ibid., Aug. 16, 1867; Flora Warren Seymore, Indian Agents of the Old Frontier, 40; Martha Buntin, "Difficulties Encountered in Issuing Cheyenne and Arapaho Subsistence, 1861–70," Chronicles of Oklahoma, Vol. XIV (March, 1936), 37–45.
[28] Atchison Daily Champion, Oct. 10, 1867.
[29] Montgomery, "Fort Wallace and Its Relationship to the Frontier," Kansas Historical Collections, Vol. XVII (1926–28), 190f.

the ration deadlock, he sent a rider out of Larned in search of the on-coming Peace Commission.[30]

No one at the Commission meeting could explain why Sherman had stopped the rations. Certainly 150,000 meals had not yet been consumed. This is what 50,000 rations would provide, and food in this amount had been ordered by Sherman. Whatever the reasons, Taylor told the Commission something had to be done quickly. Even if Butterfield and his party were not attacked by the irritated and hungry Indians, a lack of food at the treaty grounds would certainly do nothing to keep the tribes from wandering away. If that happened, the Commission trip to Kansas would be even more dismal than the one up the Platte had been.

Sanborn offered to ride through the darkness to Fort Larned and try to persuade the post commander that rations should be released to Murphy's waiting wagons. If he rode all night, there was a chance of getting a load of rations started by dawn, which would be a full day ahead of the time the Commission could reach Larned. Taylor gave his consent, and Sanborn left the camp, riding out with the courier who had brought Murphy's call for help.[31]

The energetic Sanborn showed considerable courage that night. He had been on the plains enough and he knew enough of Indians to realize that riding in darkness was extremely dangerous. As he rode toward Larned, he unquestionably knew that Plains Indians conducted a considerable portion of their combat operations at night —patroling, raiding, ambushing.

Perhaps Reynolds had stayed nearby after the courier rode in, or he could have been watching the fires still burning on the prairies. In any event, he saw Sanborn leave, and he mentioned it in his next dis-patch to the *Chicago Times*. However, he did not say why the com-missioner was leaving nor did he indicate that an evening meeting had been held.[32] None of the other correspondents reported any part of the incident.

This was the second time the Peace Commission had denied access

---

[30] "Journal," Oct. 10, 1867.   [31] *Ibid.*

[32] *Ibid.*, Aug. 7, 1867; *Chicago Times*, Aug. 8, 1867.

to a meeting. The first time—in St. Louis—the newspapers had reported it. The meeting near Mule Creek was never reported, and likely never known of by anyone in the press party.

Obviously, the Peace Commission did not consider the Sherman order anyone else's business. Had the correspondents known, they could have used it to embarrass Sherman—and there was every indication that most newsmen of that time would have welcomed such a chance. When Sherman left the Commission and returned to Washington, Hall wrote: "We missed—Ah, how we missed—the pleasant face and outstretched hand of the Lieutenant General. We had not the privilege of falling onto that beloved neck." Any student of Sherman's attitude concerning the press—and particularly reporters —can appreciate Hall's sarcasm. Stanley was less biting but more direct: "The corps of correspondents," he said, "feel immensely relieved and bless their stars that Sherman is gone."[33]

The dangers involved in cutting off the ration supply for the Medicine Lodge Indians would have made strong copy for anyone waiting for the chance to discredit Sherman. But there were no press stories, and the only possible conclusion is that the correspondents were unaware that any story existed. Whether they intended it or not, the Peace Commission had effectively throttled the press on that October night.

As for Sanborn, he made it to Larned without misadventure. Fires had been seen to the southwest—the direction in which he traveled— and the moon was nearly full. He made the trip in one of the ambulances, his only protection the mounted courier riding alongside and the soldier driving the vehicle. It was a bad time for the lonely traveler—war parties from any number of tribes could have been riding. But if they were, they missed Sanborn—or perhaps they did not miss him. Perhaps they saw him and let him pass, for reasons only they could know. It was a successful ride. Sanborn had the storehouses opened at the fort, and Stanley reported that just prior to the Peace Commission's arrival at Larned yet another wagon train of supplies had been dispatched to Medicine Lodge Creek.

[33] *Chicago Tribune*, Oct. 19, 1867; *Missouri Democrat*, Oct. 15, 1867.

FOUR

"STINK TOO MUCH WHITE MAN"

—Kiowa

The dangers of the open plains were forgotten as the column neared Fort Larned. In the late afternoon, as the fort came in sight, Thomas Murphy, the Indian superintendent, and Jesse Leavenworth, Kiowa-Comanche Indian agent, rode out to meet the train. Stanley knew Leavenworth from the Hancock expedition, and the correspondent noted that the Indian agent was as irascible as ever. Apparently everyone who met Leavenworth in 1867 was similarly impressed with his temperament. When the agent had begun his tour of duty with the Comanches and Kiowas, according to most observers, he had been a dedicated and not unpleasant man—but a few months trying to keep track of those wildly independent tribesmen south of the Arkansas had soured him. No matter how troubled he was over his Indian charges, Leavenworth got little sympathy from Stanley, although the *Democrat* correspondent had to admit some admiration for Leavenworth's determination to continue in a difficult job.[1]

After a short pause, the Commission column passed between the fort and the Arkansas, moving six miles upstream to cross to the south bank. Commissioner Taylor, Senator Henderson, the Kansas delegation, and two new arrivals stayed with the train. One Commission ambulance—with Harney and Tappan—turned out of line and headed for the fort. The ambulances with the correspondents fol-

[1] Carolyn T. Foreman, "Colonel Jesse Henry Leavenworth," *Chronicles of Oklahoma*, Vol. XIV (March, 1936), 14–29; *Missouri Democrat*, Oct. 21, 1867.

lowed. Fayel told his driver that there was no need to go into the fort, but the soldier replied that he had orders to follow General Harney, no matter where the tall, white-haired soldier went.[2] The press party vehicles all went to Fort Larned, and as a result, the words spoken by Taylor and the others who remained with the train were never reported.

Larned had changed a great deal in the few months since Stanley had been there with Hancock. It was a scattering of buildings on the open plains—nothing imposing or impressive. But since Stanley's last visit there had been much construction, and new frame barracks were standing where there had been nothing but buffalo grass before. The fort was filled with soldiers, as Harker had been, but here there was none of the festive air, with ladies offering lemonade for the dusty travelers. Larned had become a critical link in the army's chain of frontier defenses. Stationed there were units from two infantry regiments, one cavalry regiment, and a Kansas militia cavalry regiment, for a total of eight companies.[3] This was a considerable concentration of power for one post in 1867.

At the sutler's store and saloon, Sanborn and E. W. Wynkoop were waiting to greet the press. The correspondents were ushered into a rear room where Wynkoop offered them a drink from his private liquor chest. They discussed the efforts made by Wynkoop, Leavenworth, and Murphy in collecting the Indians and then holding them at Medicine Lodge. Wynkoop said that some of the work had been done by friendly Indians. He added that at one point he had been threatened with death by the famous Cheyenne warrior, Roman Nose. This may have surprised any of the reporters who had read a *Harper's* account of late June raiding against the railroad. One story told of a soldier shooting Roman Nose in the chest at point-blank range with a .50-caliber Spencer repeating carbine.[4] A chest wound from a .50-caliber projectile would have been fatal in most cases.

[2] *Missouri Republican*, Oct. 21, 1867.

[3] *Ibid.; Sec. of War* 67, 44; Elliot Report; the Larned visit taken from *Chicago Times*, Oct. 22, 1867; *Cincinnati Commercial*, Oct. 21, 1867; *Cincinnati Gazette*, Oct. 22, 1867; *Missouri Democrat*, Oct. 21, 1867; *Chicago Tribune*, Oct. 23, 1867.

[4] *Harper's Weekly*, July 27, 1867.

Although Wynkoop had had his share of troubles with his Cheyennes and Arapahoes, the experience had not destroyed his good humor, Stanley said. The Welshman had met Wynkoop on the Hancock expedition. At that time, he had not been favorably impressed with the Cheyenne-Arapaho agent, but as the group sat in the sutler's saloon and the agent talked, Stanley changed his mind—he reported that Wynkoop was a fine mannered gentleman and a good Indian administrator.

The correspondents learned that a number of tribal leaders were at Larned and that they would meet the Indians before resuming the trip. In fact, the Indians would travel to Medicine Lodge with the Commission. Wynkoop and Sanborn explained that Superintendent Murphy had asked certain chiefs to meet the Commission so that the group could ride into the treaty grounds with a native escort. The correspondents learned that the tribesmen at Medicine Lodge were not overly trusting of the Commission. No one was sure how the Indians might behave when the Commission appeared, and having a few Indian leaders accompany them into the council area was a measure of insurance against sudden violence. Generally, Southern Plains Indians were hospitable in the extreme. But the Peace Commission came with two companies of cavalry and Gatling guns. Even as the correspondents sat in the saloon and talked, infantry troops were preparing to leave Larned to join the Commission escort.

It was some time before the Indians were brought into the small room. S.F. Hall—who appeared to keep close watch on such things—noticed that one of the correspondents was feeling the effects of the liquor Wynkoop so liberally poured into their glasses. Finally Sanborn led about ten Indians into the room. They stood for a few moments blinking in the dim light after having come in from the sun. The reporters stared back at them from across the narrow room.

Satanta, the Kiowa war leader, was there, and Little Raven, the Arapaho chief who enjoyed great popularity in Denver, Colorado.[5] These and the others were named off by Wynkoop. Stanley recog-

[5] Hafen and Hafen, *Reports from Colorado*, 67, 210.

nized Satanta as one of the Kiowas with whom General Hancock had talked during the May expedition. Apparently Satanta recognized Stanley as well, for he crossed the room and greeted the *Democrat* reporter before speaking to anyone else, throwing his arms around the Welshman and laughing.

Satanta may have awed the press corps. Only the most uninformed could have been unaware of his many exploits in Texas and along the southern border of Kansas. He was a large man, and on this occasion his face was painted. From a long rawhide ribbon about his neck, a brass bugle dangled at his waist. There were stories on the frontier about the big Kiowa playing the battered instrument at the slightest provocation. He held a blanket around his body as he moved from reporter to reporter, hugging each one in turn and shouting salutations that no one could understand. Although he knew some English, Satanta spoke his greetings in Kiowa—one of the strangest sounding of all Indian tongues. When the tall Indian came to the small, goateed Reynolds, the contrast must have been amusing. Reynolds did not indicate in any of his copy that he knew Satanta personally or that he had ever met him before. At any rate, the Lawrence editor was impressed with the Kiowa's size, although he had reservations about the hugging: "The embrace was more prolonged than one cares to receive from lately hostile Indians bedaubed with paint and covered with blankets, unless it be strictly in the interest of God and Humanity."

Following Satanta's lead, the other Indians also passed among the correspondents, embracing them and speaking short greetings in their native tongue. Budd watched all of this, and if the Cincinnati reporter's scorn and contempt did not show in his face, it certainly showed in his dispatches. "All white men who think more of Indians than they do of white men," he said, "enjoyed it hugely."

In the close room, quite an odor of smoke and grease must have prevailed. Even Brown, who seemed to be obsessed with Indian vermin and who mentioned it many times during the trip, failed to comment on the Indians' personal cleanliness or other delicate subjects.

He seemed carried away with the proximity of the tribesmen, and he said that it seemed impossible these same people were capable of such bloody deeds against the whites. Perhaps in honor of the event, the chiefs had staked their blankets to an anthill for delousing prior to the meeting. But such a procedure could hardly take the place of soap and water, and in these close confines, the impact on sensitive and unaccustomed nostrils could have been overwhelming. However, the only remarkable thing about the meeting was that of all the correspondents, only Budd found anything uncomplimentary to say about the Indians.

Satanta was the center of interest—a state he obviously enjoyed. As soon as the big Kiowa had walked into the room, Reynolds decided that he was drunk. Drunk or sober, Satanta made a deep impression on the reporters. Hall, Fayel, and Brown were interested in the size of his head—although he was big all over, his head seemed out of proportion. "It is only one inch less than Daniel Webster's," Fayel commented, "about the cranium."

Sanborn and Wynkoop offered the Indians a small drink of whisky, and all accepted. Satanta explained to everyone that he was leader of the Kiowas. Of course, there were a good many warriors among the Kiowas, not to mention other chiefs, who would have disputed the claim, but they were not present. Satanta was as outspoken as the reporters had been led to believe he would be. In broken English, he said that he wanted to get away from Larned because it "stink too much white man." From time to time, the happy Kiowa asked for another drink of whisky.

Satanta was one of the principals to the Medicine Lodge proceedings who would come to a violent end, a victim of the plains war—Major Elliot was another. In 1871, the Kiowa's quick tongue and weakness for bragging would lead to his arrest and trial. He claimed to have led a Texas massacre of seven teamsters, although there was doubt about his real part in the incident. When told he would be tried in Texas for murder, he said he would rather be shot. He was confined in the Texas state penitentiary, later released, and later still returned to prison as the Kiowas' part in the Southwestern wars ebbed and flowed. He would die a suicide in the Huntsville, Texas, prison in 1878.[6]

Satanta occupied so much of the reporters' attention at Larned that the other Indians received but brief mention in the dispatches. Best known of the other tribesmen was Little Raven, whom Stanley said was fat and good natured. Stanley might have added that Little Raven was the social lion of the assembled tribesmen. He had often visited in Denver and seemed honestly to enjoy the company of white men.

Brown later wrote that Little Raven was the orator of the Plains, but he was apparently confused because no one else ever accused the Arapaho chief of being particularly outstanding in council. Budd's report of the Larned meeting contained a remarkable passage "Little Raven of the Kiowas, fat and sassy, laid upon his back, the commissioners passing forward one by one, laying their venerable hands on his heaving bosom." The little ceremony, Budd wrote, was an indication of mutual friendliness. The Cincinnati reporter did not explain what the rite was supposed to mean. There was something obscene about the affair, as Budd described it. Such a bizarre event could hardly have escaped the notice of other correspondents, yet none of them mentioned it, and the incident of the heaving bosom must be classified as fabrication. At Larned, Budd obviously fell into the myth-maker mold—he manufactured his own facts for the sensation seekers among his readers. Perhaps it is too harsh to call Budd a liar, but to say only that he rendered a disservice to his fellow journalists—at Larned and later—would be an understatement.

At any rate, Budd's dispatch to the *Cincinnati Gazette* concerning the Larned visit destroyed his credibility as an Indian "expert"— a term applied to him by the other Ohio reporter, Brown. The "fat and sassy" Little Raven was not a Kiowa as Budd represented him to be, but an Arapaho. Confusing the tribes of particular Indians

[6] H. D. Corwin, *The Kiowa Indians: Their History and Life Story*, 64; Paul I. Wellman, *Death on the Prairie*, 96–100; Dan W. Perry, "The Kiowas' Defiance," *Chronicles of Oklahoma*, Vol. XIV (March, 1936), 30–36.

53

was not an uncommon error, but it was not a mistake one would expect from an "expert."

The party lasted for about one hour after the Indians arrived. No one was dismayed that Wynkoop and Sanborn continued to give the tribesmen a sip of whisky from time to time. Everyone except Budd seemed to enjoy the affair. The Ohioan stayed in the background, and if his account of the event can be credited, he saw nothing about Wynkoop, the Indians, or anybody else present that deserved his admiration—or even his friendship.

Satanta became louder with each drink. He laughed a great deal. William Fayel found the big Kiowa particularly fascinating. There was some reluctance to leave the sutler's saloon, but finally Sanborn moved the party outside. Horses and the ambulances were waiting. A few of the correspondents may have been slightly tipsy, and some confusion resulted as they climbed into the ambulance. The Indians mounted their ponies. At least one of the Indians had an American saddle of fine leather, and all of them had blankets hanging from their horses. As the party rode slowly out of the Fort, soldiers working on new buildings stopped and watched. Although there was loud talking and laughter among the correspondents and the Indians, the soldiers they passed were silent. Soon, they were away from the buildings and picked up the trace of the Peace Commission train, following it upstream along the Arkansas.

The crossing was well used, and there was no problem in driving the ambulances down into the bed of the river. Vegetation that marked the north and south banks of the Arkansas was separated by more than one mile of sand and a few hundred feet of water. The Arkansas—as it does today—meandered between its banks over a wide path of sand in all but flood-stage seasons. The water itself was more grit than wet. Stanley was disappointed that the mighty Arkansas, the waters of which he had seen foaming in the Royal Gorge of Colorado, was no more than two feet deep at mid-stream. The crossing was unexciting.

On the south side of the river, the little caravan found where the tracks of the Peace Commission party had cut into the deep buffalo grass. William Fayel was greatly impressed with the possibilities this country had for raising cattle. The reporters began to realize why the area immediately south of the Big Bend of the Arkansas was a favorite place for Indians to graze their winter-starved war ponies each spring. The grass stood hock deep to the horses, and the wind blowing across it made ripples, like green waves on an ocean.[7]

A few yards from the river, they saw peel-pole markers sunk in the ground by Superintendent Murphy's crew, marking the way toward Medicine Lodge. One mile from the Arkansas was the Peace Commission camp. As the reporters pulled into the campsite, the sun was setting, and it was not until later—when the sun's brightness had left the western sky—that they noticed another red glow. Once more, someone had set fire to the prairie, this time south of the Arkansas.

The evening meal was being prepared by orderlies as the newsmen dismounted from their ambulances and gathered around the cook fires. With sunset, it had turned cold, and they ate sitting near the fires. Information was passed to the correspondents from the official party that there would be a Peace Commission meeting that night. The Indians who had accompanied them from Fort Larned were in their own tentless camp nearby. Some of the reporters heard Satanta laughing early in the evening, but as the Commission meeting began, there was no other sound to indicate that Indians were in the camp.

The Commission meeting on the open prairie south of the Arkansas was mentioned by every correspondent except Bulkley of the *New York Herald*. All the correspondents except Bulkley used long letters to their editors to report the progress of the Commission. These documents—handwritten and often bulky—were dispatched to their destination by mail, and as a result it was always quite some time before the stories were printed. Apparently the *New York Herald* valued speed over detail. Bulkley sent only one letter, which contained a number of separate dispatches, but the rest of the story he told with short telegrams. This was a step toward modern news reporting, and only one of many areas in which the *Herald* led the way.

[7] *Missouri Democrat*, Oct. 21, 1867; *New York Tribune*, Oct. 23, 1867.

Bulkley may have dispatched letters as well as wires, but if he did his editors failed to print them. The *Herald* told the story of the Peace Commission trip from Harker to Medicine Lodge in thirty-eight lines. In the *New York World*, Milton Reynolds' copy fared even worse. Of all the New York papers, only the *Tribune* covered the Commission movements with more than a few sentences.[8]

The contrast between the *Herald* and the *Tribune* coverage of the treaty was indicative of the differences between those two great newspapers in 1867. In the *Herald*, the story was sharp, to the point, and with a minimum of color. Horace Greeley's paper—with Stanley supplying the copy—was long-winded and eloquent, with every story squeezed for each drop of emotional juice that was in it. The *Tribune* was still hanging onto the old ways of personal, individual journalism; the *Herald* was bringing in the dynamic era of fast-moving news and emotionless reporting. The two men who wrote for these papers were well suited for the task. Stanley, for the *Tribune*, produced human documents; Bulkley, of the *Herald*, was as impersonal as a telegraph key.

That first night south of the Arkansas, the Kansas delegation had the opportunity to put their views on record. Before the Peace Commission came to the Kansas plains, a letter had been sent Governor Crawford asking for his ideas on the Indian situation. With officials of the Commission and some of the correspondents gathered around the fire, Taylor called the meeting to order, and Senator Henderson rose to address the Kansans. On the trail from Harker, Crawford and his friend Senator E. G. Ross had asked certain questions concerning the Peace Commission's intentions regarding the Indians of the South Plains. Henderson was now ready to answer the Kansans' questions.

As chairman of the Senate Indian Affairs Committee, Henderson probably knew as much about legal obligations to the tribes as any other man on the Commission. Along with Tappan and Sanborn, the

[8] *New York Herald*, Oct. 9, 1867; *New York Tribune*, Oct. 7, 15, 23, 1867; *New York World*, Oct. 7, 19, 1867.

Missouri Senator was an expert on the treaty promises the United States had made to the various tribes. He told Governor Crawford about previous treaties and how they affected the Medicine Lodge negotiations. Crawford was somewhat impatient with this dialogue, failing to see the connection with former treaties and the one about to be made. Some of the correspondents agreed with the Governor.[9] Crawford explained that his state was very concerned about the number of Indians wandering about. They were even more concerned about the possibility that the Peace Commission would take additional Kansas lands and make federal Indian reservations on them. Too much land in Kansas was already in Indian hands, Crawford said, and the state had an unfair share of tribes. One might meet Cheyennes, Arapahoes, Kiowas, and any number of "tame" Indians on a trip from Fort Harker to Lawrence. The Osage reservation—which extended from Indian Territory into southern Kansas—should be returned to state control.

After Henderson had finished his outline of previous treaties—a discourse interrupted often by the Kansas governor—Crawford presented a written report to the Commission. The entire text of the document was printed in the *Chicago Times* and *Cincinnati Commercial* essentially as it later appeared when Crawford published it. It was a curious document.

The report started with a short description of what had happened on the frontier since the Sioux uprising in Minnesota during the war. From that time, Crawford claimed, all the Plains Indians had been members of an alliance to wage a general war against the whites. The Indian army was "powerful, well organized and equipped." Such a comment must seem remarkable to any serious student of the Plains Indians. Most accounts would lead one to believe—and certainly the Indian fighting itself and the results thereof—that the tribes were

[9] Crawford, *Kansas*, 265–72; account of Oct. 11 meeting taken from *Chicago Times*, Oct. 13, 1867; *Chicago Tribune*, Oct. 17, 19, 26, 1867; *Cincinnati Commercial*, Oct. 28, 1867; *Missouri Democrat*, Oct. 21, 1867; *Missouri Republican*, Oct. 21, 1867; *New York Tribune*, Oct. 23, 1867.

never noted for their ability to co-operate with one another, even in the simplest endeavor.[10] Raising a well-organized and well-equipped army is not a simple matter. To attribute to the Plains warriors the administrative- and organizational-management abilities required to create an allied army and wage a general war appears somewhat over optimistic of their real capabilities.

Most of the Crawford paper was taken up with a list of depredations, many by Comanches and Kiowas but the majority by Cheyennes. Both General Hancock and Agent Leavenworth had claimed that neither the Kiowas or Comanches had broken any treaty in Kansas since the peace councils on the Little Arkansas.[11] If Crawford and others on the frontier disagreed on what had been happening in Kansas, it appeared that all were aware of depredations elsewhere. There was no lack of evidence that Comanches and Kiowas had been active south of Red River. It was a time of war parties west of the Brazos—stolen horses, shattered families, captured children, missing travelers, and deserted ranches. Yet, for some unexplained reason, the Peace Commission seemed unconcerned with what had happened in Texas. When Leavenworth and others spoke before the Commission, they made great to-do about the purity of the Comanches and Kiowas in Kansas while admitting that there were captive women, children and grisly trophies—from Texas—in Comanche and Kiowa lodges.[12] It was as though the Red River was more than a political boundary; what was criminal north of the line was acceptable behavior to the south. It would be a few years yet before outrages occurring in Texas were of concern to the nation as a whole.

Governor Crawford felt that raids were taking place in Kansas too frequently and that they were too big to be caused by Cheyennes alone. This was one of the few times the Governor ever had anything good to say about Indians—that the Cheyennes were incapable of making all the misery with which they were charged. But in addi-

[10] *Sec. of War 67*, 67; Crawford, *ibid.*; Lindquist, "Indian Treaty Making," *Chronicles of Oklahoma*, Vol. XXIV (Winter, 1948–49), 416–48.

[11] *Sec. of War 67*, Sherman Report, 29–37; Commissioner *Report 67*, 314–16.

[12] *Ibid.*

tion to the wild tribes, the Kansas Governor accused the Osages of engaging in hostilities. He claimed that much of Kansas' problem was the result of the inefficiency of Agent Leavenworth and graft, disinterest, and thefts among government employees on the Osage reservation.[13]

Listening to all of this, the correspondents in the group were split in their opinions of the value of Governor Crawford's report. For obvious reasons, the newspaperman most interested in what Crawford had to say was Milton Reynolds, of the Lawrence *State Journal*. He was acid in his criticism of the Governor, Senator Ross, and the views of these two men. Supposedly, Reynolds had made the trip for the same purpose as the other newsmen—to report the business of the Peace Commission. But his real reason appeared to be local—to tell his Lawrence readers what the Kansas governor was doing. There was no question where the goateed editor stood in regard to Governor Crawford's policies. Everything Crawford or Senator Ross said, Reynolds pounced on with a verbal fury that was at once disconcerting and magnificent. The general theme of the Crawford-Ross line was constructed around the probability of an Indian war and involved raising more Kansas troops for federal service on the frontier. Reynolds was opposed to putting more Kansas militiamen on duty, and he thought the idea of a "general Indian war" was preposterous. He frankly admitted that Indian depredations and raiding could become general across the frontier, but he did not for a moment believe that the tribes were capable of a "general war" in the sense of coordinated action against the whites.

The subscribers to the *Chicago News* read this Reynolds' paragraph after the Crawford paper was presented to the Peace Commission:

> The politics of this state are terribly muddled and mixed and a systematic attempt has been made by Governor Crawford and his partisans to drag the Indian question into the dirty pool. Political aspirants induce the government to proclaim the Manifest Falsehood that white settlers had a right to go onto the Indian lands

[13] *Ibid.*, 8; Graves, *River*, 113.

in spite of treaty stipulations. . . . It is not to be presumed that either is a scoundrel or would steal anything from the government or the Indians—of course not!

This outburst was the result of the Crawford-Ross contention that white Kansans needed all the land in the state, whether previously set aside for Indians by treaty or not. The most remarkable thing about the tirade is not the libel of Governor Crawford's character, but Reynolds' views on Manifest Destiny and the Indian problem.

Reynolds was particularly protective of the Osages—who were not involved in the business of the Peace Commission, as both Reynolds and Governor Crawford knew. He accused the Kansas chief executive of lying in an attempt to influence a policy that would return Osage lands to state control. Even before the October 11 meeting south of the Arkansas—when Crawford read his paper—Reynolds wrote:

> There has been no hostile spirit manifested by the Osages in spite of the persistent presentations of Governor Crawford and his friends to the contrary. . . . A few months since, it was reported that a railroad train had been thrown off the track above Ellsworth. Immediately one of Crawford's spies and informers at Topeka telegraphed —and the lying dispatch was published all over the country—that the Osages committed the outrage, when every intelligent man in Kansas knows that the Osages were not within 200 miles of Ellsworth at the time.

Crawford and Ross may have been working honestly for the welfare of their state, and on the other hand they may have been as black-hearted as Reynolds painted them. Osage sources claimed that Crawford encouraged white men to move onto Osage lands—and saw to it that they went well armed. It was no secret that both Crawford and Ross were interested in a new railroad to the southwest, one that would traverse Osage country.[14] Extinguishing Osage land titles could mean a new railroad, with enormous profits for stockholders in critical government positions.

14 *Cong. Globe 67*, 703; Mathews, *Osages*, 659–60.

At that first meeting with a Kansas delegation, there was no hint that Senator Henderson would side with Crawford in his advocacy of moving the Osages out of Kansas and returning the Indian lands to the whites. But there was evidence that the rest of the Peace Commission took seriously and literally the wording of the bill creating the commission on which they served. They were there to deal with tribes hostile to the United States, and the Osages did not fit the description. The Commission's refusal to act on Crawford's accusation against the Osages was an indication that the commissioners took his charges with some of the same grains of salt Reynolds insisted upon.

Criticism of Crawford was not confined to Reynolds' copy. Henry Stanley reported that the Governor's testimony before the Commission was strongly tinged with prejudice. Hall—who had spent some time in southern Kansas himself—was almost as brutal as Reynolds in his treatment of Crawford in his columns to the *Chicago Tribune*:

> Governor Crawford does not breathe all peace but favors hostilities which will require enlistment of 10,000 Kansas troops. He has much to say about the rascality of the Indians. To him, the life of one male inhabitant of Ellsworth is worth more than the lives of all the aboriginals that ever lived in America, including all those who tolerated and protected white men 300 years ago.

The Chicago correspondent was not satisfied with an attack on Kansas politicians alone—he went after Kansas newspapers as well. Reynolds had written that false reports of Indian depredations had been printed all over the country, but Hall was more specific. He accused the *Leavenworth Conservation* and the *Atchison Champion* of spreading wild tales known to be untrue. He added that all of this was done to further Crawford's aims and to deceive the honest seeker of fact. Hall said that many high-ranking army officers had been duped by such publications into believing that there was more trouble on the Plains than really existed.

Hall and Stanley explored many background elements in the Kansas situation, but one they missed would have been obvious to a modern reporter trying to discredit the Governor—the profit motive. It would have been easy to publish facts that would have damaged Crawford's image of purely moral wrath against savagery. There was money to be made in war, as any Leavenworth merchant could have testified.

For example, a single army contract made in 1867 in Leavenworth called for hauling supplies to various posts throughout the state. The rates ranged from $1.54 to $1.65 per hundredweight per hundred miles. This single contract involved "about" 1½ *million pounds* of supplies. In addition to the freight rate, had this contract called for hauling nothing but hay—about the cheapest commodity sold in Kansas in 1867—more than $11,000 would have changed hands. One good cavalry horse cost an average of $159 in Kansas during that year.[15] To operate in the field, a cavalry regiment needed one thousand horses. Obviously, Kansas shippers and merchants were making fortunes—and could make larger ones—and certainly Crawford was aware of this. Each garrison strengthened meant payrolls, more paving bricks, more coal, more oats, more of everything. Kansans stood ready to sell or haul. But hard as they tried to discredit Governor Crawford, Stanley and Hall did not mention the economic reasons for his policies.

William Fayel, of the *Missouri Republican,* did not commit himself on the Crawford paper. He said in his St. Louis column that the Governor and Senator Ross were urging with all their official influence for troop strengths to be maintained in Kansas. He quoted Ross: "Give us the military to complete the roads, then the buffalo and Indians will leave."

Brown and Budd were both in sympathy with Crawford's views. Budd did not deal with the October 11 meeting—probably he was in bed—but there was no doubt about his sentiments in regard to the Indians. He wrote:

> While the pioneer men of our country are opening to civilization this country, they are met and scalped by the Noble Red Men, with

[15] U.S. Congress (HR), *Report of the Quartermaster General* (1867), 534.

a dishonest Commissioner (Taylor) who has swindled them out of a large fortune, sitting and drinking with pride his shame and demanding "the Indians want peace."

What Budd meant specifically in this paragraph is anybody's guess. Although he constantly attacked the members of the Peace Commission for being dishonest, he never gave any details.[16]

The other Cincinnati correspondent—Brown—was impressed with one portion of the Crawford report. He wrote at length on the Indian depredations Crawford described.

There was one other thing Crawford discussed with the Commission. He wanted Leavenworth removed from his job as the Comanche-Kiowa Indian agent. Henry Stanley was present when the commissioners discussed the problem among themselves. They spoke of replacing Wynkoop, too, because he was in bad standing with the Cheyennes. Perhaps both agents should be removed, they said, so that the treaty negotiations could proceed. But after a short while, they decided that such a move was not justified. It would have been a terrible blow to both Leavenworth and Wynkoop to relieve them just before the treaty council—a meeting they had both worked hard to organize. The commissioners undoubtedly understood this, as did Stanley. There was no indication that either agent was ever told that the Kansas governor had suggested changes in their administration. Wynkoop had not joined the camp, and Leavenworth had returned to Larned and would not rejoin the party until the following morning. At any rate, Commissioner Taylor's good opinion of both men remained steadfast.[17]

Stanley was steadfast, too. During the Hancock campaign, he had not been favorably impressed with the Indian agent's viewpoint—either Wynkoop's or Leavenworth's—but from his report of the Kansas delegation meeting on October 11 throughout the remainder of the trip, he wrote of both men in glowing terms.

Nothing was settled at the meeting. Crawford and Ross wanted assurances that no reservations would be established in Kansas and

[16] *Cincinnati Gazette*, Aug. 9, 1867. Italics are Budd's.
[17] Commissioner *Report 67*, 309f., Commissioner *Report 68*, 62f., 65.

that troop strengths would be maintained. The Peace Commission was not ready to commit itself on either point. Senator Henderson continued to speak diplomatically with Crawford as the Kansan continued to protest Indians' living in his state. General Harney was becoming more and more blunt, and it was obvious to Henry Stanley that the tall white-haired soldier was developing an intense dislike for Crawford. The fact that Henderson did not deal roughly with Crawford appeared to make Harney even more angry. As it later turned out, the October 11 meeting may have been the beginning of bad feelings between the two Commission members—Harney and Henderson—that would later cause tense moments for everyone. Stanley saw at least a part of this. He wrote, "The situation presents serious difficulties."

As the meeting was breaking up, Indian Superintendent Murphy called Commissioner Taylor and others of the official party aside and spoke to them of another problem. William Fayel was standing nearby. Murphy was concerned about the military escort. In a letter to Commissioner Taylor on October 5, the Indian Superintendent had emphasized that the military escort should be small and made up of well-disciplined regulars.[18] Now, having seen the temper of the tribes as they were collected on the Medicine Lodge, Murphy felt that perhaps the Peace Commission should take no escort at all. He was afraid the sight of armed riders might disturb the Indians—they might disappear into the vast prairie, or they might start shooting.

It was apparent to Fayel that the comment disturbed the members of the Commission who heard it. On the one hand, they were anxious to fulfill their obligations by meeting with the tribesmen and making a treaty. But on the other, they had little desire to go into a huge Indian camp without army protection. Murphy said he was sure the Indians would remain friendly so long as the Commission did not come among them with soldiers and weapons. The Commission was not so confident. Taylor refused to consider leaving the army units behind. No purpose could be served if the members of the Commis-

[18] "Journal," Oct. 10, 1867.

sion were all slaughtered. "Matters look a little squally," Fayel reported.

There was good reason for the commissioners to be uneasy about the prospect of entering a camp of some four thousand Southern Plains Indians without soldiers. And fifty soldiers were able to offer but little protection. The Cheyennes had stopped raiding, but most of them were still staying away from the treaty grounds—assembled within easy striking distance. The Kiowas were traditionally unpredictable, and certainly Harney must have been aware of their reputation. These fine, delicate-featured horseman were claimed to be the most vicious, ruthless, unprincipled Indians on the Great Plains.[19] If trouble should develop, most assuredly the Comanches would throw in their lot behind Indian friends—although they were not overly fond of the Cheyennes, their loyalty to the Kiowas was already well known. Only the Arapahoes could be considered trustworthy, and many of them were not resigned to peace.

Against this force of potential savagery there stood only a handful of soldiers and two Gatling guns. But the Peace Commission was determined to go on their way to Medicine Lodge. And of course, the correspondents were bound to go with them—that was their assignment. Not all the brave men on the Great Plains carried a lance or a carbine. Many of them carried only a handful of well-used pencils.

If Murphy's words had brought on the specter of violence as a result of any mishandling of the treaty talks, the sight of burning prairies could have done little to ease tension as the commissioners and the correspondents went to their beds. It was late, and most of them were quickly in their tents, but George Brown stood in the darkness for a while and watched the distant fires.

[19] Mooney, "Calendar History," 233f.; Corwin, *Kiowa Indians,* 64; Josiah Gregg, *Commerce of the Prairies,* 250; M. Morgan Eastergreen, *Kit Carson: A Portrait in Courage,* 49.

FIVE

"WE LOOK ON YOU
WITH GREAT GLADNESS"
—Comanche

On the morning of October 12, the Peace Commission waited for Leavenworth and Wynkoop to join them before taking the trail south to Medicine Lodge.[1] When the agents arrived, near noon, they brought with them thirty additional wagons loaded with Indian gifts and two companies of infantry riding in army ambulances. The troops were Company "F," Third Infantry, and Company "K," Fifth Infantry. At Harker, Bulkley had spoken with one of the commissioners and learned that infantry troops would join the party at Larned. Both Brown and Stanley noted the addition to the escort, but neither of them identified the units.

Bulkley's dispatch to the *New York Herald* concerning the infantry escort gives us additional information. After the meeting of the evening before—when there was tension and talk of Indian violence—one might suspect that General Harney or Commissioner Taylor asked the Larned commander for the additional troops. This was not the case however, because Bulkley's report of the addition to the escort had come days before the extra troops actually arrived. The use of two infantry companies had been planned all along, and they just happened to come at a time when spirits needed bolstering.

As the column got under way, Reynolds counted 211 vehicles in

[1] Material for the Oct. 12 account taken from October and November issues of all newspapers represented except *Harper's Weekly* and *Leslie's Illustrated Newspaper*.

66

the line, but Stanley reported only 175. Possibly the *Missouri Democrat* reporter did not count the ambulances of the official party and the escort, but he missed little else. He wrote that there were 1,250 animals in the column and "about 600 men, counting camp followers." Stanley continued to speak of camp followers throughout the trip, but he never clearly identified them.

Medicine Lodge Creek was over sixty miles distant. The road staked out by Murphy was straight, and it dipped down sharply into the shallow valleys that were becoming more numerous farther south of the Arkansas. The rolling prairie was covered with a thick carpet of buffalo grass. On the flanks, Major Elliot had increased the number of outriders, and on the rolling terrain, the riders often dipped out of sight.

There was more here to interest the correspondents than there had been north of the river. For one thing, the land had a richer look. Trees appeared along the small streams, and the grass was often belly deep to the horses. Alongside the official party ambulances rode the Indians the reporters had met the day before at Larned. From time to time, the newsmen could see Satanta talking with General Harney in the lead ambulance. Behind them, the correspondents could see the heavy wagons cutting ruts in the soft sod and beating down the grass. Each wagon was drawn by three spans of mules. The drivers' language was remarkable enough to be mentioned in a number of dispatches.

Word was passed along that the party would camp on Rattlesnake Creek that night. It was mid-afternoon when one of the outriders came back toward the column and shouted that there was buffalo ahead. The reporters stood up in the ambulances and tried to see. Soon a large herd of buffalo was sighted, and as the wagons drew nearer, the animals continued their quiet grazing, ignoring the passing train. A hunt was quickly organized, amid a great deal of excitement. Horse holders rode up to the ambulances with spare cavalry mounts. Commissioner Taylor's son and *Harper's* artist John Howland jumped from the ambulance and scrambled onto horses. As he rode off, his buckskin fringes flying, Howland was cheered by the other correspondents. Extra wagon drivers in the column joined the hunt, and some of the soldiers rode into the herd. Gunfire soon sounded, and the herd began moving away from the column.[2]

Most of the hunters dismounted and cut the tongues from animals they had shot. Others took the time to cut hump steaks from their buffaloes. Some just shot the animals and left them, riding on to continue the hunt. Hunters began to return to the train. As young Taylor and Howland rode up to one of the newsmen's ambulances, Brown described the scene: "They soon came in with bloody hands and the red tongues of their victims hanging from their saddle pommels." While Taylor and Howland told the press party about their prowess with a rifle, the shooting continued on the prairie. The hunt was turning into a slaughter.

Satanta was furious. The big Kiowa's disposition was probably not too sweet at best, now that the effects of the sutler's whisky had worn off. Both Stanley and Fayel noticed Satanta observing the buffalo hunt with a deep scowl. When the Indian started to complain to General Harney, everyone on the train noticed his displeasure. He was loud, and he expressed himself in most emphatic terms. Harney was hardly less disturbed than was the Kiowa. He ordered the shooting stopped, and he ordered Major Elliot to place certain of the hunters under arrest. Elliot rode into the herd a second time— he had been hunting earlier—and soon all the hunters returned to the column.

Most of the correspondents saw Harney's action as reasonable, but Brown wrote:

> Why was this? Because we were in hostile country and because Satanta and the Indians with us found fault with the killing of their buffalo, since it was their country and their game, and since the animals were some of them left to rot on the prairie to stench up the air that the *Noble Red Man* was to breathe![3]

[2] The buffalo account taken from *Chicago Tribune*, Oct. 22, 1867; *Cincinnati Commercial*, Oct. 21, 1867; *Missouri Democrat*, Oct. 21, 1867; *Missouri Republican*, Oct. 21, 1867.

[3] Italics are Brown's.

Brown ignored the reason for Satanta's anger. The Kiowas might butcher a man for the fun of it, but never a buffalo. Brown must have understood this as well as anyone else, but the incident offered a good opportunity to show Peace Commission subservience to Indian whim, and the reporter from Cincinnati took advantage of it.

In less than an hour, the column reached Rattlesnake Creek, and the night's camp took form as it had since the Commission left Fort Harker. But here the various elements of the encampment—official party, wagon park, and escort—were set closer together than at earlier campsites, and soldiers patrolled throughout the area, cavalrymen on horseback around the perimeter and infantrymen on foot among the tents. After the orderlies had the tents pitched and the fires started, many of the reporters wrote dispatches with the dateline "Rattlesnake Creek." Some of them noted that the wind south of the Arkansas did not seem to blow with the same persistence as it did farther north. By the time the newspapermen gathered around the fires for the evening meal, the sun was down, and it had turned cold. They were in high spirits, however, as they ate hump steaks and roast tongue. There is no record of Satanta's eating anything.

Beyond Rattlesnake Creek, the plains were wild and empty. Fayel looked for ranch and farm buildings, but he saw none. But if there were no signs of human habitations, there was game. Hall saw geese flying south, and the column passed a number of buffalo herds. No one rode out to shoot any of the big animals, and they continued grazing as the column passed by. Toward evening, someone pointed to smoke on the southern horizon. The prairie was on fire once more.

That night, after everyone was in bed, a small party of horsemen rode into camp. There were calls from a number of sentries as the group rode to the official party tents. Major General C. C. Auger and a small group of aides had just come from the end of the track at Harker on horseback. The General carried a letter to the Peace Commission outlining the Presidential order appointing him to serve in Sherman's absence.[4] Now the party was complete, and Medicine Lodge Creek was only a part of a day's ride away.

[4] Augur, LS; Everett Rich (ed.), *The Heritage of Kansas*, 22f.

On October 14, the Peace Commission pushed on, and although no one in the column saw Indian riders watching them, the coming of the train was known in the tipis along the Medicine Lodge. Early in the day, tribal leaders were gathering at one end of the Indian camp, their ponies ready for the ride out to meet the commissioners.

When the head of the column was within a few miles of the Indian encampment, Harney signaled Major Elliot, and the escort commander rode in to confer with the General. After a short talk— Elliot riding his horse alongside Harney's ambulance—the escort officer returned to his troops and moved them to the rear of the column. Outriders were called in, and the infantry ambulances also were dropped back. Stanley noted that Harney was doing everything he could to avoid annoying the Indians or provoking them to hasty action.

None of the press representatives mentioned any quickening of the heart beat as the entourage neared the Indian camp. The camp, though still out of sight, lay just ahead. The detachment was coming in naked, its armed protection behind, its flanks unguarded. Crossing the last rise, the men entered the small natural basin where Medicine Lodge and Elm creeks joined. To the left rose the gentle, wooded rise of ground that gave the place its Indian name—Timbered Hill River. Ahead stood a small band of painted Indians.[5]

Tension lessened as Harney and the other commissioners dismounted and met the Indian leaders on foot. Embraces and handshakes were exchanged. The interpreters, who always stayed near the commissioners, hurried up, and the Indians, too, had a number of interpreters. The tribesmen were still welcoming the Peace Commission as the correspondents moved forward and stood a short distance away, watching and listening.

The most notable member of the Indian welcoming committee was Black Kettle. He was known to both Sanborn and Tappan, and

---

[5] Valley and camp descriptions taken from *Atchison Daily Champion*, Sept. 17, 1867; *Chicago Times*, Oct. 22, 1867; *Chicago Tribune*, Oct. 24, 1867; *Cincinnati Commercial*, Oct. 24, 1867; *Cincinnati Gazette*, Oct. 22, 1867; *Missouri Democrat*, Oct. 21, 1867; *Missouri Republican*, Oct. 24, 25, 1867.

the reporters listened to what the Cheyenne chief was saying. The journalists knew the chief from the various reports they had heard of his efforts to promote peace, but as far as is known, this was the first time any of them had seen him.

As Black Kettle talked with Taylor, Sanborn, and Henderson, S. F. Hall noted the Missouri Senator's appearance, finding it amusing; "His nose was a bright yellow while a red streak adorned one cheek and a few green patches the other." The Senator's colorful decorations were the result of too many close and enthusiastic hugs from the tribesmen. As the chiefs stood before the Commission, General Harney was probably looking closely at the Indians' paint to detect anything that might mean trouble, but apparently no black paint was present on any of the faces. Although the paint held little meaning for the gentlemen of the press, Harney knew that black was associated with death, and any number of other unpleasant things.

A different account of this initial meeting, largely disprovable, was apparently created by A. A. Taylor, son of the Indian Commissioner. Writing his account of the treaty meeting some twenty years later, Taylor claimed the Indians rode out en masse to meet the commissioners. They were in a vast circular formation, Taylor said, with each successive ring of horsemen riding in opposite directions to create the illusion of a pinwheel. As this circling continued—all at full gallop—the whole mass of horsemen moved closer to the head of the Peace Commission column. When the edge of this horse-and-human pinwheel came within one hundred yards of the commissioners, the turning suddenly ceased, and the Indian horsemen drew aside to form an aisle from the rim of the wheel to its center. Through the opening thus created the commissioners passed to be greeted in the center of the wheel by the Indian leaders.[6]

Such a maneuver would have been an accomplishment for even a a highly disciplined body of cavalry—for Plains Indians from several

---

[6] Taylor, "The Medicine Lodge Peace Council," *Chronicles of Oklahoma*, Vol. II (June, 1924), 103. Taylor's account appears in a number of secondary sources among which are Carl Coke Rister, *Border Captives*, 138; Clyde and Grace Jackson, *Quanah Parker*, 61; Stanley Vestal, *Warpath and Council Fires*, 121.

71

different tribes, it would have been remarkable. Such a performance would certainly have caught the attention of the reporters in the party, but none of them mentioned the incident.

The correspondents—particularly Stanley—were examining the area as the Indian welcome speeches to the Peace Commission continued. Throughout the valley stood scattered stands of trees—cottonwood, elm, sassafras, and persimmon. The leaves of the smaller trees were already turning red and gold, but there had been no heavy frost yet, and the fruit on the persimmon trees was still bright orange in color.

The Commission had entered the valley at its northwestern end, and the nearest Indian encampment was that of the Arapahoes—at the base of the Timbered Hill. Directly ahead of them, near the Medicine Lodge, was Butterfield's ration camp; across the stream was a small Cheyenne camp. The Cheyenne camp and the ration camp were about all the reporters could see as they rode into the valley, but from their talks with Indians later in the day, many of them were able to reconstruct the entire encampment for their readers. On the near side of the Medicine Lodge and beyond the Arapahoes were the Plains Apaches.

Directly across the creek from the latter were the Comanches, and farthest downstream—on the south side—was the Kiowa camp. Although most of the site was not visible to the correspondents, the area which they could see through the groves of trees was covered with tipis, horse herds, and Indians.

Stanley used a great deal of space to describe the camp, but he may have been mistaken in one important respect. He placed the small Cheyenne encampment of Black Kettle at the far end of the treaty ground—some ten miles away. Later, Cheyennes told George Bird Grinnell that the initial Cheyenne camp was directly across the stream from the site of the Peace Commission camp.[7] This site seems more likely because throughout the meetings, Black Kettle stayed near the commissioners, talking with them each night. Also, it would have been logical for the Cheyennes to camp near their allies the

[7] Grinnell, *Cheyennes*, 207–49.

Arapahoes rather than beside the Kiowas. Except to the Comanches, Kiowas were uncertain friends to say the least.

During the course of this conversation with the Indians, the Commission members were shocked at Black Kettle's warning that the Cheyennes camped on the Cimarron might decide to attack the peace meeting. The commissioners knew about the Cimarron camp. Black Kettle explained that, although he was in favor of peace, a great many other Cheyenne leaders were eager to get on with the war. According to the correspondents, the Cheyenne's words put a sudden stop to the leisure good humor of the meeting. Brown said Black Kettle's comments caused "no inconsiderable panic."[8]

General Harney quickly moved to establish the Peace Commission camp. He issued orders to have the ambulances drawn up to form a ring barricade, with cook fires and tents in the center. No one would leave the enclosure after dark without a pass from Harney. As the ambulances pulled into position and the teams were being unhitched, the wagon train assembled nearby, and the escort rode into camp a short distance upstream. The Negro orderlies pitched tents and started campfires in the hollow square of ambulances. The reporters could hear mules braying and trace chains rattling as the teamsters picketed their animals in the wagon park. From downstream, dogs were barking in the Indian camps. Although the welcoming party of chiefs had disappeared among the lodges, there were a great many Indians watching the Peace Commission camp as darkness settled along the Medicine Lodge.

Brown and Hall spent the evening writing dispatches, but they were the only correspondents thus engaged on that first uneasy night in camp. Once the animals in the wagon park were quiet and the Indian dogs had stopped yammering, the waters of the Medicine Lodge could be heard flowing between its banks. It is not difficult to imagine the thoughts that came to Brown as he looked between the ambulances and beyond the firelight to see the dark shapes of warriors in the trees across the stream. The Indians had only recently been engaged in hostilities, he wrote, and "their hands [were

[8] *Cincinnati Commercial*, Oct. 24, 1867; *Missouri Democrat*, Oct. 25, 1867.

73

still] reeking with the blood" of innocent victims. But curiosity, not murderous intent, brought the Indians to stand in the dark and watch. There were no alarms during the night, and the guard was not called on to prevent the white men's being butchered in their sleep. Except for the slow tread of the passing soldiers, or the occasional howl of an Indian dog from down river, the night was quiet, and to Hall unseasonably cold.[9]

Allowing the Peace Commission to rest undisturbed for a moment, we should now give some attention to the difficult and dangerous job which had been done in assembling the tribes for the negotiations.

No head count of the Indians at Medicine Lodge was attempted, but Superintendent Murphy estimated there were about 3,126 in the Medicine Lodge camp and another 1,200 on the Cimarron.[10] Additional bands arrived at the treaty grounds throughout the course of the treaty councils, and there were a number of tribes camped on the prairie nearby—Indians who had no part in the meetings but had come to watch. At any given time, the total number in the immediate area was probably well over 5,000. It was very nearly a standard procedure to overestimate the numbers of Indians involved in frontier incidents—not only by newspapermen but by settlers and the army as well—but the correspondents' reports from Medicine Lodge were on the conservative side. They accepted Murphy's estimate and used the number 5,000 in many of their stories.[11]

Collecting these Indians—many of them hostile, most of them skeptical—was no small task. The success of the operation was due almost entirely to the efforts of Murphy and his two major subordinates, Wynkoop and Leavenworth, who had sent runners among the Indians in August with news of the coming treaty talks.[12] The

[9] *Chicago Tribune*, Oct. 22, 1867; *Cincinnati Commercial*, Oct. 21, 1867.

[10] "Journal," Aug. 12, 1867.

[11] Watson, "The Indian Wars and the Press," *Journalism Quarterly*, Vol. XVII (December, 1940), 301–10; Aug. 12, Sept. 12, 1867; *Chicago Times*, Oct. 9, 1867; *Cincinnati Commercial*, Oct. 21, 1867; *New York Herald*, Oct. 28, 1867.

[12] Commission *Report 67*, 314f.; "Journal," Sept. 19, 1867; *Atchison Daily Champion*, Sept. 12, 1867.

runners had been friendly Indians—mostly Arapahoes—who had made a habit of hanging around the Indian agencies and army posts for just such an assignment. Some of these Indians who had attached themselves to the whites eventually ended up scouting against their own people, and in some bands this had caused a great deal of internal bitterness.

Information had been sufficiently circulated by September 9 for a number of chiefs to be waiting for Murphy when he arrived at Fort Larned from his Atchison headquarters. Apache, Arapaho, Cheyenne, and Kiowa leaders talked with Murphy at that time and were told to assemble on Medicine Lodge Creek where they would be fed until the Commission arrived.

South of the Arkansas, Leavenworth found a large Comanche and Apache village on the Canadian River. This group learned of the proposed treaty and spread the news throughout the High Plains area to other widely scattered Comanche bands. Murphy probably did not expect to have all the Comanches represented at Medicine Lodge, but Leavenworth's efforts were effective enough to bring in members of every band except the Staked Plains Kwahadi, who since the early eighteenth century had been raiding white settlements from the Cross Timbers to deep inside Mexico. The Kwahadi never made a treaty with the whites.

The identity of the Apaches in the Canadian River camp that Leavenworth visited, of those who saw Murphy at Larned, or of the ones who signed the treaty at Medicine Lodge was never fully documented. After the Comanche-Apache war for domination of the Southern Plains, only the Lipans remained permanently east of New Mexico. The Apaches involved with Medicine Lodge, however, must have been Plains Apaches, a group of Indians splintered from the major Apache tribes. They wandered through Comanche land, a relatively docile and peaceful people. It is doubtful that there were any Lipan Apaches at Medicine Lodge because of the bitter and constant enmity between them and the Comanches.[13] When the

[13] For other details on Comanches and Lipans, see Grant Foreman, *The Last Trek of the Indians*, 286–92; Col. W. S. Nye, *Bad Medicine and Good: Tales of*

Lipans—who had often fought on the side of the Texans—were finally placed on a reservation in the Indian Territory in 1880, neighboring Comanches promptly massacred most of them. At any rate, there were about five hundred Apaches in the treaty camp when the Peace Commission arrived. This large number probably rules out their being Kiowa-Apaches.

When Murphy talked to the Indian leaders at Fort Larned, he learned that the Kiowas were already near the council grounds. The tribe was neither so large nor so scattered as the Comanches, and shortly after they learned of the treaty talks, they moved to the council grounds to await the coming of the Peace Commission.[14]

Because of the hostile attitude of the Indians under his supervision, Wynkoop had a difficult and often dangerous job in passing the word of the Indian meetings. Many Arapahoes were anxious to stop war on the Smoky Hill, but the majority of Cheyennes were in no mood for peace talks. In October, 1867, only Black Kettle, of all the major Cheyenne leaders, was actively speaking for peace—and a great many white men did not trust him. Black Kettle's role as peace leader was ironic in view of the events that were to follow Medicine Lodge. In 1868 he suffered a second Sand Creek type attack when his camp on the Washita River was struck by the Seventh Cavalry. Black Kettle was killed in this attack. He must be counted as yet another of the principals of the great Medicine Lodge council who subsequently died violently in the frontier war the treaty was supposed to end.[15]

Wynkoop enlisted the aid of two men who were as safe among the Cheyennes as any white man could expect to be in the fall of 1867. They were D. A. Butterfield and William Bent. Butterfield was well known among the Cheyennes, but this tribe's temper was so raw that he found it necessary to recruit Arapaho bodyguards to protect

---

the Kiowas, ix; Frank Bryan, "The Llano Estacado," *Panhandle and Plains Historical Review*, Vol. XIII (1940), 21–37.

[14] Mooney, "Calendar History," 227–30; Perry, "The Kiowas' Defiance," *Chronicles of Oklahoma*, Vol. XXIV (March, 1936), 30–36.

[15] Commissioner *Report 67*, 319; *Peace Commission*, 6–11; Hoig, *Sand Creek*.

his party as it moved from camp to camp and later at Medicine Lodge when rations were issued. Bent was particularly useful in the collection plan because the Cheyennes considered him a part of their tribe. He had lived on the Great Plains for years, had taken at least two Cheyenne wives, and had sired three half-Cheyenne children. The two oldest of these—George and Charlie—were valuable as runners and interpreters.[16]

Even though members of their own tribe extended the invitation for peace talks, many of the more militant Cheyennes could not forget Sand Creek and the Hancock campaign. Roman Nose, the famous Cheyenne warrior who was later killed at the Battle of Beecher's Island, was so bitter he threatened physically to attack Wynkoop. When the Peace Commission arrived at Medicine Lodge, Black Kettle's band of about 150 persons was the only Cheyenne representation immediately at hand. To the Peace Commission, it was obviously sinister to have the bulk of the Cheyennes ignoring the invitation to the treaty grounds, yet assembled a short day's ride to the south.

The Cheyennes' reluctance to take part in the negotiations actually was because of factors more complex than we have indicated. Internal disagreement existed among the Cheyenne leaders, stemming as much from personal enmity, warrior society politics, and plain stubbornness as from any bitterness toward white policy. The Medicine Lodge newsmen were not knowledgeable or concerned with warrior societies, tribal customs and tradition, or petty political quarrels within the various bands. Although extensive research has since provided a vast literature on such subjects, the men at Medicine Lodge were left to their own devices. The story background of the newsmen's dispatches was often reduced to its simplest form, not because the background was irrelevant or unimportant but because the correspondents could only write of what they saw.

[16] Special Report 13, 24, 53; David Lavender, *Bent's Fort*; C. B. McClure, "The Battle of Adobe Walls, 1864," *Panhandle and Plains Historical Review*, Vol. XXI (1948), 18 ff.; Harold H. Dunham, "Governor Charles Bent," *Denver Westerners Brand Book*, Vol. VII (1951), 222–36.

The details of the Indian collection effort failed to arouse much interest among the correspondents. They reported in great detail the more dramatic incidents—Roman Nose's threatening Wynkoop, the agent's subsequent hasty flight, and the use of Arapaho bodyguards. The reporters generally felt no responsibility for giving their readers an account of things which had happened before their arrival on the scene. With the possible exception of Milton Reynolds, they all considered themselves reporters in the strictest sense of the word, and not analysts or commentators. Even so, not only Reynolds but many of the others gave credit where it was due, stating that any success at the councils would be a direct result of Murphy's energy and persistence.[17]

Some of the tension in the Peace Commission camp may have evaporated by the morning of October 15, the first full day among the Indians. With dawn, the Indian camps came alive with routine activities, and there was no indication that danger might be waiting only a few miles away on the Cimarron. Many of the correspondents found the Indian camps extremely interesting, and some of the most detailed and well-written reports to come out of Medicine Lodge were those describing family life as it went on near the tipis.[18]

Indian women were preparing food, scraping buffalo hides, and repairing buckskin garments or saddle gear while they constantly waved packs of dogs and naked children aside. Older boys from all the bands rode out to the open prairie and drove in pony herds to water in the Medicine Lodge, then ran them out again to graze all day in the deep buffalo grass. Most of the horse herders were very young boys who stayed all day with the ponies.

Fayel, more than any other correspondent, spent his time going through the Indian camps. He was never molested nor threatened, and his passing was always the signal for hordes of children to run out and look at him, touch him, or try to talk to him in some Indian

[17] *Chicago Times*, Oct. 26, 1867; *Missouri Republican*, Oct. 24, 1867.
[18] *Cincinnati Commercial*, Oct. 24, 1867; *Missouri Democrat*, Oct. 21, 1867; *Missouri Republican*, Oct. 24, 1867.

tongue he could not understand. He watched two Indian youths cleaning a revolver in one of the camps, and he noted that there was no urgency in their movements as they discharged the weapon, rubbed it with heavy blanket cloth, and reloaded the chambers. He and the other reporters noticed that any talk of the Cheyennes coming to raid the council grounds excited the assembled tribesmen as much as it did the whites. If the Cheyennes did come, no one was sure which side the various bands would take if there was fighting, but it was assumed that none would remain neutral. As he went through the Indian camps on the morning of October 15, Fayel could see no signs of apprehension nor of preparations for a battle. Perhaps the St. Louis reporter would not have recognized such signs even if they had been present.

The *Republican* correspondent reported a flurry of excitement in one of the camps across the river from the Peace Commission, probably a Comanche camp. While loading a Colt revolver, a young Indian accidentally discharged the weapon and wounded himself. It was only a flesh wound, and after the Indians in the immediate area saw the source of the shot, they went about their business as though nothing had happened. To the Indians—including the boy who had shot himself—the incident was not at all remarkable. It amazed Fayel that the Indians accepted as a matter of course incidental shootings that came with young boys' handling heavy firearms.

George Brown visited extensively among the Indians, too, and on that first morning in camp he observed a delousing operation, which he reported in clinical detail. The procedure fascinated him, and though he disclaimed an interest in watching the squaws clean their children, he seemed constantly to return to the subject.

While some of the reporters were being delighted or disgusted at the way of life in the Indian camps, tribal leaders visited the Peace Commission to talk. The press members remaining with the commissioners reported that deliberations were casual, unhurried, and accompanied by a great deal of smoking and handshaking. Everyone understood that these early meetings were purely the preliminaries; formal talking could begin only after a decent time had elapsed. The Peace Commission did not hurry the Indians.[19] This was the tribal way of making a peace council—or any other kind for that matter—and the commissioners respected the tradition. But at least one of them was not happy about it.

The first days at the council grounds marked the beginning of what the correspondents viewed as a feud between Senator Henderson and General Harney. The disagreement between the two men lasted throughout the meetings and was sometimes punctuated with harsh language. Henderson was in a hurry. He saw no reason for delay, and he wanted to send a message to the Cheyennes on the Cimarron to come in at once. Commissioner Taylor, apparently anxious to avoid aggravating what was already a tense situation, insisted on doing things the Indian way. Harney strongly argued that the worst thing the Peace Commission could do was start sending ultimatums to the Cheyennes. He was aware of yet another touchy problem—the presence of armed troops in the peace camp. He, like Taylor, wanted to move cautiously. To this end, he ordered the soldiers of the escort to remain close to their camp, and when Henderson urged speed, Harney disagreed emphatically.[20]

On that first afternoon, Taylor called what he termed a "little talk" about a quarter of a mile from the Peace Commission camp. Everyone appeared on time except the Comanches. Their interpreter, Phillip McCusker, rode down the river to fetch them while the others waited, Peace Commission, Apache, Arapaho, and Kiowa alike. Often independent to the point of insolence, perhaps the Comanches were taking the opportunity to show Taylor that they could not be ordered around, even for "little talks."[21]

In his usual prolific style, Henry Stanley described the Peace Commission as they sat under the large tent fly that had been put up to keep the sun from shining too brightly on the delegates of the

[19] *Sec. of War 67*, 67.

[20] *Cincinnati Commercial*, Oct. 24, 1867; *Missouri Democrat*, Oct. 23, 1867.

[21] The account of the first meeting taken from *Chicago Times*, Oct. 25, 1867; *Cincinnati Commercial*, Nov. 4, 1867; *New York Herald*, Oct. 30, 1867; *New York World*, Oct. 21, 1867.

United States. Tappan sat with his head lowered, his drooping mustache almost touching his belt buckle, as he whittled on a stick. Other reporters throughout the treaty meetings discovered that Tappan was always whittling on a stick. According to the Cincinnati correspondents, whittling was the only contribution he made. Beside Tappan was Taylor, his head covered by a wide-brimmed felt hat. His great bulk dwarfed the folding camp chair in which he sat. General Harney was next to Taylor, sitting stiffly as though at attention. Terry was prim and neat, and Stanley noticed the cut of the General's uniform and the flatness of his stomach. Augur sat smoking a cigar, the breeze ruffling his muttonchop whiskers. Senator Henderson stood to one side, impatiently watching downstream for some sign of the Comanches.

The Lords of the South Plains finally appeared, left their ponies standing nearby, and took their places among the other Indians before the commissioners. Taylor gave a short speech of welcome. Some of Butterfield's ration gang were there, and Taylor had them break out articles of clothing as presents for the tribes. There was a short period of confusion as the Indians talked among themselves and the presents were distributed. Taylor had the work crew bring enough suits so that each tribe represented would have twenty. There was laughter among the Indians. Two of the Arapahoes who had acted as guards for Butterfield cut the seat out of the new trousers just presented them, pulling the garments on over their leggings. The bodyguards told Commissioner Taylor they would stand by him even if the Cheyennes came looking for a fight. As they moved back into the small crowd of Indians who had gathered on the sidelines to watch, the Arapaho braves presented the correspondents with an amusing display of Plains stylishness, wool pants without seats.

After each of the tribal leaders had made a speech of welcome to the Peace Commission, the discussion turned to the Grand Council and when it should begin. The Comanches and Kiowas wanted to talk seriously only after the Cheyennes came in from the Cimarron. Black Kettle rose and explained that his people on the Cimarron were making medicine to restore the tribe's strength after the recent hostilities along the Smoky Hill River. He said it would require about five days. Satanta said he wanted to make peace and get his people moved into winter camps before the frosts came. The Kiowas, he said, were impatient with the Cheyennes for taking so long to restore their strength.

It was obvious to most of the press corps that Senator Henderson was even more impatient than the Kiowas. He said to the other commissioners that he felt the Cheyenne medicine-making was nothing more than a ruse, but this remark was not interpreted for the Indians. At that time, no one on the Commission rebutted the Missourian. As for the correspondents, few of them had made up their minds about what was happening on the Cimarron, but Brown told his readers the Cheyennes were involved in orgies of blood lust, whatever that meant. No one ever rode to the Cimarron to see what the Cheyennes were doing, but whatever it was, it took a good deal longer than the five days Black Kettle had mentioned.

After a discussion among themselves, the Kiowas and Comanches agreed to talk in four days, on October 19. Ten Bears, an old Comanche who wore gold-rimmed spectacles when he spoke, said his tribe was willing to talk when the Kiowas did. He explained to the Peace Commission that he was not new to white men's peace talk. He had been to Washington City where he had met President Lincoln. He wanted the commissioners to look on him as a friend and to show him the proper road to travel. He ended by saying, "You laid out the road once before and we traveled it." The reporters failed to see the barbed nature of that comment, but before many days had passed, they came to expect sharp but diplomatic remarks from old Ten Bears.

When the Arapahoes and Apaches also agreed to meet on October 19, Black Kettle rose once again and gave them all a warning. He said the Cheyennes on the Cimarron might be hungry when they came in, and it would not be advisable to let them arrive and find nothing to eat. Apparently his words had little impact on the other Indians. A number of correspondents reported the following day that Murphy issued supplies, and there was no reluctance on the part of the other tribes to take whatever was offered them. After a few more expressions of good will, the meeting closed. It had taken all afternoon, and William Fayel agreed with Henderson that most of it had been time wasted. The Indians rode back down the valley to their camps, and the commissioners walked to their ambulance compound as the sun was setting. Senator Henderson hurried to his tent and spent the entire evening preparing his opening remarks for the Grand Councils.

SIX

"THAT COUNTRY IS OURS"
—Cheyenne

In the twilight after the October 15 meeting, the correspondents saw a group of about eighty mounted Indians on the far side of Medicine Lodge Creek, directly opposite the Peace Commission camp. When they heard chanting—which served to excite everyone in camp —they moved to the edge of the ambulance compound to watch and listen.[1] General Harney and a few other commissioners were already there, also looking across the stream. The tribesmen pushed into the water, still chanting, and rode directly toward the Commission camp. An armed sentry, his carbine on the ready, moved out and stood near General Harney. The Indians crossed the stream at a trot and rode to within a few yards of the sentry and General Harney, drawing rein and quitting their singing. The Indians' faces were painted, and feathers hung from their ponies' tails. The heavily armed warriors were all Cheyennes who had ridden in from the Cimarron.

General Harney recognized Gray Head and Tall Bull, two Cheyenne leaders he had known on the Northern Plains in years past. Harney greeted the Indians with handshakes and embraces, and they responded warmly, laughing and slapping the tall General on his back. Gray Head showed a worn bit of paper, and for a time the group laughed and talked together. The paper was a safe conduct pass signed by General Harney on July 17, 1858. The Cheyenne

[1] Information concerning the Cheyenne visit taken from *Missouri Democrat*, Oct. 23, 1867; *Missouri Republican*, Oct. 24, 1867.

leaders had first met Harney during the General's 1855 Platte River campaign against the Sioux, a punitive expedition brought on by that tribe's Oregon Trail depredations.[2]

Ominously, only a few of the Indians dismounted. Friendly talk and laughter notwithstanding, a false move could cause the war to start again right on the banks of the Medicine Lodge. The tension eased, however, when Harney invited Tall Bull and Gray Head to his tent and the soldier and two chieftains faded back into the shadows.

General Harney had assessed the situation, and he obviously thought it best to speak with the Indian leaders in private. Whether private discussions were his wish or the specific desire of the Indians, the correspondents could not tell. Conversations continued for some time inside Harney's tent, and when the group reappeared they were exchanging expressions of friendship. Tall Bull and Gray Head shook hands with everyone they could reach as Harney escorted them back to their horses. The mounted Cheyennes were still waiting just beyond the circle of the Peace Commissioners compound.

Mounted once more, Gray Head said he and his party were hungry. It had been a hard ride from the Cimarron. They were told that rations waited them in Black Kettle's camp across the river. With friendly shouts, the Cheyennes wheeled about on their ponies and dashed back into the stream, disappearing into the trees across the creek. Late that night, some of the newsmen heard the Cheyenne party leaving Black Kettle's camp, the sound of their horses fading slowly as the warrior band returned to their own camp on the Cimarron.

The first contingent from the Cimarron camp had come and gone without incident. Even so, nerves remained taut. The correspondents made it known to their readers that the inadvertent discharge of a weapon at the wrong time or the wrong place could have caused disaster. But if the Cheyennes' departure left the white men temporarily relieved, the sudden and unexpected appearance of the plains warriors had certainly done nothing to quiet Commission nerves. At

[2] Wirth, *Soldier*, 11–12.

least one of the writers with the group—Fayel—wrote bitterly about the incident. He regretted that the Commission had to feed the Cheyenne warriors, whom he called the marauders of the Smoky Hill.

No one really understood the purpose of the Cheyenne visit. General Harney had little to say to the reporters concerning this subject, and whether, during the discussions in his tent, Harney learned the Cheyennes' real purpose remains a mystery. Many felt that the Cheyennes were scouting the encampment position preparatory to an attack. The Commission gained at least one benefit from the visit. When Harney invited Tall Bull and Gray Head to return to the Peace Commission camp for hearings to be held on the Hancock expedition the following night, both of the chiefs accepted and they did show up as promised.

One of the Peace Commissions' functions as specified by Congress was to determine causes of war on the Great Plains. To this end, hearings were conducted in Fort Leavenworth and up the Platte River.[3] Now, three days before the first Grand Council was scheduled to begin, Taylor decided to continue taking testimony on the Hancock campaign, one of the most important historical incidents of that time in Kansas.

The correspondents now learned at firsthand the conflicting nature of the reports of the Hancock campaign. The most pressing unresolved question before the Peace Commission was not in connection with Hancock's movements during the campaign, nor with his military competence in the field. Rather, it concerned the accuracy of his interpretation of the Indian situation in Kansas at the time he had taken the field.[4] One of the incidents preceding the engagement of Hancock's forces in hostilities involved the Kiowas and had occurred near Fort Dodge in March, 1867. Fred Jones, an army interpreter at Dodge, reported that he, Major Daniel Page, and an-

[3] "Journal," Aug. 3, Oct. 16, 1867.

[4] This account of the Hancock affair taken from Commissioner *Report 67*, 8f., 309–30; Commissioner *Report 68*, 4; "Journal," Aug. 12, Oct. 16, 1867; *Sec. of War 67*, 36f.; *Special Report 13*, 3, 53, 81, 94–101; *Special Report, 60;* Hancock "Reports," 106f.

other white man had been threatened, insulted, and intimidated by a band of Kiowas in the vicinity of the fort. The Kiowas told Jones that a general war was about to begin in Kansas and that all white settlers would have to move out or suffer the consequences. Jones said the Indians claimed they had killed seventeen Negro soldiers in Indian Territory or in Texas, and they had scalps to prove their claim.

When Major Henry Douglass, Fort Dodge commander, heard the Jones story, he wired its details to General Hancock at Headquarters, Department of the Missouri, Fort Leavenworth. About this time there had been a number of raids on livestock along the Smoky Hill, and in several instances Indians had attacked trains and crews. Throughout this period, reports were current that a general war was approaching, and Governor Crawford, of Kansas—as has been seen—was convinced that such a war was imminent.

Hancock alerted the Seventh Cavalry and seven companies of the Thirty-seventh Infantry, and these military units began preparations for taking the field in early March. Bad weather prevented the expedition's going onto the plains until March 21, by which time Hancock had notified Indian Agents Leavenworth and Wynkoop of his intentions to "encourage and confirm the friendly and deter the refractory." In his wire to Leavenworth, Hancock claimed the Kiowas were guilty of a serious offense, and he repeated the Jones story. Leavenworth and Wynkoop joined the Hancock expedition, and both denied any hostile intent on the part of the tribes for which they were responsible. Wynkoop was convinced that depredations had been committed by renegade warriors and not entire tribes. Leavenworth accused some of the Kiowas of raiding in Texas, but he denied that they committed depredations in Kansas.

On the Pawnee Fork of the Arkansas River, north of Fort Larned, Hancock's column surprised a Cheyenne and Sioux village. The leaders of the village rode out to ask Hancock not to bring his soldiers any closer to the camp because the approach of armed troopers would panic their people. Hancock held two conferences with the chiefs and insisted upon marching to the village. As these talks continued, the women and children slipped out of the camp. Hancock indicated his displeasure at their leaving and demanded that they be brought back.

After a short search in the darkness, the Indian braves returned, saying they were unable to locate the persons who had fled. Lieutenant Colonel George Custer was ordered to surround the village with the Seventh Cavalry, but by the time the orders were issued the village was deserted, and Hancock sent Custer in pursuit of the departed Indians. Within a few hours, information was sent back to Hancock that a station on the Smoky Hill route had been attacked by Indians, and the General assumed the fight had been made by warriors from the Pawnee Fork Village. He ordered the village burned. In the village, the soldiers found a young girl whom Hancock reported as white. She had been raped, and within a few days she died.

Reporting to the Commissioner of Indian Affairs, both Wynkoop and Leavenworth condemned Hancock's actions. They said the Jones story was untrue and that the Pawnee Fork village had been a camp of peaceful Indians. The two agents' charges and other information were available to the Peace Commission when it reopened the Hancock hearings at Medicine Lodge. Details of Hancock's campaign were generally known to the reporters as well, although Fayel said he had never heard of Jones or his story. It is difficult to understand how Fayel missed the story of the Kiowas and the Negro soldiers' scalps. The story had been carried in many eastern newspapers.

Most intimately acquainted with the details of the campaign was Henry Stanley, who had accompanied Hancock. During the days of the expedition itself and later when the Peace Commission, staying at Fort Leavenworth, was investigating the campaign, the *Democrat* reporter had been a staunch supporter of Hancock. During early hearings concerning the incident, Agent Leavenworth had produced two witnesses in his attempt to prove the Jones story false, but still

---

[5] Hancock "Report," 106f.; Stanley, *Travels*, 38–40; *Missouri Republican*, Oct. 24, 1867.

Stanley remained loyal to Hancock, telling his readers that the General had acted on accurate information.[5]

On October 16, when the Peace Commission began calling witnesses in the hearings at Medicine Lodge, there seemed little doubt that General Hancock had acted in good faith during his Kansas expedition. None of the correspondents ever questioned his motives, nor was his character or competence in the field assailed in the official records of the Peace Commission.[6] The unresolved questions concerned the reliability of Hancock's sources of information. The General's integrity was not questioned, but his judgment, perhaps, was.

Wynkoop, the first witness, insisted that Hancock had been misinformed about the Kansas situation from start to finish. The Cheyenne-Arapaho agent's words were attended closely by five of the correspondents, and they reported what he said verbatim. What appeared in their newspapers was essentially the same as Wynkoop's own official report and the report of the Peace Commission, solid evidence of the newsmen's ability to report a story straight.

Wynkoop refuted the Jones story, claiming the Pawnee Fork village had been friendly, and finally—causing a stir of excitement among the reporters—he said the girl who had been raped was actually a Cheyenne who had been found and attacked by soldiers of the Seventh Cavalry. Such an outrage could have occurred. Soldiers had been in or near the edge of the village for some time after most of the warriors were gone. However, none of the correspondents accepted Wynkoop's story in full—they reported his words without comment, except for Budd, who said the whole story was fantastic.

Throughout their testimony, neither Hancock nor Wynkoop said anything that proved their contentions—each simply refuted what the other said. Even so, Wynkoop made a highly favorable impression on most of the press gang, and Stanley—whose previous evaluation of Wynkoop had softened somewhat at Fort Larned—was becoming an outright Wynkoop admirer. At this point, it must have

---

[6] Official testimony from Commissioner *Report 67*, 310–14; *Peace Commission*, 12–14; Hancock, "Report," 27. News reports from *Cincinnati Commercial*, Oct. 24, 1867; *Missouri Democrat*, Oct. 23, 1867; *Missouri Republican*, Oct. 24, 1867.

been interesting to Stanley's readers to guess how the *Democrat* correspondent would eventually resolve the conflict of his loyalties between Hancock and Wynkoop. Throughout the Hancock hearings, the bulk of the press corps at Medicine Lodge reported the story as interested bystanders, but bystanders nonetheless. Stanley, however, became so involved in the negotiations that his dispatches became reflections of his personal feelings. He became as personally entangled in the Hancock hearings as Reynolds had been in the meeting of the Kansas delegation.

After Wynkoop's testimony came that of Major Douglass, the Fort Dodge commander. In his testimony, he retold the Jones story just as it had been related to him and as he had relayed it to General Hancock. After listening to Douglass' testimony, Stanley was convinced that Wynkoop—although a good man—was wrong, and that General Hancock had indeed acted on correct information. Point by point, the *Democrat* reporter criticized Wynkoop's testimony. There had been a war on the Smoky Hill before Hancock took the field, he said, and the Pawnee Fork village had been hostile. There was no doubt that the girl in the burned village had been white. As evidence that all of this was true, he wrote: "The readers of the *Democrat* can not have forgotten how graphically and distinctly Hancock's expedition on the warpath was described by the Special Correspondent." Who had been that special correspondent? Stanley, of course.[7]

With the hearings unfinished, the correspondents who reported the testimony were split in their opinions. Fayel and Reynolds made no speculative comment, reporting only what was said. Hall wrote in the *Chicago Tribune* that Hancock's arguments appeared questionable and that he may have "acted rashly." Although Hancock was not at Medicine Lodge, the correspondents had heard him at Fort Leavenworth. Brown, Budd, and Stanley supported Hancock. Budd said the commissioners would do their best to injure General Hancock and thereby "get a beef contract" for "our cousins and friends." Budd did not explain how this would take place, nor did he say who

[7] *Missouri Democrat*, Oct. 23, 1867.

"our cousins and friends" might be, but while he was at it, he took the opportunity to say that Tappan was useless and that Sanborn was interested in nothing but money.[8]

When the first day's hearings were adjourned for the evening, it was still early. Fayel, Hall, Howland, and Stanley got passes from General Harney to leave the Peace Commission camp. They had been invited to a dance in the village of the Arapahoes, and with a number of other unidentified white men they walked the short distance to Little Raven's cluster of lodges.[9] Although the Arapahoes were as trustworthy as any tribe at Medicine Lodge, some of the reporters carried revolvers. Howland, the *Harper's* artist, wore his new Navy Colt. Near the Arapaho camp, the group was met by Little Raven, who escorted them into his village and to the spot where the festivities were to be conducted.

Pushing their way through a crowd of women and children on the outside of a large tent, the correspondents squeezed through the door and found themselves in a smoky cavern filled with half-naked Indians. In the center of the tent was a fire, and around it were dancers in two rows, men nearest the fire and women forming the outer ring. Shortly after they arrived, Little Raven gave the signal to begin the party. Up to then, the tribesmen and their women had stood, staring in silence as Little Raven seated his guests at one end of the tent. At his indication, however, the Indians began to laugh and shout, and with the dancing under way, many of them were obviously showing off their best steps for the admiration of the visitors.

Small hand drums—which Fayel called skin tambourines—were struck with sticks to provide rhythms. The dancers moved around the fire uttering various shouts and cries which none of the correspondents could understand. The tempo increased, and shortly the nearly naked bodies were glistening with sweat. Everywhere, horns, rattles, and bone whistles punctuated the general din.

---

[8] *Cincinnati Commercial*, Oct. 24, 1867; *Missouri Democrat*, Oct. 23, 1867; *Missouri Republican*, Oct. 23, 1867.

[9] Material for these accounts taken from *Chicago Tribune*, Oct. 26, 1867; *Missouri Democrat*, Oct. 25, 1867; *Missouri Republican*, Oct. 25, 1867.

Stanley was fascinated with the dancers. But as the hysteria grew, his attention was suddenly focused on his white companions. Fayel and Hall had joined the circle of dancing Indians, exerting themselves until they were dripping with perspiration. The Indians were delighted, but no more so than Henry Stanley, who wrote about the episode in the greatest detail. Following the example of his friends, Howland also abandoned himself to the frenzy of the moment, leaping into the swaying circle around the central fire.

It is difficult to tell how much of Stanley's account was true. The dance definitely occurred, and the correspondents were there. Stanley's story about the occasion, however, makes it seem that he grasped an opportunity to make fun of his competitor from St. Louis. For his part, Fayel reported the Arapaho festivities, but if he really did join the dance, his enthusiasm had cooled noticeably by the time he wrote about it, for he made no mention of white participation. Nor did Hall describe himself as a dancer. On the other hand, every description of the Medicine Lodge correspondents indicated that these gentlemen of the press were capable of rowdyism, particularly after drinking a little whisky. There were no reports of any liquor being involved at the Arapaho party—but no one reported its absence. Whether or not the Indian camp contained a supply of the potable, there was plenty in the correspondents' tent at the Peace Commission camp, where the thoughtful Sanborn had provided the reporters with a keg of their own.[10]

Drunk or sober—dancers or spectators—the guests finally said good night to Little Raven and his band. Men and boys crowded around the correspondents, patting their backs and laughing. There were close embraces. The party of white men moved outside the tent, where there were more embraces. Little Raven and a group of his braves escorted the party of reporters to the edge of the camp. As the correspondents were about to walk the short distance to their camp, Howland—the killer of buffalo, the buckskin-clad frontiersman who spoke Spanish and told tales of the border—discovered that someone had stolen his Colt revolver. There were quick In-

[10] *Missouri Republican*, Oct. 24, 1867.

dian conversations as the *Harper's* artist searched his own clothing, finding nothing but an empty gun belt. Little Raven expressed extreme regret that one of his people had defiled his hospitality. The Arapaho chief offered Howland one of his two Navy Colts, both of which were in excellent shooting order according to Stanley. Later, Fayel reported that Howland refused the offer. Stanley said the artist took the Indian's revolver.

With or without the pistol, Howland and his companions returned to the Peace Commission camp, as Little Raven continued to express his regret from the edge of his encampment. The correspondents, now somewhat subdued, showed their passes to a sentry and entered the ambulance compound. It had been a cheerful interlude. But Fayel noticed that the sentry guards had been doubled in anticipation of Cheyenne hostilities.

The day following the Arapaho dance was a tense one in the treaty camps. The reporters who filed copy on that day reflected on the jumpy nerves, not only in the Peace Commission inclosure, but throughout the Indian encampments as well. As the commissioners were preparing their notes for continuing the Hancock hearings, a panic swept the tribal camps nearest the Commission.[11] Indians were trying to strike tipis and run their pony herds in from the open prairie. Fayel soon discovered that a rumor of approaching soldiers had started the frantic rush.

At the time, the Peace Commission escort was at its camp site upstream, and their horses were standing along picket lines. If other United States military formations were in the area, General Harney knew nothing of them. But within a few moments, a large body of mounted men appeared from the west, riding toward the treaty grounds with no baggage or women visible. Soon the sight of long lances and streaming hair made it apparent that the riders were not soldiers but Indians. Turmoil continued in the camp as fear spread that the Cimarron Cheyennes had come to attack the Peace Commission. But when the cavalcade started into the basin, some of the interpreters with the official party recognized the mounted men as

[11] *Ibid.*

93

Comanches. When Indians along the valley realized they were not being attacked by hostiles, their furious activity ceased, and everyone stood and watched as the High Plains horsemen rode along the stream to find camp sites near their kinsmen. Hall reported that the intruders were Nakoni and Paneteka Comanches who had recently heard of the treaty talks and had come in to join the council.[12]

Excitement in the treaty camp remained high, however, because of the presence of the uninvited tribesmen. Little Raven, very much disturbed according to the newsmen, came to the Commission camp and reported that his pony herds had been raided.[13] Pawnees had driven off a number of his horses, the Arapaho chief said, and this action was a breech of tribal etiquette. The Arapahoes organized a pursuit party, and General Harney sent a civilian scout with the Indian posse. After the war party—for that was essentially what it was—rode out, Little Raven became sullen and refused to speak with anyone.

Little Raven regained his good disposition, however, when the posse returned four days later with all the Arapaho horses. The raiders had been caught and punished—a number of them had been killed. Arapaho warriors had fresh scalps to show, all of them taken from Kaw Indians, the tribe after which the state of Kansas had been named. Stanley wrote that General Harney was delighted to hear that a few "tame" Kansas Indians had been slaughtered by Arapahoes.

With evening of October 17, Tall Bull and Gray Head returned to the Peace Commission camp, and the Hancock hearings. The two Cheyenne chiefs entered the camp quietly, without the fanfare of chanting or the escort of warriors they had brought on their first visit.

Major Douglass, the Fort Dodge commander who had transmitted the Jones story to Hancock, was cross-examined by members of the Peace Commission. As the questioning proceeded, it became

---

[12] *Chicago Tribune*, Oct. 26, 1867.

[13] "Journal," Oct. 15, 1867; *Chicago Times*, Oct. 29, 1867; *Missouri Democrat*, Oct. 28, 1867; *Missouri Republican*, Oct. 28, 1867; *New York Herald*, Oct. 30, 1867.

clear to the correspondents that Jones had been considered untrustworthy by everyone in the Fort Dodge garrison, including Major Douglass. Before the major had sent the dispatch on the Kiowa threats and the Negro scalps, he had questioned Major Page, who was present with Jones at the time of the alleged incident. Page denied that the Kiowas had been abusive, and he denied seeing Negro scalps or hearing the Kiowas brag of taking any. But despite what Major Page had said, Douglass sent the Jones story on to Hancock. We find no indication from either newspaper dispatch or official report why Douglass ignored Page's comments. All the correspondents except Hall viewed the whole matter as just one more frontier incident which defied explanation. Hall found it astonishing that Douglass would relay to his superior a story which was so obviously without foundation.[14]

Next, Gray Head testified that Hancock's troops had frightened his people at the Pawnee Fork village.[15] Ever since the Sand Creek massacre, the Cheyenne chief testified, the Indian women and children had been difficult to convince that there was any such thing as a friendly formation of white troops. The Indian leader claimed that his tribe was not hostile, although he could not speak for all the young men who had been in the camp, nor for the Sioux. Gray Head explained that his band had been on the Pawnee Fork preparing for the spring buffalo hunt. He further stated that the girl in the village was an idiot Cheyenne and that any physical abuse of her had occurred after the Indians had gone.

The Cheyenne chief's words were reported by most of the correspondents. None of the reporters said outright that they believed his story, yet they did not malign him—he was given their respect, and even admiration. No one said he was lying.

There was some discussion among the commissioners as the reporters sat waiting to see if the Cheyenne chief would be cross-

[14] *Chicago Tribune*, Oct. 24, 1867; *Missouri Democrat*, Oct. 25, 1867; *Missouri Republican*, Oct. 24, 1867.

[15] Commission *Report 67*, 310–14; *Peace Commission*, 12–14.

examined. Suddenly a violent disturbance in the nearby wagon park disrupted the meeting. Shouts and curses were heard, and one of the soldiers claimed there was a knife fight between two of the teamsters.[16] Sanborn rushed off to calm his teamsters. Reynolds reported the fracas with some relish, but Fayel was disgusted by it. Order was eventually restored, most of the commissioners went to the wagon park, and the Indian witnesses drifted off into the darkness. Reynolds went to the wagon park, too, and he reported that the disturbance had developed between two mule drivers when an Indian woman wandered into the area. No one was injured severely in the evening, but the next morning, when the argument was resumed with Colt revolvers, one teamster was seriously wounded. None of the correspondents bothered to mention whether the wounded man lived or died.

The wagon-park scuffle, which put an end to the hearings, also brought to a close a wild and exciting day. "We have rather lively times down here on the border," Reynolds said.

This was the last of the Hancock hearings, and as the correspondents reflected on the testimony—once the camp's calm had been restored—two of them agreed with Hall that Hancock had acted rashly. Stanley reversed himself, admitting that his own graphic reporting during the Hancock campaign had been in error on a number of occasions. Hancock had been deceived, the *Democrat* reporter wrote, first by Major Douglass, then by the interpreters at the Pawnee Fork village, and finally by those who led him to believe the girl in the Indian camp had been white. Hall continued to maintain—as he had from the first—that Hancock's case had been seriously injured. William Fayel simply called the Jones story a lie. The *Republican* reporter never became personally involved in Peace Commission controversy as Stanley and Reynolds often did. If his copy was less colorful, it was also closer to modern standards of objective reporting than was most of the other material written at Medicine Lodge. Of all the correspondents who expressed their opinion, only Budd and Brown failed finally to agree that Hancock may have been

[16] *Chicago Times*, Oct 29, 1867; *Missouri Republican*, Oct. 23, 1867.

96

a victim of misinformation. Their reports of the hearings did not extend beyond the Wynkoop testimony.[17]

The sentiments expressed by Hall, Fayel, and Stanley were shared by the Peace Commission.[18] In their final report to the President, the Peace Commission stated that Hancock's expedition had been ill conceived and that until his forces took the field, there had been no general war in Kansas. On the Jones story, an inspection of the Washington files of the Army Adjutant General later in the year disclosed no record of seventeen Negro soldiers' being killed at the time Jones made his charge—in Texas, the Indian Territory, or anywhere else. Commenting on an incident in which Jones had been shot at by an Indian, the Commission said it was unfortunate the bullet had missed. Further, in his official army report for the year, General Sherman deplored the circulation of false reports and rumors on the frontier by those who, apparently, wanted to start Indian trouble.[19] Although he was not at Medicine Lodge, Sherman later helped write the Peace Commission report which reflected the same thinking.

Concerning the Kiowas and Comanches, the Peace Commission said they found no evidence that either tribe, with the exception of the Box family raid, had violated the 1865 Treaty of the Little Arkansas. In early 1867, a Comanche-Kiowa war party raided the James Box family ranch in Montague County, Texas. A sensitive issue in the controversy between Leavenworth and Hancock concerned the prisoners taken in this raid.[20] The Indian agent claimed Hancock had allowed the guilty Indians to loiter around Fort Dodge despite the general knowledge that Box family captives were being held in their village. Satanta and Kicking Bird, rivals for Kiowa leadership, became involved in the argument and made accusations against each other. Kicking Bird said Satanta had a white captive girl in his camp at the time of the Medicine Lodge councils. Satanta accused Kicking

[17] *Chicago Tribune*, Oct. 25, 1867; *Missouri Democrat*, Oct. 25, 1867; *Missouri Republican*, Oct. 24, 1867.

[18] *Peace Commission*, 6, 12–14; Wirth, *Soldier*, 37f.

[19] *Sec. of War 67*, 36.

[20] *Special Report 13*, 12–14; *Special Report 60*, 3.

Bird of having led the Box raid. If any of these claims or counter-claims were aired at the Medicine Lodge hearings, they went unreported by the newsmen. Here was a rather striking example of the Peace Commission's being unconcerned about what had happened—and was happening—south of the Red River. Obviously, the Peace Commission was concerned with the Kansas frontier.

Directly as a result of the Hancock hearings at Medicine Lodge, there was a reconciliation between Agent Wynkoop and some of the Cheyenne leaders. Many of the warriors who had been in the Pawnee Fork village had assumed Wynkoop led the Hancock expedition to their encampment. But with the conclusion of the Hancock testimony, the reporters noted with obvious satisfaction that Tall Bull and Gray Head went to Wynkoop and shook his hand. Fayel could detect no hypocrisy in the gesture, and he wrote that the expression of friendship was warm and real.[21]

This show of affection was no indication that the Cheyennes on the Cimarron were ready to come in. The newspapermen learned that on the same evening, Tall Bull and Gray Head went to Black Kettle's camp where they held a hearing of their own.[22] Later, Black Kettle was willing to talk about the meeting with the reporters. Tall Bull told Black Kettle to come to the Cimarron and tell everyone there what he expected to gain from remaining at peace. To emphasize his words, Tall Bull said if Black Kettle did not feel it necessary to make the trip to the large encampment to the south, the Cimarron Cheyennes would ride in and kill all his horses.

[21] *Missouri Democrat,* Oct. 23, 1867; *Missouri Republican,* Oct. 24, 1867.
[22] *Ibid.*

SEVEN

"I WILL KEEP ANY GOOD TALK
YOU MAY GIVE ME"

—Comanche

H. J. Budd was a most unflattering reporter. He had little good to say about anyone. Taylor, Tappan, and Sanborn were his particular targets, and he accused them all of being impractical, useless, and corrupt. Brown agreed with his Cincinnati companion concerning Tappan, but he said Taylor and Sanborn were well-qualified for the task of Indian treaty making. He described Taylor as "a most estimable man."[1]

Stanley wrote a great deal about the commissioners. With his usual flare—his was the kind of writing that was attracting the attention of James Gordon Bennett in New York—the Welshman described the members of the official party in personal, human terms: "Look with me between the wheels of this wagon, examine each feature, and tell me what you see." The *Democrat* reporter saw a dedicated, hard-working group of men, with Sanborn their outstanding intellectual leader. Both Brown and Reynolds agreed that in addition to being the most energetic member of the Commission, Sanborn was the legal genius on the Indian situation. Stanley characterized Commissioner Taylor as a philanthropist, Tappan as a quiet man who seldom became involved in Commission discussion, and Henderson as the party's spokesman—a man of business with no taste for nonsense or time wasting. Stanley pointed out that Henderson was not only the Commission spokesman but also the public relations or publicity man. The Missouri Senator was the primary contact between

[1] *Cincinnati Commercial*, Oct. 22, 1867; *Cincinnati Gazette*, Sept. 27, 1867.

press group and official party. He issued statements, answered questions, and kept the press group informed of Peace Commission plans. When there was uncertainty or doubt, "we all [felt] an inclination to ask Senator Henderson," Stanley said.[2]

With the exception of Harney, who always sympathized with the Indians, the military members of the Commission were apparently so taciturn that no opinion of them took shape among the correspondents.[3] Stanley said newspaper readers across the nation remembered Terry because of his part in the battle of Fort Fisher during the Civil War, an engagement which Stanley had covered as a newsman. Some of the other reporters were obviously not as intimately acquainted with the military leader's accomplishments. The general impression of Terry was that he was well groomed, quiet, and a good soldier.

In his official escort report, Major Joel Elliot claimed that General Augur made serious remonstrances about the terms offered the Indians during the treaty talks, but that his protests were ignored. If Augur made his objections in public meeting, he must have done it very quietly because no hint of protest was reported by any one of the press party. Indeed, Augur may as well have remained at his Omaha headquarters for all the attention he attracted among the correspondents.

The newsmen were never as closely associated with the Indian leaders as they were with the members of the Peace Commission, and their impressions of the native delegations came almost entirely from the speeches at the various meetings. A great deal of time was spent describing the tribes before the Grand Councils began, however. The interests of the newsmen were so varied that comparing their reports is difficult. Budd, for example, concerned himself with descriptions of Indian savagery, while Reynolds was interested in where the tribes made their home and the language they spoke. No important formal studies of Plains Indians had yet been made, and

[2] *Chicago Times*, Oct. 21, 1867; *Cincinnati Commercial*, Sept. 27, 1867.
[3] Elliot, "Report"; *Missouri Democrat*, Oct. 19, 1867.

the Medicine Lodge news reporters did not have the benefit of works
by James Mooney, George Bird Grinnell, and the other scholars
who have gone among the tribes to study their culture. The reporters' opinions were probably formed from hearsay and the literature of the day, much of which was sensational, sentimental, and
highly inaccurate. Otherwise, they had only the evidence available
at Medicine Lodge to provide authority for their reports. This would
have been adequate for description alone, but none of the Medicine
Lodge correspondents who wrote about Indians confined themselves
to description. They assigned characteristics, traditions, and customs
to the various bands, and in doing so they gave a rather confused
picture of each tribe. Brown's description of the Cheyennes, for example, was in many ways identical to Hall's report on the Kiowas.
But if they were at odds on background, their reports on eyewitness
incidents were remarkably similar.[4]

Budd, who enjoyed belittling the members of the Peace Commission, was equally unkind to the Indians. He found them distasteful, and he said so. He reported that the Plains Apaches had a great
many Mexican wives, "whom they call Mexicanos and who are the
most degraded people on earth." He also, mistakenly, stated that the
Apaches were the only Plains Indians who wore mustaches. Actually
most of the Plains Warriors did pluck the hair from their lips, chin,
and eyebrows, but it was only the Indians of the Kiowa tribe who
frequently grew mustaches. Satank, one of the most famous and influential Kiowas, had a long, silvery mustache at the time of Medicine Lodge, and Budd saw him at close range at least once.[5]

Reynolds, too, was inaccurate in saying that the languages of the
Comanches and Kiowas were much alike. His experience on the fron-
tier should have kept him from advancing this thesis. The Kiowa
Indian tongue was unlike any other language spoken on the Great
Plains in the nineteenth century. Of particular interest to Reynolds
was the use of sign language among the tribes, and he said the Kiowas

[4] *Chicago Tribune*, Oct. 18, 1867; *Cincinnati Commercial*, Nov. 4, 1867.
[5] Nye, *Carbine and Lance*, 109; *Cincinnati Commercial*, Oct. 24, 1867.

had developed the art to a state of perfection. Obviously, he did not understand the relationship between the Kiowas' use of sign language and the difficulty of their spoken word.[6]

Hall's description and background of the tribes indicate that he may have done some research before coming to the treaty meetings. Prior to his arrival at Medicine Lodge, the Chicago reporter gave a long account of the tribal units which would be represented. Of all the correspondents, he alone explained the informal organization of the Comanches, and, quite correctly, he described them as a loosely related tribe of many independent bands sharing general traditions and customs but at the same time maintaining certain distinctions. Even the language varied from group to group, Hall said, an astute comment considering the scant information available to him at the time. The Kiowas Hall described in words remarkably similar to those James Mooney would use in later years, after his extensive study of the tribe. The Kiowa Indians lacked all the better qualities of the other Plains Indians except bravery. Hall—like Mooney after him—said the Kiowas were best known for their vicious savagery.[7]

On three points there was general agreement among the correspondents at Medicine Lodge: Comanches were the best horsemen on the Great Plains, Arapahoes were the most peaceful of the wild tribes, and at the time of the peace councils the Cheyennes were the most dangerous.

How did the writers move all their copy from Medicine Lodge back to civilization? According to Stanley, the only dependable link with the outside world was a daily courier to Fort Larned who carried both telegrams and letters for the reporters. Regular mail runs connected Larned with Fort Harker, where rail and wire services were available. Although there was a military wire to Fort Larned, it was never used by the correspondents.[8] About four days was required

[6] Mooney, "Calendar History," 162; Perry, "The Kiowas' Defense," *Chronicles of Oklahoma*, Vol. XXIV (March, 1936), 31; *Chicago Times*, Oct. 25, 1867.

[7] Mooney, "Calendar History," 233f.; *Chicago Tribune*, Oct. 18, 24, 1867.

[8] Downey, "Frontier Army," *Army*, Vol. XIII (February, 1863), 48–52.

for a telegram to reach New York from Medicine Lodge, eight to ten days for letters. Dispatches reached nearer cities in considerably less time, and the press associations were generally faster than the special correspondents. For example, the first news in the *Missouri Democrat* of a treaty's being signed did not come from Stanley at the council grounds, but from Washington by wire. A. S. H. White, Peace Commission official secretary, had telegraphed the news on the army wire from Fort Larned to the Department of the Interior in Washington. The Department of the Interior released the story in Washington, where it was picked up by all the press associations and special Washington correspondents. It appeared in St. Louis as a small wire dispatch.[9] The story scooped Stanley because his account of the signing was in letter form and had to be carried to St. Louis by horse and rail.

The style of the Medicine Lodge correspondents' letters was distinctive, yet there were many similarities. The obvious likeness lay in the use of verbatim accounts of speeches made at the treaty meetings. Even Bulkley, who usually made use of short wire dispatches to the *New York Herald*, included some letters with verbatim copy once the first treaty was signed. Stanley said he took shorthand notes at the councils, and some of the other reporters may have done the same. The similarity in the verbatim accounts possibly may be explained by an exchange of notes between reporters after each speaking session.

However, the most logical explanation for the similarity in speech reports appears to be that correspondents had access to the notes of the Peace Commission stenographer. One of the stenographers, it will be remembered, was a correspondent himself—Howland of *Harper's*. Additionally, nothing has been found that would suggest any attempt or reason for the Peace Commission's keeping their records and transcripts of the meetings secret.

Another Commission stenographer was George Willis. He had

[9] *Missouri Democrat*, Oct. 26, 1867; *New York Herald*, Oct. 30, 1867; *New York World*, Oct. 25, 1867; *New York Tribune*, Oct. 23, 1867.

been hired in St. Louis and like Howland was under the direct supervision of A. S. H. White. Verbatim accounts taken by Willis were used on a day-to-day basis for framing replies and rebuttals to Indian speeches. All the shorthand notes were later used in writing the final report, but no quotations were included in the report nor in the "Journal of Proceedings" of the Commission. Major Elliot's official report of the escort included quoted accounts of the Kiowa and Comanche grand councils. Altogether, it was obvious that the reporters had no trouble in obtaining Peace Commission documents on the speech making.[10]

Whatever method the correspondents used to make their notes on speeches, a third party was always involved when the Indians spoke— the interpreter. Each of the reporters recognized the importance of the interpreters, but none stated the basic problems of interpretation as well as Robert M. Utley:

> Exact meaning is extremely difficult to convey from one language to another and the average [frontier] interpreter . . . was scarcely proficient in the science. . . . Even the honest seeker of truth encountered enormous obstacles stemming from the differences in cultural background.[11]

Seven languages were spoken by the principals in the Medicine Lodge councils. American history provides a few examples of treaty making under such complex circumstances, but at Medicine Lodge there was an additional barrier to understanding, a barrier common to all negotiations with Indians. While many European languages have similarities, the Indian languages exhibited at Medicine Lodge were widely disparate, and the bridges between them were Comanche, the nearest thing to a *lingua franca* of the Plains, and the sign language, which had almost universality. From such complexities and the admittedly frontier level of interpretation, it is clear that, while the reporters present left no evidence that they questioned the

---

[10] "Journal," Aug. 7, 1867; *Peace Commission,* 1–24; Elliot, "Report"; Kappler, *Treaties,* 982, 984, 989.
[11] *Custer and the Great Controversy,* 86f.

accuracy of interpretations, they had no choice but to accept the interpreters' word.

The correspondents mentioned a total of five interpreters at Medicine Lodge. Two were listed in the payment ledger which Sanborn kept. Three signed the treaty as witnesses, and four were named by A. S. H. White in a letter written to General Sherman announcing the ending of the treaty councils. The only persons mentioned by the reporters and not accounted for in one or more of the Peace Commission documents were Ed Guerrier, named by Brown and Budd as a Cheyenne interpreter, and Fishermore, a Kiowa listed by Hall and Fayel.[12]

The man most prominent in all accounts of interpreters was Phillip McCusker. He was one of the few South Plains frontiersmen to marry a Comanche woman. Many Northern Plains tribes allowed white traders to winter with them and take Indian wives, but the Comanches—although hospitable—did not usually welcome adult white men into their families. Traders conducted their business and left, but McCusker was not a trader. He had scouted and acted as interpreter for the army and the Department of the Interior for several years. At Medicine Lodge he was a Comanche interpreter, and indications exist that he also spoke Kiowa and Kiowa-Apache.[13]

The Comanches were a Shoshoni people, but they had lived in the Southwest for so long they had assimilated into their language many words and phrases of that area, giving their speech a sound much like Mexican Spanish. Comanche was the trade language of the Southern Plains—like Swahili in parts of Africa—and was understood and spoken by Indians as far north as the Platte River. An

[12] "Accounts"; Kappler, *Treaties*, 982, 986, 989; White Letter; *Chicago Tribune*, Oct. 24, 1867; *Cincinnati Commercial*, Nov. 4, 1867; *Cincinnati Gazette*, Oct. 29, 1867; *Missouri Democrat*, Oct. 23, 1867; *New York Herald*, Oct. 30, 1867; *Leslie's Illustrated Newspaper*, Nov. 16, 1867.

[13] For a discussion of the use of the Comanche language, see Francis Gilmore and Louisa Wade Weatherill, *Traders to the Navahos*, 7; for additional accounts of McCusker, see Harry Drago, *The Red River Valley*, 33–35; R. T. Jacobs, "Military Reminiscences," *Chronicles of Oklahoma*, Vol. II (March, 1924), 12; Taylor, "The Medicine Lodge Peace Council," *Chronicles of Oklahoma*, Vol. II (March, 1924), 106.

effect of Comanche domination of the Southern Plains for over a century was reflected in this widespread use of the Comanche spoken word.[14]

The language least known by whites and Indians at Medicine Lodge was Kiowa. Kiowa was an ancient tongue, possibly originating in the Tano language of the oldest Pueblo peoples of the Southwest.[15] Considerable debate continues among students of the Kiowas concerning the roots of this tribe's speech. Because of the difficulty of communicating in their own tongue, many Kiowas learned Comanche and English as well. I-See-O, a Kiowa who was at Medicine Lodge and who later became a sergeant in the U.S. Army, said the Kiowas had no interpreter of their own at Medicine Lodge but used Mc-Cusker. He failed to indicate whether McCusker interpreted from Kiowa or Comanche. Hall said Fishermore interpreted for the Kiowas, but Fayel disagreed, reporting Fishermore to be a Comanche interpreter. No evidence has been found to support either claim. In defense of the two reporters, there was unquestionably a great deal of multilingual conversation between tribes as the councils progressed. Fishermore could have been one of the middlemen, interpreting Kiowa speeches for McCusker. Bulkley commented on the confusion when he reported that Satanta had to pause after each sentence of his speech so that his words could be interpreted into three different languages.[16]

Cheyenne interpreters were plentiful. All the Bents were at Medicine Lodge—including Julia, sister to George and Charlie—and each of them was capable of interpreting for the Cheyennes. Both George and Charlie were listed in the Peace Commission "Ledger of Accounts" as runners, but this probably entailed a great deal of inter-

[14] R. G. Carter, *On the Border with Mackenzie*, 86; Richardson, *Comanche Barrier*, 16; Wallace and Hoebels, *Comanches*, 22.

[15] Mooney, "Calendar History," 143–46; Alvin M. Josephy, Jr. (ed.) *American Heritage Book of Indians*, 377; Nye, *Bad Medicine*, 4; Perry, "Defiance," *Chronicles of Oklahoma*, Vol. XXIV (March, 1936), 36.

[16] "Accounts"; Kappler, *Treaties*, 982; Mayhall, *Kiowas*, 166; Morris Swett, "Sergeant I-See-O: Kiowa Scout," *Chronicles of Oklahoma*, Vol. XIII (September, 1935), 344.

pretation as well. George was specifically mentioned in White's letter to Sherman, and he also signed the Cheyenne treaty as a witness. Charlie had been reported on the Smoky Hill, riding with hostile Cheyennes, but Fayel spoke with the half-blood Cheyenne and wrote that the reports of misconduct were not true. According to Charlie, when the Smoky Hill trouble started, he had ridden south into Indian Territory specifically to stay out of any war that might develop.[17]

John Smith is also mentioned as interpreter for the Cheyennes. Smith was cited by a number of correspondents, but his origin and qualifications were ignored by the press reports, though he was undoubtedly present. Ed Guerrier, identified by both Cincinnati reporters as a Cheyenne interpreter, is not mentioned in any official record.[18] Even so, his name is well known to frontier historians.

Like the Cheyenne tongue, Arapaho was an Algonquian language, but the two are so dissimilar that only a philologist could detect the similarities. Cheyenne interpreters were useless to the Arapahoes. Little Raven brought his own—Mrs. Margaret Adams, who attracted a great deal of attention among the reporters. Brown, Bulkley, Budd, Fayel, and Stanley wrote of her in detail, and she was the central theme for one of James Taylor's drawings for *Leslie's*. Budd, Stanley, and Taylor called her Virginia in their stories, confusing her name with that of her thirteen-year-old daughter, who was with her. Mrs. Adams was properly identified in the White letter to Sherman.[19]

At the time of the treaty negotiations, Margaret Adams was about thirty-three years old. Her father had been the French-Canadian trader, John Poisal, her mother an Arapaho. The first of her three

[17] Homer W. Wheeler, *Buffalo Days*, 8; Lavender, *Bent's Fort*, 363; Meyers, *Deaths*, 414; *Missouri Republican*, Oct. 24, 1867.

[18] *Cincinnati Commercial*, Nov. 4, 1867; *Cincinnati Gazette*, Oct. 29, 1867.

[19] Berthrong, *Southern Cheyennes*, 8; Hyatt Verrill, *The Real Americans*, 131; Vestal, *Warpath*, 137; the major source for material on Mrs. Adams is LeRoy Hafen and W. J. Ghent, *Broken Hand: The Story of Thomas Fitzpatrick; Cincinnati Commercial*, Oct. 28, 1867; *Cincinnati Gazette*, Oct. 29, 1867; *Missouri Democrat*, Oct. 29, 1867; *Missouri Republican*, Oct. 28, 1867; *New York Herald*, Oct. 30, 1867; *Leslies' Illustrated Newspaper*, Nov. 16, 1867.

marriages was to Thomas Fitzpatrick, a mountain man and the first U.S. agent to the Arapahoes in the area of Fort Laramie. Fitzpatrick was Virginia's father. Throughout her life, Mrs. Adams had lived near or among the Arapahoes and earlier had interpreted for them at the treaty of the Little Arkansas. When she appeared at the first Grand Councils at Medicine Lodge, wearing a red satin dress, she created a sensation—particularly among the Indians. Brown's comment on Mrs. Adams was to the effect that she came to all the meetings drunk.

Official records did not specify anyone as interpreter for the Plains Apaches or the Kiowa-Apaches. The correspondents made no distinction between the two bands, although the two groups spoke different dialects. Both tribes were Athapaskan, but the Kiowa-Apache Indians had lived in an area where Athapaskan languages were unknown, and over a period of years their speech became unintelligible to the Southwestern Apaches. At some time in their history, the Kiowa-Apaches had migrated away from the rest of the Apache peoples and established a family relationship with the Kiowas—hence their name. Bulkley said the Apache speeches were translated into Arapaho by an Apache-speaking member of Little Raven's tribe. Mrs. Adams in turn translated the Arapaho into English. This answers the question of Plains Apaches' understanding the negotiations, but yet unexplained is how the Kiowa-Apaches said or understood anything. If the tribal potentates were unable to speak or comprehend, they probably were the least confused group at Medicine Lodge—uninformed, perhaps, but not confused.[20]

The Comanche language played a critical part in the discussions. Once a speaker's words had been translated into Comanche, an interpreter from each of the other tribes could translate for his own people. In this process little of the speaker's original meaning could have been preserved, but it was the only method available. As Comanche interpreter, McCusker's role could hardly be exaggerated.

[20] Mooney, "Calendar History," 143–46; Mayhall, *Kiowas*, 144; *New York Herald*, Oct. 30, 1867.

The Peace Commission agreed, paying him more than they paid any other interpreter—$583.65.[21]

Ironically, the reporters could be accurate to a fault yet miss the point an Indian speaker tried to make. What they were reporting was not what the Indian said but what an interpreter *said* the Indian said. Of all those who were involved in the frontier wars—or of all those who since have claimed knowledge of the fighting—in the final analysis only one group really knew what the Indians were trying to say: the Indians.

[21] "Accounts"; Stanley, *Early Travels*, 65f.; J. B. Thoburn, "Horace P. Jones, Scout and Interpreter," *Chronicles of Oklahoma*, Vol. II (Dec., 1924), 380–91.

EIGHT

"I HAVE NO LITTLE LIES HIDDEN ABOUT ME"

—Kiowa

On the first day of the treaty meetings, the interpreters led the tribes to the grove of cottonwoods and elms where the negotiation site had been prepared. The place was about one mile from the Peace Commission camp, downstream along the Medicine Lodge and on the north bank near the large Arapaho encampment.[1] Close by, across the stream, lay the lodges of Black Kettle's Cheyennes.

Superintendent Murphy and his crew had cleared a large area of its underbrush and removed some of the bigger trees, building a twenty-foot-high brush arbor in the center of the cleared space. Folding tables and camp stools had been arranged under the arbor for the commissioners, and on either side were tables and stools for the press party. Logs were placed on the ground around three sides of the arbor to serve as benches so that the Indians could sit facing the Commission. When the Commissioners and correspondents arrived at the council site, many of the Indians awaited them, and the newsmen could see long lines of mounted Indians still streaming in from various parts of the encampment. The grove filled rapidly with blanketed tribesmen as the commissioners found their places under the awning of brush and sat down.

Speakers from each tribe moved to the arbor and seated themselves

---

[1] Treaty site description from the *Chicago Times*, Oct. 29, 1867; *Chicago Tribune*, Oct. 23, 1867; *Cincinnati Commercial*, Oct. 28, 1867; *Missouri Democrat*, Oct. 25, 1867; *New York Herald*, Oct. 30, 1867; *Harper's*, Nov. 16, 1867; *Leslie's Illustrated Newspaper*, November 16, 1867.

on the first line of logs. They were garbed in their best blankets and fine buckskin jackets, and many wore neck pieces of bear claws and elk teeth, while others sported breast plates of polished quills and bones. Some were fitted out in army coats, and a number of the bronzed necks were decorated with medals strung with rawhide thongs. Behind the tribal leaders the lesser chiefs and warriors took their places. In the deep shade of the grove the women tended children and horses.

Hall described in detail the half-circle of Indians facing the commissioners. The Kiowas were on the left, with Satanta sitting in front on an army campstool, probably commandeered from some frontier post. The chief wore an army coat General Hancock had given him earlier in the year. Behind him were Kicking Bird and old Satank. Satank wore about his neck a silver medal with the profile of President Buchanan. The old Kiowa was sixty-seven years old, and streaks of gray marked his long, straight-hanging hair. His mustache was a dirty white.

To Satank's left were the Comanches, and Phillip McCusker squatted in front of them. Ten Bears was wearing his eyeglasses, and Hall noticed the old Comanche squinting his one good eye as he watched the commissioners. The old warrior's thin white hair was pulled tight on either side of his face, and two wrapped braids hung down his chest. Following the style of most of his tribal fellows, he wore a bandanna knotted tightly under his chin.

Black Kettle and Gray Head represented the small group of Cheyennes, and sitting directly behind the two Cheyenne leaders were the Bents. Next came the Arapahoes, with Margaret Adams sitting before them in a folding chair provided by Superintendent Murphy. The lady wore a small red bonnet that matched her billowing dress. Little Raven was there, too, but if he was wearing his revolvers, Hall failed to mention them. Finally, on the far right, were the Plains Apaches with their chief, Little Bear.

The Bents' half-sister, fifteen-year-old Julia, was on the forward edge of the crowd of women. Stanley and Hall noticed her but disagreed concerning her physical appearance. Hall described her as fat and ugly, and he said she had "sunk to barbarism" after running away from the St. Louis boarding school to which her father had sent her. Stanley said the girl had a charming laugh and he wrote that her feet were "the most diminutive size." And, "A peep at her trim ankles might drive an anchorite insane."

As the chiefs found their places, the crowd quieted. Stanley said Fishermore moved among the warriors, making faces, laughing and telling everyone to keep still and behave. When the Kiowa was satisfied with the deportment of his braves, he moved to the brush arbor to shake hands with all the commissioners. Once this demonstration was completed, Fishermore moved to take his place next to Satanta, and with one more warning to all that they should remain still, he turned, facing the commissioners as he seated himself. Everyone watched Commissioner Taylor.

Senator Henderson was the only commissioner absent. Taylor told the Indians that Henderson would speak for the United States and that as soon as the Senator arrived, the official talking could begin. Gray Head, taking advantage of the lull, rose to say that the Cheyennes could not talk until the rest of the tribe arrived from the Cimarron. However, he would listen while the others talked. The newsmen made note of Black Kettle's silence.

While Gray Head's words were being translated, Senator Henderson arrived. He did not sit but stood before the other commissioners as the last of Gray Head's speech was relayed to the Peace Commission and tribesmen. When the Cheyenne chief sat down, Henderson said, "The government of the United States and the Great Father have sent seven commissioners to come here and have a talk with you." Negotiations were finally under way.[2]

Henderson wasted no time on greetings. Omitting the usual expressions of good will and friendship, he went to business, telling the Indians of the 1865 treaty made on the Little Arkansas and re-

[2] News reports of speeches from the *Chicago Times*, Oct. 29, 1867; *Chicago Tribune*, Oct. 26, 1867; *Cincinnati Commercial*, Oct. 29, 1867; *Cincinnati Gazette*, Oct. 29, 1867; *Missouri Democrat*, Oct. 25, 1867; *Missouri Republican*, Oct. 25, 1867; *New York Herald*, Oct. 30, 1867.

minding them of the subsequent war. Reports had gone to Washington that the Indian treaty signers later attacked "peaceable people building a railroad." Women and children had been carried away and men killed, Henderson said. This treaty violation had disappointed United States leaders, and the Peace Commission sought to find those responsible and learn the reason for their acts. The Commission wanted to know whether soldiers or agents had mistreated the discontented tribes, the Senator continued, so action could be taken to prevent such things' happening again. "We have come to correct these wrongs," he said.

Telling the assembled chiefs and warriors what they might expect, Henderson explained the President's desire to house and educate the tribes. The Senator talked at length about one of the Peace Commission's major purposes—to civilize the untamed tribes, but he used more tactful terms. The United States wanted to give the Indians "all the comforts of civilization," Henderson said, including domesticated cattle, farm equipment, and arable land. The Senator pictured for the wild hunters barns, hospitals, and churches. "What have you to say? Tell us, and then we will tell you what road to go," Henderson concluded. He sat down to complete silence.

Satanta arose, holding his army coat about his shoulders like a cloak, and passed along the line of commissioners shaking their hands. The big Kiowa's hair had been carefully groomed. Falling on either side of his head, it had been brushed back to expose the right ear, and from beneath the dark mane there hung a number of small, tightly woven braids. The hair style emphasized a short, bull neck and square jaw. Bulkley, who was not usually interested in details—said Satanta was "very grand."

Replying to Henderson's comments on the war in Kansas, Satanta denied knowledge of hostilities between United States soldiers and Kiowas. Satanta said he had run from the Smoky Hill as soon as trouble started. If wrongs were committed by a few Kiowa young men, he did not know of the acts, nor could he be expected to know everything that happened. The Cheyennes were making war, he continued, not the Comanches and Kiowas. "I would not hide it. I would tell you. Two years ago I made peace with General Sanborn and General Harney and Colonel Leavenworth, and I have not broken that peace yet."

Like Senator Henderson, the Kiowa chief spent most of his time talking about barns, hospitals, and churches. He left no doubt that the Kiowas disliked even talking of permanent homes, farming, and other devices of civilization. His people disapproved of houses, he explained, because when a Kiowa was placed in a pen he died. He wanted to roam the prairie where he was born, free as his fathers had been and as he wanted his children to be after him. He loved the buffalo and the wild country and the open spaces free of barns and hospitals. Stanley appeared pleased that Satanta's closing remarks stunned the commissioners. "I have no little lies hid about me," Satanta said. "But I do not know how it is with the commissioners."

When the Kiowa resumed his place, wild shouts and grunts of approval came from the assembled Indians. The speech had been impressive. Even Budd was swept up in Satanta's powerful personality, and he broke his rule of saying nothing good about Indians— taking, at the same time, the opportunity to belittle the commissioners:

> Satanta is a powerful speaker. . . . Even the commissioners could not help expressing their admiration at his magnificent figure. . . . Savage-like as he is, there is a specimen of nobleness in him which two or three of the Commission might do well to imitate.

Reynolds, also impressed with Satanta's bearing, was more interested in what the Kiowa chief had to say. In these first peace talks, the Lawrence editor distinguished himself as something a little more than a newspaper reporter. He was making an effort to probe, understand, and explain more than obvious words and actions. In the story that he filed, he said these "Bedouins" of the plains could not comprehend a system restrictive of their nomadic lives. Satanta's words came from the heart of the wild tribal philosophy, and he explained their natural resistance to "civilizing" influences. The Kansas editor recognized the basic problem when he said "[Our civilization] is contrary to their whole way of life." In 1867, few people understood this tragic problem.

Little Raven, offered the honor of speaking next, declined on the grounds that he was too disturbed over certain recent horse thievery. Ten Bears, the bespectacled Comanche, rose. He was slightly stoop shouldered, and following Satanta, he presented a rather drab physical appearance. The younger Comanches in the crowd wore long braids greased to a bright shine, and others a scalp lock down their back, but Old Ten Bears retained too little hair for these styles.

He, like Satanta, wanted to remain free, to roam the plains and hunt buffalo. War had persisted in Texas for so long that peace could scarcely be remembered south of the Red River. Ten Bears claimed the Comanches had been forced from their lands in the south, and many white women, he said, had been left crying after Comanche raids left their husbands dead. But no Comanche war existed in Kansas, he added. Ten Bears, perhaps, lacked the fire and force of Satanta, but the correspondents took note of his use of irony and the sparkle in his eye as he concluded, "Of myself, I have no wisdom. But I expect to get some from you." Finished, the old man passed along the line of commissioners, shaking each hand as the various tribes shouted their approval, and even some of the correspondents applauded.

Silver Brooch, a Panateka Comanche, spoke somberly of his band's long history of persecution in Texas. The Panatekas, at one time, had been a powerful band, raiding into Mexico as far south as Durango. The first Comanche band to have close contact with white civilization on the Texas frontier, they had suffered the degenerating effects of whisky and smallpox. A group of their leaders had been massacred attending a supposed San Antonio peace conference in 1839; the Panateka band were the first Comanches forced onto reservations in Texas. Since the Texas reservation period of the mid-1850's, their strength had steadily declined.[3]

[3] *Ibid.*, all newspaper sources cited in fn 2 above; for details on Comanche background, see Richardson, *Comanche Barrier*, 125–32; Kenneth F. Neighbours, "The

Silver Brooch was blunt. He complained that though his people had been promised many things, they had received little. "My band is dwindling very fast," he declared, "I shall wait until next spring to see if these things shall be given us. If they are not, I and my young men will return with our wild brothers to live on the prairie."

Hall and Reynolds recognized Silver Brooch's threat to join the Staked Plains Kwahadi. By other newsmen, however, the Comanche's words were not treated as a threat but rather as the desperate plea of a man whose people were being destroyed. Later, when Congress failed to provide money for reservation buildings promised in the treaty of Medicine Lodge, many Comanches went on the war trail.[4] The hostilities should not have surprised anyone who heard Silver Brooch.

When the Comanches finished speaking, Apache Chief Poor Bear spoke, holding a war shield in one hand. Stanley said Poor Bear was threatening in his demeanor. According to the *Democrat* representative, Chief Poor Bear claimed his shield had made enemies tremble with fear, and he warned that the commissioners, too, should fear him. Some confusion in translation occurred at this point. The only reporter who emphasized the threatening nature of the Apache's speech was Stanley, who mistakenly called Poor Bear an Arapaho. This is one of the few instances when the Medicine Lodge correspondents disagreed on what was said at the Grand Councils. Poor Bear, in a gesture of reconciliation, offered his war shield to Commissioner Taylor before seating himself, and Taylor showed pleasure in accepting the trophy.[5]

Most of the day was consumed by these first speeches. In midafternoon, after Poor Bear's speech, the meeting was adjourned until 10 A.M. the following day. The white men returned to camp in

---

Assassination of Robert S. Neighbors," *West Texas Historical Association Yearbook*, Vol. XXXIV (October, 1958), 38–49; Rupert N. Richardson, "The Comanche Reservatoin in Texas," *West Texas Historical Association Yearbook*, Vol. V (June, 1929), 46–47.

[4] *Sec. of War 68*, Sherman Report.

[5] *Missouri Democrat*, Oct. 25, 1867; *Missouri Republican*, Oct. 24, 1867; *New York Herald*, Oct. 30, 1867.

the army ambulances that had brought them out that morning. They spent the remainder of the day discussing the morning's negotiations and preparing the final drafts of the proposed treaty. Fayel was able to report definitely on Indian sentiments: the warriors wanted nothing to do with reservations or white civilization. Bulkley offered one of his infrequent personal opinions, saying that Satanta's attitude could complicate matters if the Kiowa leader continued to disagree. Stanley agreed but was much more optimistic. The Kiowas and Comanches, he averred, would accept whatever terms the Commission specified.[6]

While the official party discussed the next day's plans, the correspondents prepared their dispatches. The newsmen now had material from an Indian peace conference, and they took advantage of it writing long and detailed columns on what they had heard and seen that first day. The reporters now knew a great deal about Indians in council. Only Reynolds had earlier seen such a gathering. The diplomacy and fine manners of the tribesmen, it was obvious, had impressed the newspapermen. Now doubting previous tales of Indian savagery, some members of the press corps failed to differentiate between Indians on the war trail and Indians in council.

Before evening of October 19, the commissioners completed work on the treaty they would present to the Comanches and Kiowas the following day. The correspondents looked at the document, but, as Fayel and Reynolds explained, it could not be copied verbatim until ratified and proclaimed. Most of the reporters outlined the treaty terms essentially as they were to appear in the finished document. Reynolds' account was most complete, and although the Peace Commission had expressly forbidden a verbatim report of the treaty much of Reynolds' October 21 story follows the wording of the treaty as it was ratified nearly one year later. The newsmen probably made a copy of the draft and sent it out on the first mail run.[7]

The Kansas editor broke the treaty terms down into eight major

[6] *Ibid.*, all sources.
[7] *Chicago Times*, Oct. 29, 1867; *Missouri Republican*, Oct. 28, 1867; *New York Herald*, Oct. 30, 1867.

parts. The first three clauses provided for peace and guaranteed resti-
tution for any Indian loss at the hands of white men. The Indians,
in turn, were required to turn over to U.S. authorities any warrior
becoming involved in raids or other depredations. The next three
clauses dealt with civilizing the tribes, providing for construction of
houses, barns, blacksmith shops, hospitals, and schools on the reservation.

Reynolds defined the reservation boundaries as they later appeared
in the ratified document. He listed the various persons who would
take up residence on the reservations to assist the Indians, including
agents, millers, farmers, blacksmiths, and doctors. Finally, annuities
were guaranteed the tribes according to population and willingness
to settle down and farm. Annuity funds would be spent for clothing
and farm implements, Reynolds said, with all expenditures closely
supervised. Major differences between this and earlier treaties lay in
provisions that the Indians must take reservation lands and farm
them, guaranteed against white encroachment, in order to be eligible
for treaty benefits, and that tribes would no longer be allowed to
reside anywhere except on the established reservation. As long as the
buffalo lasted, they could hunt in those areas specified in the Cheyenne
treaty of the Little Arkansas. The hunting ground, essentially, was
the Arkansas Big Bend country in Kansas. Other treaties gave Indians title to reservation lands, but this was the first time they had
been required to give up all right to live on traditional tribal lands
outside the reservation boundaries. Although Reynolds did not fore-
see the effect, this restrictive clause made legally possible confine-
ment of the tribes to their reservations by force. In less than one
year, the clause proved useful.[8]

In addition to formalizing treaty terms, the commissioners filled
most of the evening framing answers to the Indian speeches made at
the first Grand Council. General agreement was that the Indian way
of life on the Great Plains depended on the buffalo, and once these
animals ceased to exist, the nomadic ways of the tribes would end as

[8] Kappler, *Treaties*, 887–92, 977–89; Richardson, *Comanche Barrier*, 262.

well. Circuitous logic, perhaps, but the important point is that the Peace Commission and correspondents believed that the buffalo would soon disappear. The extinction of the animals was taken for granted, and no one discussed saving the herds. Such a lack of concern appalls a conservation-oriented society, for just such attitudes of the nineteenth century made conservation necessary in the twentieth.[9]

Much thought concerning the reservations system hinged on the vanishing herds; without buffalo to chase, the Plains Indians would be happy to settle on farms and follow a plow. No one seemed to realize that the buffalo had far greater significance for the Plains Indians than as a source of food and clothing. Indeed, when the buffalo were gone, a whole way of life would cease to be.

After dark, the men at Medicine Lodge were warned of Indians on the plains nearby, Indians not invited to the treaty talk. A group of about twenty Osages came into the official party camp, causing considerable stir among the newsmen. To Reynolds, these tall, well-built men of the prairies were a familiar sight. But to the other correspondents, they were unique. Many of the reporters described the Osage: their heads were close cropped except for a long roach which was laced with turkey wattles and dry skin; their ears were pierced at the top and bottom and hung with beads and copper rings; their language seemed unique, too, after listening to the other tribes all day. They spoke a Siouan tongue and evidently had no interpreter. The Osages told the commissioners they had come in to see what was happening. They also wanted to be fed.[10]

According to Bulkley, General Harney distrusted the Osages and was unhappy about their visit. This was not the only instance of Harney's showing dislike for the "tamer" Indians of the frontier. He could not have disliked the Osages because of their being less than capable fighters, however. Most Plains Indians feared these

[9] *Chicago Times*, Oct. 29, 1867; *Missouri Democrat*, Oct. 28, 1867.
[10] *Ibid.*; *Chicago Times*, Oct. 29, 1867; *Cincinnati Commercial*, Oct. 28, 1867; *New York Herald*, Oct. 30, 1867.

tall people who once had lived throughout most of Missouri and Arkansas, spilling over into the tall grass prairie along the Kansas and Arkansas rivers. Perhaps the most vicious feud on the frontier was between the Osages and Kiowas.[11] Harney, certainly, was aware of all this. Apparently he did not respect any tribe that had not mounted a full-scale war against the United States. Or, perhaps he simply found more to admire in the buffalo-hunting blanket Indians of the Plains. None of the several correspondents who mentioned this quirk of Harney's explained the reason for it.

Apprehensive as the negotiating tribes were, the coming of the Osages caused no noticeable excitement in the camps nearest the Peace Commission compound. Likely the Osages had not been seen as they rode into the Commission camp under cover of darkness. General Harney muttered to the press corps that the Osage band probably wanted to trade whisky for wild horses. At any rate, the Osages ate the food given them, squatting just outside the ring of Commission ambulances, and then they quietly disappeared into the night. No one saw them again throughout the remainder of the peace meetings.

Harney was nervous most of the evening, checking the sentries often. Reynolds reported that others on the Peace Commission also were uneasy. Unlike Harney, however, most of the commissioners were concerned over Satanta's reaction to the peace terms mentioned in the Grand Council. Stanley wrote that despite possible trouble spots ahead, the Peace Commission seemed in high spirits. No one could completely ignore the continuing Cheyenne problem; everyone was well aware of the Plains warriors on the Cimarron watching and waiting. Not a dispatch written from Medicine Lodge at this time failed to point out the threat of a Cheyenne attack.[12]

The outcome of the Comanche-Kiowa Grand Council would certainly be reported to the Cheyennes, and if the warriors of Gray Head and Tall Bull did not like what they heard—if they felt the

[11] Corwin, *Kiowa Indians*, 18f.; Mathews, *Osages*, 556f.; *New York Herald*, Oct. 30, 1867.

[12] *Chicago Times*, Oct. 29, 1867; *Missouri Democrat*, Oct. 28, 1867.

Peace Commission was improperly treating with the other tribes—
they might well ride in with war paint. But whether the atmosphere
of the camp was one of foreboding or forced optimism, no chances
were taken. The compound guard remained at double strength, and
Harney restated his order that everyone would stay in camp.

NINE

"WHY DO YOU INSIST ON THOSE HOUSES?"

—Kiowa

On Sunday, October 20, the commission waited for the Indians. Although the meeting had been set for late in the morning, none of the tribesmen were present when the Peace Commission arrived at the council grove. The delay caused another flare-up between Senator Henderson and General Harney, and the spat was reported in detail by both Stanley and Reynolds, who seem to have worked their way into the midst of Peace Commission discussions. They were consistently more attentive to the push and pull of Commission personalities than the other correspondents.

For once, Henderson seemed undisturbed about waiting, and he speculated that the tribes were probably attending church. Reynolds pointed out that Henderson had been eager to provide Christian services for the Indians, but there was never any suggestion by Reynolds or anyone else that the Peace Commission was trying to force Christianity on the Indians. No mention was ever made, for instance, of assigning missionaries to the reservations. Most of the commissioners were probably aware that white man's religion had never been spectacularly successful among the tribes of the Great Plains. The Spaniards had discovered—often too late—that Comanches were interested in Christian missions, but not for spiritual reasons; missions meant tame Indians, and tame Indians meant livestock, women, and children to be easily taken by Comanche raiders. Destroyed missions were a monument to the uninvited Spanish religious invasion of the Co-manches' country.[1]

Senator Henderson's desire to provide Indian church services appeared to be more of a gesture of friendship than one of missionary zeal. If he was successful in having religious services for the Plains braves, none of the correspondents mentioned who preached, where the services were held, or if the Indians showed any interest.

When the Indians finally appeared, many were drunk, and others suffered from too much liquor the night before. When Harney saw their condition, he was furious. He was contemptuous of Senator Henderson's hope that the tribesmen had been in church. The old soldier laid the blame on the Osages who had been in the Commission camp the night before. He had expected liquor trading by the Osages, he told Stanley, and added that a tame border Indian was beneath a white man's respect. As Harney continued to speak of Osages, whisky, and the foolish idea of Plains warriors in church—speaking loud enough for all to hear—Henderson was becoming quite angry. However, Stanley said the Missouri Senator held his tongue, at least for the moment.[2]

Noon had almost arrived before all the tribal chiefs had taken their places around the brush arbor, but happily they were not under the influence of the whisky which was making some of their warriors loud and unruly. The seating arrangement was identical to that of the first day, but the Indian spokesmen had established a different speaking order. When Commissioner Taylor opened the meeting, Ten Bears rose to make the initial address to the council. It was soon apparent that the chiefs had come prepared to speak frankly.[3]

---

[1] Richardson, *Comanche Barrier*, 15–74; Simpson, *San Saba Papers*, 153; *Chicago Times*, Oct. 29, 1867.

[2] *Missouri Democrat*, Oct. 29, 1867.

[3] Newspaper accounts of the Comanche-Kiowa meeting in the *Chicago Times*, Oct. 29, 1867; *Chicago Tribune*, Oct. 29, 1867; *Cincinnati Commercial*, Oct. 28, 1867; *Cincinnati Gazette*, Oct. 28, 1867; *Missouri Democrat*, Oct. 28, 1867; *Missouri Republican*, Oct. 28, 1867; *New York Herald*, Oct. 30, 1867; *New York Tribune*, Nov. 6, 1867; *Harper's*, Nov. 16, 1867; *Leslie's Illustrated Newspaper*, Nov. 16, 23, 1867.

None of the Comanches, Ten Bears said, wanted anything to do with wooden barns or medicine houses. They wanted to roam free on the prairie, following the buffalo as they had always done. "I wish you would not keep insisting on putting us on reservations," the old Comanche said. There was little need for it. In the past, it had always been the white man who broke treaty promises. Particularly had this been true in Texas, and once again Ten Bears recalled lost Comanche lands south of Red River. The Indians showed their approval of the speech with loud shouts, and as the Comanche sat down, a number of heated conversations among the rear ranks warriors disturbed the meeting momentarily. When Satanta rose, the Indians fell silent, waiting for his talk.

Everything was said yesterday, the big Kiowa began, but he remembered a few additional things he wanted to tell. He did not like agents to hide treaty annuities from him. At the councils on the Little Arkansas, Satanta said, firearms and ammunition had been promised, as well as other things of less importance, and these things were being held in some storeroom. He wanted his annuities now. As he continued standing before the Peace Commission, the Indians shouted their approval once more.

Despite the good impression Satanta had made upon the press party until then, his unsubtle accusations against his agent, Leavenworth, were extremely distasteful to Hall. The Chicago correspondent said the Kiowa chief was lying, trying to get more than was his due under the Little Arkansas treaty provisions. Hall, apparently, chose to ignore Commissioner Taylor's reply to Satanta. Taylor explained that the Commission was aware that many annuities had not been issued for the year 1867; the goods were in the Peace Commission camp and would be distributed at the end of the treaty talks. Although Taylor did not bother with a detailed explanation, the Commission had decided on August 7 that annuities then in transit should be brought to Medicine Lodge by Superintendent Murphy—and not issued until Taylor gave the order to do so. Indian annuities were generally distributed in summer and fall, and the Peace Commission holding order reached the agents before much of the clothing and equipment had been received by the intended tribes. Hall questioned Satanta's claim that some of the Kiowa annuities had not arrived. After Taylor's statement, it was obvious that Satanta had spoken the truth. Before they left Medicine Lodge, Satanta's Kiowas had their full share of 1865 treaty goods.[4]

All accounts of what happened next indicate a complete breakdown of order. Satanta and Ten Bears became involved in a heated argument, and Senator Henderson, too, tried to speak. Snatches of the Indian conversation were interpreted, and the newsmen finally were able to make some sense out of the babble. Satanta began by saying that the Kiowas needed to discuss among themselves what Taylor had said. Ten Bears told McCusker it was too bad about the Kiowas' having to do so much talking among themselves before they decided anything. Ten Bears' slur must have touched a raw nerve in the big Kiowa. Despite their friendship, Kiowas and Comanches frequently became irritated at each other because of their different ways of decision making. According to certain Indian sources, Comanches thought Kiowas talked too much, and Kiowas felt that Comanches rushed off on depredatory attacks without sufficient discussion.[5] With Henderson still on his feet, trying to restore order, Satanta left the council. For a moment the meeting was in danger of disintegrating.

Whisky in Indian bellies did little to help the situation. A great deal of noise came from the braves standing in rear of the log benches, but Henderson, with the help of McCusker and other interpreters, finally got the Indian delegation quiet. Before anyone else spoke, Henderson and other Peace Commission members spoke together, but the reporters could not hear what was said. Another flurry of movement was heard in the rear ranks, and the warriors moved aside as Satanta stalked back up to the brush arbor. Everyone was waiting for him to resume his speech, but he waited for a long period, looking around at the Peace Commission and the Indians.

Obviously still angry, the Kiowa launched a bitter attack against Agent Leavenworth, this time leaving no doubt about the man of

[4] "Journal," Aug. 7, 1867.
[5] Alice Marriott, *Ten Grandmothers*, 165.

whom he spoke—he called Leavenworth by name. Satanta said the Kiowas could no longer trust their agent because of his blatant favoritism, and they wanted another agent. Before anyone on the Peace Commission could answer Satanta's charges, Ten Bears came to his feet. The old Comanche claimed his people liked Leavenworth, and they would not hear of his being moved. For a moment it appeared that Satanta would leave the council a second time. Instead, after a few moments of glaring about, he sat down. Ten Bears had already resumed his place and was watching the big Kiowa.

Satanta and Leavenworth had been at odds before. After the Hancock campaign, the Kiowa agent had bitterly complained about Satanta and his activities in Texas. When Hancock accepted Satanta's show of friendship—even giving the Indian presents—Leavenworth denounced the army for not arresting the Kiowa for his depredations south of the Red River.[6] From all accounts, during 1866–67, Agent Leavenworth had been driven nearly mad from the Kiowas' duplicity. At the time of Medicine Lodge, the agent had had little trouble from the Comanches. By the following spring, he was to learn that Comanches could be as obstinate, uncontrollable, and treacherous as the Kiowas.

Reynolds held the opinion that Satanta's ill temper at the Grand Council had nothing to do with Leavenworth or with Ten Bears' sharp remarks. The Kansas editor asserted that the tribes could no longer be allowed to roam and the Indians began to comprehend this thinking as the council progressed. Any Indian leader worth his salt would have to object violently. "Much care and caution must be exercised to carry out the new policy," Reynolds wrote. Clearly, Reynolds understood the sensitive nature of the negotiations. A wrong word or a hasty action at any point could bring on a full-scale war with the southern tribes; or at this tense time, perhaps the southern tribes might even begin fighting among themselves.

Henderson may have agreed with Reynolds. At any rate, when the chiefs had finished their speeches, the Senator ignored the attack on Leavenworth, replying instead to the Indians' frequent com-

[6] Commissioner *Report 67*, 35; *Special Report*, 60, 3.

ments that they wanted to remain free to follow the buffalo. His next speech was another one recorded rather accurately by the reporters. Stanley, Bulkley, Budd, and Brown agreed on all except three minor words:

> You say you do not like the medicine houses but you do like the buffalo and that you wish to do as your fathers did. We say to you that the buffalo will not last forever. They are now becoming few and you must know it. When that day comes, the Indian must change the road his father trod, or he must suffer and die . . . we offer you the way . . . Before all the good lands are taken by whites we wish to set aside a part of them for your exclusive use . . . On that land we will build you a house to hold the goods we will send you when you become hungry and naked. You can go there and be fed and clothed.[7]

Reading from the notes he had prepared the evening before, Henderson outlined the treaty terms. In the sullen silence that followed, he asked if anyone had a comment on the treaty provisions. Satanta, controlling his temper once more, said, "I ask the Commission to tell the Great Father what I have to say. When the buffalo leave the country, we will let him know. By that time we will be ready to live in houses."

The day's business ended on an uncertain note, but with darkness settling in the basin, Taylor adjourned the meeting. He told the Indians to come to the council grove prepared to sign the treaty the following morning. The tribesmen silently moved away from the brush arbor to their horses in the trees. Riding back to the Peace Commission compound in their ambulances, the commissioners and correspondents remained quiet, too. Darkness had fallen by the time they reached their camp.

On the morning of October 21, the Peace Commission presented a copy of the treaty for the Indians' signatures. But the document was not exactly as Henderson had explained it the day before. One change

[7] This is Stanley's report, which was identical to Bulkley's and Budd's and differed from Brown's in only minor wording.

had been incorporated the previous evening—after the turbulent second day of the Grand Council. Once again, Senator Henderson spoke to the tribes, explaining the new provision. It was an important one, allowing the Comanches and Kiowas to hunt on their old lands south of the Arkansas—the Texas Panhandle, as well as the Arkansas River Big Bend country in southern Kansas. The government agreed to bar white settlement in the Arkansas Big Bend for three years. William Fayel outlined in his dispatches the Texas Panhandle hunting area exactly as it had been defined in the 1865 treaty of the Little Arkansas.[8]

From the beginning, Reynolds reported Sanborn's concern about using any plan that would force the Indians to give up title to the Southern Plains south of the 36th parallel and west of the 100th meridian. Apparently, after the Indian speeches of October 20, the Peace Commission was convinced that to come to terms with the tribes, they would have to allow continued hunting in the Texas Panhandle as long as that area's buffalo herds were large enough to justify the chase. This provision made the treaty a bit ambiguous. The Indians were specifically denied the right of making permanent homes outside the reservation. Yet, the tribes could spend the major part of any year following buffalo off the reservation and still be in compliance with treaty terms. If the Commission intended the treaty as a confining document, forcing the tribes to a pastoral status, the hunting clause weakened chances of establishing such an arrangement.

How much the Indians understood is impossible to determine, but Stanley was convinced that the tribesmen had little comprehension of what was happening. One thing was certain: the Indians understood they had been promised continued hunting in Texas. Of course, trouble came later when white men denied the promise. The continued movement of Indians through the Texas Panhandle after the treaty presented a constant irritation to whites, who claimed the tribes were more interested in raiding than hunting. The situation grew worse year by year, as in the past, until the Red River War of 1874 forced the Indians from Texas. Only then were the confining measures of the

[8] Kappler, *Treaties*, 982.

treaty realized.[9] By then, hunting rights had little meaning anyway; the buffalo were nearly gone.

After a short discussion of the new provision on hunting rights, Commissioner Taylor asked the Indians if they had any questions. They told him they had discussed the treaty the night before and that with the addition of the new clause, it was acceptable to them and they were ready to sign. Kicking Bird, of the Kiowas, said there had been enough talk. Time had come for the commissioners to pass out presents. No indication was given that the Indians had changed their minds about the reservation system, and as Satanta moved up to the folding army table where the treaty lay, he said, "Why do you insist on those houses?" Silver Brooch liked the idea of houses, but for the second time he warned that the dwellings should be completed by the following spring at the latest.

Ten Comanches and nine Kiowas made their mark on the treaty. Most correspondents reported names of a few signers; Fayel listed all of them. He was incorrect in naming two Kiowas—Crow and Stumbling Bear—as Comanches. The signers were: for the Comanches, Ten Bears, Painted Lips, Silver Brooch, Standing Feather, Gap in the Woods, Horse Back, Wolf's Name, Little Horn, Iron Mountain, and Dog Fat. For the Kiowas: Satanta, Satank, Kicking Bird, Stinking Saddle Cloth (Fishermore), Woman's Heart, Stumbling Bear, One Bear, Crow, and Bear Lying Down.[10] Any list of Indian names is interesting to speculate upon. Although little profanity was included in their language, the Plains Indians spoke obscenely by European standards, and proper names were no exception. Some humor might have been added to an otherwise somber moment if the interpreters had translated Indian names literally.

Stanley, obviously optimistic and light hearted up to the point of treaty signing, became depressed about what the piece of paper really meant to the Indians—not what they thought of it but rather the effect it would have on them. The treaty began, "From this day

[9] Wirth, *Soldier and Brave*, 47f.; Chapman, "The Claim of Texas to Greer County, Oklahoma," *Southwest Historical Review*, Vol. XVIII (July, 1949), 19–34.
[10] Kappler, *Treaties*, 982.

forward," but Stanley observed that the phrase really meant until such time as the white man wanted to take more land. By touching the feather, Stanley said, the chiefs had ceded 60,000 square miles of territory that had always been the Indian home.

Considerable evidence exists that after the 1865 councils on the Little Arkansas, the provisions of that treaty were changed after the document reached the U.S. Senate—without being referred back to the Indians involved. There has been no indication that anything of this nature occurred with the Comanche-Kiowa Treaty of Medicine Lodge.[11] The draft treaty, at least according to newspaper accounts, was very nearly identical with the ratified document. Variations occurred in the amount of detail supplied by the correspondents, but over-all few sentences in the entire treaty escaped examination by someone in the press party at Medicine Lodge.

The United States and the Comanches and Kiowas pledged their honor to maintain a lasting peace on the frontier.[12] In reporting the pledge, Fayel said the Indians specifically promised to maintain peace in Texas. None of the other newsmen mentioned such a provision, and such a definitive area was not a part of the final treaty.

The reservation was outlined, and although none of the press party attempted to define its exact boundaries, they adequately indicated its general location. Taylor wrote that the Comanches and Kiowas had been given 6,000 square miles of land, certainly an exaggeration. The area actually was about 4,800 square miles. Howland was guilty of the most obvious inaccuracy in claiming the reservation was larger than the one provided by the Treaty of the Little Arkansas. In fact, it was much smaller. The reservation included all of present-day Kiowa, Comanche, Cotton, and Tillman counties, and parts of Caddo, Grady, Stephens, and Jefferson counties in southwestern Oklahoma.

[11] Commissioner *Report 67*, 309f.; Brill, *Conquest*, 87; Jackson, *Century of Dishonor*, 90; Grinnell, *Fighting Cheyennes*, 236.

[12] Kappler, *Treaties*, 977–82; newspaper discussions of treaty terms in *Chicago Times*, Oct. 25, 1867; *Cincinnati Commercial*, Nov. 4, 1867; *Cincinnati Gazette*, Nov. 4, 1867; *Missouri Democrat*, Oct. 28, 1867; *Missouri Republican*, Oct. 28, 1867; *New York Herald*, Oct. 30, 1867; *Harper's*, Nov. 16, 1867; *Leslie's Illustrated Newspaper*, Nov. 16, 23, 1867.

Also provided was at least 160 acres of tillable land per member of the various tribes authorized to live on the reservation, the article that prompted Fayel to say that the Peace Commission had established an agricultural reserve. Article IV dealt with the construction that Silver Brooch wanted completed by the following summer. The reporters were all interested in this clause of the treaty, and they covered it in great detail. Reynolds listed the buildings and their cost, and he said the total amount to be spent for improvements would be $35,000. His readers would be concerned with those figures; Kansas material and labor would go into the reservations. Although Reynolds correctly stated the cost of each individual structure, his total was too high. The treaty specified an agency building and medical facility at $3,000 each; a warehouse for $1,500; buildings for a farmer, carpenter, blacksmith, miller, and engineer costing $2,000 each; a school for $5,000; and an $8,000 saw mill and shingle factory. The total construction bill would come to $30,500. The construction program was impressive, providing the basic requirements of any new settlement. However, as Silver Brooch pointed out, having it on paper and having it on the ground were two entirely different things. None of the correspondents expanded on this basic weakness of all United States treaties with the Indians, although a few mentioned it briefly: The time it took to ratify a treaty, appropriate money, and complete construction was beyond the understanding of the Indians. But if the newsmen were naïve about this purely mechanical disadvantage of Indian treaties, they were members of a large company.

Fayel took particular note of Article V, which required an Indian agent to live on the reservation, where he could inquire into complaints, investigate depredations, and file written reports on disputes and disagreements. Previously, agents generally lived at an army post near Indian lands, and some detractors accused agents of never going near their native charges.[13]

Article VI, the major civilizing provision of the treaty, established a Comanche-Kiowa land book for keeping account of individual In-

[13] Fey and D'Arcy, *Indians*, 25–31.

dians holding legal title to their own land. To obtain title, an Indian simply indicated his desire to farm. With the agent's assistance, he would choose a 360-acre tract, which ceased to be held in common by the tribe and would become the private property of the Indian and his family. Fayel's interpretation was that the stipulation was designed to induce Indians into farming and civilization. Whether he knew it or not, the newspaperman had touched on the subject of civilizing the tribes at its most sensitive spot. Truely, if a Plains Indian could be taught an appreciation of private-property ownership, he could soon achieve a society similar to that of Western Europe.

Unfortunately, an allotment of 360 acres of privately owned farm land could hardly have been a source of delight to the Indian, who had never understood how a slip of paper could entitle a man to exclusive use of a part of the earth's surface. The concept of private ownership had little or no meaning to an Indian, especially as applied to real estate. To expect the tribesman to sell his right to hunt for the privilege of farming—was ambitious. Actually, to the Indian hunting was just as civilized as farming and more in keeping with his preference for individual independence. Perhaps it was nearsighted of the Peace Commission to expect the Indian to give up what he liked and admired in return for something he despised, all for a prize he did not understand.[14] This was what Reynolds meant when he said the Indians' idea of life was entirely different from the white man's. The Kansas editor added, "The reservation is for those who work the land." It was a concise appraisal of the entire treaty.

Article VII specified that children between the ages of six and sixteen would attend school. One teacher would be provided for every thirty children. Article VIII also covered the subject of farming, promising any beginning Indian farmer a supply of seed and implements not to exceed one hundred dollars in value. If the agent was satisfied that the Indian was serious about farming, an additional twenty-five dollars worth of seed would be provided each year for three years. Article IX gave the United States the right to with-

[14] *Ibid.*; Pearce, *Savages*, 71, 199.

draw any of the craftsmen specified in earlier articles. None of these provisions received much attention from the press gang.

Each year for thirty years, every male Indian over fourteen would receive a coat, pants, flannel shirt, hat, and socks. Women over twelve were authorized a flannel shirt, woolen hose, twenty yards of calico, and twelve yards of homespun cotton cloth. For those under the specified ages, stockings and enough cotton fabric to make a suit or dress would be supplied. The number of garments distributed would be determined by an annual reservation census. Additionally, the Secretary of the Interior was authorized to spend $25,000 annually on items to provide for the tribe's general welfare. An army officer—selected by the President—would be present to issue the annuities on October 15 of each year, and he would inspect the items for quality as well as quantity. The annuities provisions got good play from the correspondents. Howland stated incorrectly that the general welfare expenditure was authorized at $35,000, but other than that, the newspaper reports were accurate. No one mentioned the obvious reason why an army officer was specified to issue the items; with someone outside the Indian Bureau present to check inventory on distribution day, there was less chance for an Indian agent to cheat his wards.

The Peace Commission's attempts at Medicine Lodge to avert an Indian war were strikingly similar to modern techniques—for the Commissioners were trying to pacify the stable part of the tribes— the old men, the more settled and cool-headed men, and the women and children—hoping that this segment of Indian society would stop condoning and harboring the war-making braves. They hoped to remove the tribal sanctuary for war parties, giving economic aid to the tribe as a whole in return for promises to turn in terrorists. The problem facing them resembled that facing the U.S. government as it is now engaged in a guerrilla-war in Viet Nam. No one could tell the hostile from the friendly Indians when both were sitting around a council table—or for that matter on the open prairie or along the streets of Fort Larned. No one really knew who the hostiles were except the Indians themselves. As long as the Indians protected the irresponsible element in their tribe, no chance existed completely to stop Indian raiding. Nothing was harder to anticipate or to catch than a Plains war party once it had separated itself from the village and started to move, as the army learned on too many occasions. United States troops generally got to fight when and if the Indians wanted to do battle. The only way to avoid a dismal lack of initiative was to attack the villages—when they could be found— where there were always some of the innocent killed along with the guilty.[15]

All the correspondents at the councils gave an account of the restrictive treaty clause—Article XI. The Comanches and Kiowas were prohibited from taking permanent residence in any area outside the reservation, but they retained, however, the right to hunt south of the Arkansas as long as the buffalo lasted. In the Arkansas Big Bend country, no white settlements would be allowed for three years. In return for the considerations to be given them, the Comanches and Kiowas were to stop opposing railroad construction, cease attacking homes and travel routes, and show no resistance to military posts established in the western territories.

Milton Reynolds was bitterly amused at the provision designated to keep white men out of the Big Bend country. He pointed out that the army would have to be ten times larger to police such an area and keep settlers out; the Kansan claimed Governor Sam Crawford was already arming whites and encouraging them to encroach on Indian land.[16]

The last five articles of the treaty received but slight attention from the reporters, with Fayel and Reynolds, as usual, giving the most detailed accounts. These five articles provided that no part of the Comanche-Kiowa reservation could be taken from the Indians without the consent of at least three-fourths of the adult male population living on the reservation. The government agreed to pay the salaries of all reservation employees, including doctors, teachers, blacksmiths, carpenters, millers, engineers, and agricultural advisors.

[15] *Sec. of War 67*, 34; *Missouri Republican*, Oct. 28, 1867.
[16] *Chicago Tribune*, Oct. 21, 25, 1867; *Missouri Republican*, Oct. 28, 1867.

Indians were to receive employment preference in staffing the agency facilities.

Because Silver Brooch claimed he was already farming in the reservation area, the treaty authorized the construction of a $750 dwelling for him and his family. The Comanche chief thus received the distinction of being the only person whose name appeared in the body of any treaty made at Medicine Lodge. Having his name in the treaty must have been doubtful compensation for the man who had insisted to the Peace Commission that reservation construction must be completed by the coming summer. For the summer of 1868 came, and no money had been appropriated to fulfill the treaty provisions— not even the $750 for Silver Brooch's house.[17]

Undoubtedly most of the press corps at Medicine Lodge were aware of the treaty's shortcomings. Considering only the tribes south of the Arkansas, there was still the possibility of hostilities with Comanches not represented at the Peace Councils. Hall mentioned the Staked Plains Kwahadies, stating that these most inaccessible of Comanches had been at war for generations against Texas. Stanley, also speaking of the Kwahadies, said that if these High Plains warriors could be induced to enter into discussions, great areas of west Texas would be opened for settlement. Reynolds wrote that only discreet management could make the treaty work. He said that the Comanches and Kiowas had agreed to go on the reservation under protest. No matter what the inducement, they could not conceive of a "cooped-up" existence. "They can not brook restraint," Reynolds said.

Once the treaty was signed, the Indians were visibly impatient to receive their presents. Taylor told them the annuities due them under the Little Arkansas treaty would be distributed at once near the Peace Commission headquarters. Fayel said the Indians were lightened at the prospect of gifts and ". . . felt much better pleased than with puzzling their heads about various treaty stipulations."[18]

The commissioners led the Indians to the wagon park where Mur-

[17] *Sec. of War 67*, 2.
[18] *Missouri Republican*, Oct. 28, 1867.

phy and Leavenworth were preparing to distribute the merchandise.[19] On hand to help were teamsters and a few soldiers, and after a short wait, an agency roster was produced by Leavenworth, who proceeded to call the roll. The chiefs stood watching and talking with the commissioners as the people were called forward to receive the annuity goods. Among the items passed out were a number of pistols, and a few of the young Indian men, along with some of the reporters and a few teamsters, moved away from the wagon park to test fire the weapons. Understandably, the Indians were excited and happy with the guns, but when the first brave raised his weapon and fired at a tree, the pistol exploded in his hand, the pieces flying about and striking a few of the bystanders. The Indian was not as disturbed about his bleeding hand, however, as he was with the demolished weapon. The firing of a second and third pistol brought the same results. The Indians could hardly have been more indignant than Stanley and Brown, who complained bitterly in their next dispatch about the government's trying to foist off such faulty hardware on the Indians. The weapons had been manufactured by Union Arms Company, an organization Stanley said should be investigated by Congress.

The embarrassment over the exploding pistols soon passed, however, as a few Colt revolvers were issued. The Indians as well as the whites were aware of the quality of the Colts weapons, and apparently no one present speculated on how soon these weapons would be used on white men. The thought of this, however, had crossed more than one Peace Commissioner's mind. They had debated the firearms issue in a meeting not attended by the reporters. One of the official party tents had been the setting for the conference. The firearms, they found, were a part of the Little Arkansas treaty annuity held by Leavenworth since the Peace Commision order of August 7. During the commission discussion—shown in official minutes taken by A. S. H. White—the military members

---

[19] "Journal," Oct. 21, 1867; the annuities issue taken from the *Chicago Times*, Oct. 29, 1867; *Cincinnati Commercial*, Oct. 29, 1867; *Missouri Democrat*, Oct. 28, 1867; *Missouri Republican*, Oct. 28, 1867.

made no serious objection to the pistol issue. General Terry said the tribes needed weapons to hunt, and he personally made the motion that the guns be distributed. The Commission then voted to make the issue.[20]

Toward the end of the day, the wind rose, and dark clouds gathered over the treaty grounds. The last of the Comanches and Kiowa annuities were loaded on Indian ponies and hurriedly carried down along the river; some of the Kiowas had to travel ten miles to reach their tipis. The departing Indians were told that treaty presents for the Medicine Lodge Treaty would be distributed the following day.

The official party and the correspondents moved quickly to their tents, preparing to spend the night with necessary paper work and letter writing. Before dark, rain began. Reynolds described it as a typical autumn storm for the Kansas plains, with the high winds driving the chilling rain almost horizontal to the ground.

Bad weather was not enough to keep one group of Cheyennes from riding into the Peace Commission camp and asking for a conference. None of the officials knew of the Indian party's presence until a sentry reported to General Harney of their waiting in the rain outside the ambulance compound. Several chiefs were conducted into the inclosure and led to one of the Commission tents. With wet blankets still wrapped around their waists, they sat down as Commission orderlies brought more kerosene lanterns and the commissioners began assembling. Black Kettle was in the group, along with Little Robe and White Horse from the Cimarron camp.[21]

John Smith, the Cheyenne interpreter—or one of them at any rate—explained to the Peace Commission that the chiefs had a few things to discuss among themselves before they spoke with the United States delegates. Coming from the Cimarron, they had gone directly to Black Kettle's camp but had not stopped to confer. Smith

[20] "Journal," Oct. 21, 1867.
[21] The Cheyenne meeting described in the *Cincinnati Commercial*, Nov. 4, 1867; *Cincinnati Gazette*, Nov. 4, 1867; *Missouri Democrat*, Oct. 28, 1867; *Missouri Republican*, Oct. 28, 1867; *New York Herald*, Oct. 30, 1867.

explained that the Cimarron Cheyennes needed a few words with Black Kettle, and Commissioner Taylor told them to go ahead. While the Indians conversed in low tones, the rest of the Peace Commission and some of the newspapermen entered. The wind and rain audibly pounded against the tent.

Stanley watched Black Kettle. The *Missouri Democrat* correspondent reported later that the peace-seeking Cheyenne appeared very nervous as the other Indians spoke to him. Other correspondents noticed the same thing, many of them remarking that being a peacemaker among the Cheyennes in 1867 was a dangerous occupation. Finally, the Cimarron Cheyennes said they were ready to talk, and as the council proceeded, Black Kettle's discomfiture grew. Stanley reported that the Cheyenne chief seemed extremely agitated.

Smith told the Commission that the Cheyennes wanted the Comanches and Kiowas to remain with them at the treaty ground while they held Grand Council with the white man. The Cheyennes said they wanted the South Plains Indians to hear their speeches. Reporting this conversation, none of the correspondents suggested that the Cheyennes might have wanted support from the two most powerful southern tribes if trouble arose. Indeed, the correspondents' impression was that the Cheyennes needed no help in peace or war. Wet, their hair plastered down and ragged looking in the lantern light, the Cheyenne warriors were large men, and their physical appearance impressed the correspondents.

Commissioner Taylor told the Cheyenne assemblage that the tribes from the south would draw the last of their treaty presents on the following day, probably leaving after that to find suitable pasture for their pony herds before winter set in. General Augur stated further that the Comanches and Kiowas would be invited to the Cheyenne Grand Council, but he admitted there was no way of forcing the Southern Plains tribesmen to stay.

Senator Henderson was present but left the talking to Taylor and Augur. General Augur was taking his first active part in the oral deliberations with the Indians. During the Comanche-Kiowa councils, the General had remained silent, but the correspondents noted that he spoke frequently for the Commission when the Cheyennes were involved in the negotiations. Perhaps he felt more qualified to talk with these Indians because related tribesmen were in his own command along the Platte River.

Henderson did not like allowing the Comanches and Kiowas to remain in camp, and he made no effort to hide his irritation. The Peace Commission would be obliged to continue feeding them, the Senator said, and supplying rations was becoming expensive. Reynolds agreed with Henderson, and he reported an impressive daily issue of food to the Indians. Some days as many as fifty sacks of flour were distributed, and often the number went as high as two hundred. With the flour went great quantities of meat, coffee, and tobacco. There were lesser items, such as sugar—Comanches enjoyed half a cup of sugar in each cup of coffee.

Taylor was concerned that if all the other tribes left, the Cheyennes might refuse to come in at all. After a few more protests, Henderson reluctantly agreed that the Comanches and Kiowas should be invited to the Cheyenne Grand Council.

Satisfied that the Peace Commission would do what it could to have the Southern Plains tribes remain at Medicine Lodge, the Cheyenne chiefs mentioned the medicine ceremonies being conducted on the Cimarron. Taylor told them he and the other commissioners were aware of the importance of the ceremonies, but he said the United States delegation had already been waiting a number of days and wanted to go home. Smith asked the chiefs when the medicine ceremonies would be finished.

Once again, their voices low, the Cimarron Cheyennes conferred among themselves. Stanley said the Indians appeared to be talking to Black Kettle. After a few more moments of discussion, Black Kettle explained that carrying out the ceremonies to renew the strength of the medicine was a painstaking business. The ceremonies had been delayed because a number of things had gone wrong, making it necessary to begin all over again. Finally, Black Kettle said four days would be required to complete the ceremonies, and then the tribe would be ready to talk.

No one really knew what the Cheyennes were talking about. Brown became confused in his report, saying that there was a Cheyenne chief named Medicine Arrow whom the Cheyennes would follow anywhere and on any mission, no matter how dangerous. There was no Cheyenne by that name in the Cimarron village at the time insofar as could be determined. Brown probably misinterpreted the conversation about the medicine-arrow ceremonies. He was likely no worse off than any of the other newsmen, because there were few men who understood—or even tried to understand—the Plains Indians religious and social ceremonies.[22]

Black Kettle told the Peace Commission that he was eager to stop the Smoky Hill trouble as quickly as possible. If the Commission would only remain until the Cheyennes were finished with the medicine ceremonies, he said, a lasting peace could be negotiated. After Smith interpreted Black Kettle's comments, the Peace Commission engaged in a heated discussion, to the obvious enjoyment of the press gang.

General Augur suggested that the Peace Commission split, part staying at Medicine Lodge, the others going back to the North Platte to meet with the Sioux and Northern Cheyennes. This was not satisfactory to the rest of the Commission, and Taylor ended the argument by saying that the group would stay together. Senator Henderson agreed, but he said something had to be done because his time was limited. Pressing business in Missouri needed his attention. "These medicine ceremonies are humbug," Stanley and Fayel reported the Senator's saying. Immediately, Augur, Sanborn, and Harney voiced strong objections to Henderson's statement. Harney was particularly adamant, and it was apparent to the press corps that the Missouri Senator did not appreciate it when the General said Indians were truer to their religion than were white men. The words grew hotter between the two men, and both Missouri reporters were scribbling notes—they gave their readers what they claimed were verbatim

[22] Grinnell, *Fighting Cheyennes*, 42; Wallace and Hoebels, *Comanches*, 155f.; W. S. Campbell, "The Cheyenne Dog Soldiers," *Chronicles of Oklahoma*, Vol. XI (January, 1921), 90–97.

accounts of the quarrel. Henderson said he would return to St. Louis soon, no matter what the Cheyennes did. Harney lost his temper completely, according to Stanley. The white-haired soldier told Henderson if he tried to leave the peace camp soldiers would place him under arrest and detain him by force until the Cheyennes came in.

Still angry, Harney said the Cheyennes should be given five more days. Commissioner Taylor curtly said that five days were too many—Black Kettle had asked for four, and if the Commission allowed five, the Indians would take advantage of them. Taylor's comment appeared to cool Harney's temper, and he said nothing more. Taylor told Smith to inform the Cheyennes that they would be expected in four days. Little Robe replied this time, saying the medicine ceremonies would be finished by then. He said he was looking forward to making a strong peace.

Explaining that they had more business to discuss, the commissioners said good-by to Little Robe and the other Cheyenne chiefs at the entrance to the tent. Smith led them across the dark compound to their waiting ponies, and the sound of their leaving was lost in the splash of the rain as the commissioners resumed their seats.

Superintendent Murphy had two messages from the Indians who were already at Medicine Lodge. The first was from Little Raven. The fat Arapaho wanted to negotiate separately from the Cheyennes. Although the two tribes had been allies for years, their Cheyenne friends had brought them nothing but trouble, Little Raven complained. The second message came from the Apaches, whom the Peace Commission had thus far ignored. Murphy said these Plains nomads wanted to settle on the Comanche-Kiowa reservation and be confederated with the southern tribes. They had traded and lived among them for years and wanted to stay close beside their Comanche and Kiowa friends. The Apache request seemed to solve the Apache relocation problem which the commissioners knew they would have to face eventually. Quickly, Taylor instructed Henderson and Sanborn to draw up a document for the Apaches to sign, incorporating them with the Comanches and Kiowas. Actually, it was to be an appendix to the Comanche-Kiowa treaty, with all provisions identical.

The only change was an increase in annual annuities for the reservation because of an increased population. There was no report of any concern about Comanche or Kiowa objection to the arrangement. As it turned out, there was no need for concern.

As for Little Raven, Taylor dismissed his request with hardly a word. Perhaps the Arapaho had made the request because he felt it politic to disassociate himself from the trouble-making Cheyennes. No one knows. But the Peace Commission did not give a second thought to treating with Little Raven separately.[23]

When the correspondents ran back to their tents, it was still raining, with no indication that the weather would break before morning. Each newsman had dispatches to prepare, outlining the treaty that had been signed that day. There are no reports of the usual horseplay and idle conversation in the press tents. Every correspondent submitted at least one letter with an October 21 date line; the volume of copy concerning the Comanche-Kiowa treaty was greater than for any other incident of the Medicine Lodge adventure. Every newspaperman present was now a veteran of Indian treaty talking.

[23] "Journal," Oct. 21, 1867.

TEN

"THE TIME HAS COME
THAT I MUST GO"

—Kiowa

Comanches and Kiowas assembled in the wagon park on the morning of October 22 under an overcast sky. The wind was sharp and cold, and many of them were wrapped in blankets as they watched Sanborn and Murphy prepare the treaty presents for issue. The ground was soft, and water stood in the deep ruts cut by the heavily loaded wagons. In the rear of the crowd of Indian men, women held ponies on short lead ropes, ready to carry away the gifts the men would bring. Before the presents were distributed, the official Peace Commission party and the newsmen came out from the ambulance compound to join the white men unloading the wagons.[1]

The correspondents were impressed with the volume of goods Sanborn had brought to Medicine Lodge. When the canvas was taken off the wagons and the gifts were stacked on the ground, the reporters could see bundles of blankets, army coats, cotton cloth and felt hats; rows of fruit baskets filled with glass beads; heavy wooden boxes with percussion caps, paper cartridges, knives, and lead. There were eight kegs of powder, but some of these would be saved for the Arapahoes and Cheyennes. Sanborn had purchased more than one hundred Colt pistols and fifty-four Henry repeating rifles, but none of these wagons were in sight; and none were issued. When the Peace Commission finished its business on the Plains, the weapons

[1] The annuity issue described in the *Cincinnati Commercial*, Nov. 4, 1867; *Missouri Democrat*, Nov. 2, 1867; *Republican*, Oct. 28, 1867.

were still carried in the account book as items on hand.[2] Nothing in the Commission minutes or the correspondents reports indicate that a decision had been made to hold the guns, but someone obviously had decided that no more weapons should be put in Indian hands. The Indians went away from Medicine Lodge with only the weapons promised them in the Little Arkansas treaty councils.

A great many brass bugles could be seen in the piles of miscellaneous presents. None of the reporters bothered counting them, but they all mentioned the instruments in their dispatches. Actually, Sanborn had purchased 3,423 surplus army bugles, and all were issued at Medicine Lodge. Small wonder that bugles were sometimes heard during subsequent Southern Plains Indian fights.

During the morning, as the Indians were receiving their treaty gifts, various members of the Commission moved among the Comanche and Kiowa chiefs, inviting them to stay for the Cheyenne Grand Councils. No formal meeting was held and none of the correspondents commented on the Indian reaction. The time for finding winter range was growing short. Frost was expected at any time. Many of the Comanches told Fayel that it was not good to stay at Medicine Lodge. Geese had already gone south, and soon the ponies would find hoarfrost along the edges of the creek when they came down to drink each morning. Some of the Kiowas—much as they loved meetings—were impatient to go south, too. The usual winter range for the Kiowas, as well as some Comanches, was about two hundred miles to the south, along the Washita River, in the Antelope Hills or the Wichita Mountains, where rough terrain and timber helped break the force of winter winds. Some of the lodges of both bands were already being taken down. But many also remained.[3]

At about nine o'clock, the commissioners left the wagon park to meet with the Apache and Arapaho chiefs for a discussion of the next treaty. The newsmen were more interested in the distribution of treaty presents, and they remained in the wagon park watching the Indians carrying away bundles of cloth, beads, knives, and gunpowder. The

[2] "Accounts."
[3] *Missouri Republican*, Oct. 28, 1867.

Taken during the Civil War, this photo suggests the reason most of the reporters considered General Alfred Terry the smartly dressed dandy of the Peace Commission. By 1867, his beard had thinned somewhat, but his taste in clothing continued to be soldierly.

U.S. Signal Corps
National Archives

General William Harney, the senior military man to make the trip to Medicine Lodge. Old Indian fighter and veteran Great Plains campaigner, he was tall in stature and spirit to all the members of the press corps.

Brady Collection, U.S. Signal Corps
National Archives

James Taylor's sketch of the Grand Council, with Mrs. Margaret Adams in the center. The Indian with the hat, second from Mrs. Adams' right, is probably the Comanche leader Silver Brooch. Although the quality of the drawing is excellent, the original identification as "Council of the Arapahoe and Comanche Indians" was incorrect. This was the Kiowa-Comanche Grand Council, although the Arapahoes were present, as were delegates from other tribes.

Leslie's Illustrated Newspaper

On the northern leg of their venture, the Peace Commission found time to pose with this Indian woman. From the left, they are General Terry, General Harney, General Sherman, Commissioner N. G. Taylor, Samuel F. Tappan, and General C. C. Augur. Unfortunately, the photographer did not accompany the group into Kansas for the Medicine Lodge councils.

U.S. Signal Corps
National Archives

John Howland's sketches of Indian encampments (above) and the council meeting (below) for *Harper's Weekly*. A well-liked and witty artist for *Harper's,* Howland was a lively and colorful character, dressed in various

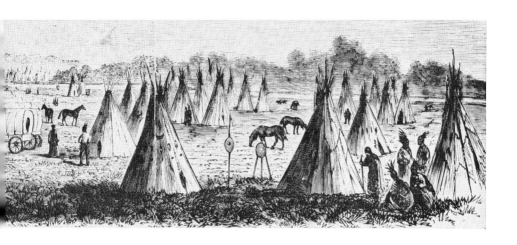

items of Western attire and wearing a navy Colt revolver. He was one of the reporters signing as witnesses to the treaties of Medicine Lodge.

Silver Brooch, the embittered Comanche who threatened to return to his wild brothers, was promised a wooden house and saw his name inscribed on the treaty paper. The newspapermen who knew him at Medicine Lodge were not present the following spring to report whether the threat was carried out when the promise remained unfulfilled.

Bureau of Indian Affairs
National Archives

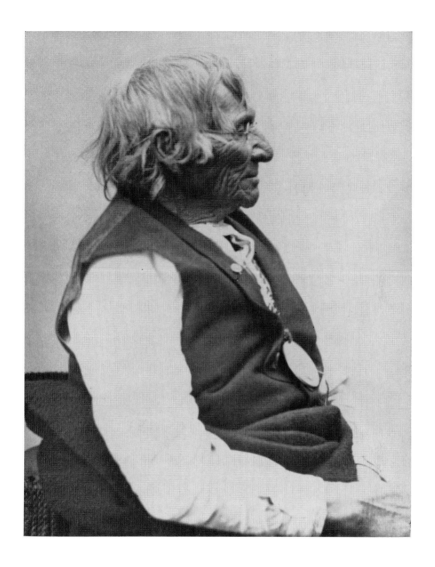

Although his Comanche idea of humor did not often appeal to the Indian Peace Commission, old Ten Bears added laughter to the council meetings which delighted the reporters.

Fat, worried Little Raven mourned his stolen horses and his close association with too-hostile Cheyennes, the Arapaho social lion whose guests were sometimes victimized by his own people.

short Apache conference was mentioned in a Fayel dispatch, but there were no meetings on the scale that there had been before the Comanche-Kiowa treaty signing, and the correspondents rather ignored it.

The Commission presented the Apache terms which were identical to those in the Comanche-Kiowa document, confederating the tribe with the two powerful groups from the South Plains. Commissioner Taylor told them they could discuss the treaty among themselves for two days before they signed the paper. Meanwhile, the commissioners would consult the Comanches and Kiowas to be sure they had no objection. No concern was expressed that the Plains Apaches might not sign. And Little Raven sat throughout the conference without being offered any opportunity to speak. The Peace Commission was making it as plain to him as they could that the Arapahoes would not be treated separately from the Cheyennes.[4]

Although the press gang was aware of Little Raven's request and the Commission's ignoring it, no one hinted that the United States delegation was being unfair. Obviously, treating the large tribes as confederates served definite purposes. Had the Arapahoes been treated separately, it would have meant putting them on the Comanche-Kiowa reservation or establishing three reservations—the Cheyenne, the Comanche-Kiowa, and the Arapaho. There was never any evidence that the Peace Commission—or Congress for that matter—considered establishing any more than two reservations in Indian Territory for the Southern tribes. Economy, as well as space, was a consideration. Confederation of tribes allowed more than one group of Indians to be served by the same expensive saw mill and hospital. One agent could watch over two tribes; one blacksmith could shoe the ponies—if the tribesmen ever decided to have their ponies shod—and make the rims and wagon bows for two tribal groups.

Putting Arapahoes on the Comanche-Kiowa reservation could have caused serious and violent objections. The Plains Apaches had for years been moving among the Comanches, and they were accepted

[4] *Ibid., Missouri Democrat*, Oct. 28, 1867.

as friends who could come and go as they pleased. But the Arapahoes were a different matter. Since 1840, an alliance of sorts had existed between Kiowas and Comanches on the one hand, Cheyennes and Arapahoes on the other. But there was little mutual trust because of the arrangement, and it was not until later that the four tribes were forced closer together by mutual war with the whites.[5]

Any of these factors, or a combination of all, could have caused the Peace Commission to decide against a separate Arapaho treaty. However, it is purely speculative to attribute the Commission's action, or lack of action, to these or any other reasons. None of the Commission records or newspaper dispatches indicated why Little Raven's request was left to wither. Whatever the Commission's reasons, Little Raven had to wait and talk peace along with the Cheyennes whether he liked it or not.

After the last of the Comanche and Kiowa presents had been hauled away from the wagon park, many of the Indians remained near the Peace Commission camp to socialize. They talked with the commissioners and watched the teamsters hitching mules to empty wagons. The empty vehicles still made deep ruts in the wet earth as the muleskinners drove them out of the encampment and started back along the road to Fort Larned.

Kicking Bird brought a hunting pony to Commissioner Taylor, who earlier had asked to buy a Kiowa horse. Kicking Bird would accept nothing for his gift. The Arapahoes had been standing all morning watching the Comanches and Kiowas carry away gifts, and some of them brought General Harney a present of buffalo meat. Harney expressed deep gratitude to the Indians, and Fayel reported that the Arapaho braves went away saying Harney was a great, fine man.[6]

The camp settled into a routine that would last until the Cheyennes arrived, and Stanley said everyone was bored. "We hankered for the fleshpots of St. Louis," he wrote, "and harped on the joys of city life." But even if it was dull, he assured his readers that he

[5] Mayhall, *Kiowas*, 74.
[6] Wallace and Hoebels, *Comanches*, 17–20; *Missouri Republican*, Oct. 28, 1867.

would be at his post.[7] Stanley's post was always near the Peace Commission. Unlike some of the other reporters, he did not spend his days wandering through the Indian camps. Even staying close to the camp, he could see plenty of Indians.

With treaties signed and presents distributed, the tribesmen from the Comanche and Kiowa camps visited the Peace Commission enclosure each day. There had been visitors from the nearby Arapaho village and from Black Kettle's camp across the stream from the first day, but until their business had been concluded, the Indians farther downstream stayed near their lodges. Now, too, the women and children came as well as the men. Stanley said they paraded through the camp in tribal groups, followed always by packs of multicolored, yapping dogs. The women wore their best dresses; Stanley considered the few Cheyenne women from Black Kettle's camp the most attractive, many of them wearing long rows of polished elk teeth down the front of their smocks. The Kiowa and Comanche women usually had their hair cropped shoulder length.[8]

The young boys parading with the women leaped and shouted to attract attention. The youngsters were allowed complete freedom of the Peace Commission camp during daylight hours, and Fayel was annoyed that they were constantly pestering him for matches. The older boys—just short of warrior age—stayed more on the fringes, watching the whites but seldom coming into the camp. They, too, were dressed in their best, and their hair was greased. Many of them had weapons.

Stanley was struck by the remarkable number of scars he saw on the limbs and faces of the Indians. He spoke with McCusker and other interpreters about Indian ills and remedies and was somewhat sickened by the pagan rituals the Indians used to cure diseases. Apparently, the interpreters did not tell the newsmen of the reputation of many Indian surgeons and doctors in each of the tribes. Indian treatment for gunshot wounds, fractures, and all diseases in horses was probably as good as anything the whites could boast—

[7] *Missouri Democrat*, Oct. 28, Nov. 2, 1867.
[8] *Missouri Democrat*, Nov. 1, 1867; *Missouri Republican*, Oct. 28, 1867.

not as clean and surely more painful in most instances, but effective.[9] A great many documented instances exist of Indian doctors—not medicine men—treating serious wounds successfully. Of course, the Indians were painfully inadequate in the treatment of such things as smallpox and cataracts of the eye. Stanley noticed that many of the South Plains Indians suffered from eye defects and other indications of congenital syphilis.[10]

While his competitor from St. Louis sat in the Peace Commission camp observing the parade of tribesmen, Fayel visited a number of tribal encampments. He discovered two white women in the Kiowa camp, both of whom had been captured in Texas.[11] Fayel noticed one of the ladies because of her blonde hair, and she directed his attention to the other one. The blonde girl was German and had been captured near San Antonio years before. Her eyes were blue, appearing exceptionally light in contrast to her sun-blackened skin. Fayel said she was about twenty-five years old. She could still speak a little English, and she told the St. Louis reporter that her mother and father were killed in the raid that struck her family's frontier ranch. A joint Kiowa-Comanche war party had raided and done the killing, and she remembered the incident quite well, having been in her early teens when it happened.

The second white woman, much older, had to speak to Fayel through an interpreter. She had been with the Kiowas since infancy. She could not remember the details of the raid resulting in her capture, and according to Fayel she did not remember where she had lived in Texas, her family name, or what had happened to her parents. Forgetful captives were the most valuable kind to the Plains Indians if they were tough enough to survive—they grew up as Indians. The woman Fayel talked with among the Kiowa lodges had been married to a Kiowa brave for many years. She had five children, but none of them were in the peace camp.

Fayel asked both women if they wanted to return to white society.

[9] Nye, *Bad Medicine,* 108f.; Wallace and Hoebels, *Comanches,* 170f.
[10] *Missouri Democrat,* Oct. 28, Nov. 1, 1867.
[11] *Missouri Republican,* Oct. 25, 1867.

The older woman had no memory of what white society was like, and she had not the slightest desire to leave her Indian home. The younger one, too, refused to consider returning. She had no place to go, and she said her place was with the Indians.

The *Republican* correspondent expressed no opinion about the refusal of these two women to come back with their own people. As usual, Fayel was reporting things as he saw them, not acting as interpreter of the news. Perhaps, too, his attitude was like the general attitude prevailing in the peace camp—an attitude that appears in an amazing number of references for this period in history; no one was particularly excited about mixed marriages and the resulting children, or even white women who had been captured years before and become, in fact, Indians themselves. At least, many people in close contact with the situation seemed to take it all for granted. To most of the men at Medicine Lodge, nothing at all seemed unusual about the two white women Fayel interviewed, nor as a matter of fact, about Julia Bent and her brothers, Mrs. Adams, and the fact that McCusker had a Comanche wife. If there was any repugnance over this racial mixing, a great many people managed to conceal the fact quite effectively.

While they were waiting, some of the official party paid social calls on the Indian leaders. Senator Henderson went to the Comanche camp and visited Ten Bears, taking McCusker along for the talking. Budd went too, at Henderson's invitation. In this small and select group, Budd's attitude seemed to mellow somewhat, and as a result of the visit he wrote some of his best copy from Medicine Lodge— it was not soured by the usual bitter comments and criticisms.[12]

Ten Bears welcomed the three white men to his lodge, and they sat smoking for some time, with Henderson—through McCusker— talking about the good things peace would bring. The conversation turned to hunting and to horses; Henderson had heard that the Comanches had many fine racing horses. While the men talked, Ten Bears' many wives stayed respectfully in the background, listening. Budd saw weapons, bundles of clothing, blankets, war shields, and

[12] *Cincinnati Gazette*, Nov. 5, 1867.

149

wood-framed saddles lying about the tipi, and eventually Ten Bears offered to show them an example of Comanche horsemanship. Senator Henderson was delighted, and the small party moved outside and to the edge of the Comanche encampment.

Speaking to a number of the men who were following at a discreet distance, Ten Bears said he wanted the white men to see how Comanches rode. A number of braves soon appeared on ponies they had tethered near their lodges. Others hurried out to the pony herd and soon rode back on small, spotted horses. Finally, about one dozen warriors were ready to perform.

The Cincinnati reporter was greatly impressed with what followed. Riding at full gallop, the Comanches swung down the flanks of their ponies, shooting arrows under the horses' necks and into a brush target as they swept past. Shouting and waving lances, they rode back and forth, full speed, hanging from their ponies' necks, rumps, or flanks, changing positions without slowing. They crawled about on their charging horses as easily as they might walk across the prairie. The well-trained hunting ponies turned and wheeled without any obvious command, and although the weight constantly shifted on their backs they never broke gait.

Budd said these were the finest horsemen on the Great Plains, and it would be difficult to find an authority to disagree with him. Rather squat and ungainly on foot, mounted Comanches had few equals. They learned to ride and tend horses almost as soon as they could walk—as did most Indians—and they seemed to have some quality which made them unexcelled with horses, whether it was capturing them, stealing them, trading them, breeding them, or riding them. Budd said they could use their fourteen-foot lances, with blade of hammered iron, from any position as they rode. Many of the correspondents had commented during the treaty meeting about this vicious looking lance, which some of them had incorrectly called a spear. The Comanches were expert in its use, often using it to kill buffalo.[13]

The Comanche horse show attracted attention throughout the

[13] Richard I. Dodge, *The Plains and the Great West*, 329f.

camp. The sound of running ponies, the shouts, and the dust cloud rising behind Ten Bear's camp started a rumor that the Cheyennes were attacking. Back in the Peace Commission camp, Fayel reported that a number of Apaches and Arapahoes were ready to bolt the treaty grounds. Soon, however, news of what was happening spread through the camp, and the Indians quieted.

The Apache treaty was signed on October 25. Stanley reported that Little Raven was still there, insisting that the Arapahoes did not want to talk peace with the Cheyennes. The Comanche and Kiowa leaders were present as well, and none of them, apparently, objected to being confederated with the Plains Apaches. Brown and Stanley wrote that the Apache document assigned the Apaches to the reservation established for the Comanches and Kiowas, and that the Apaches would enjoy the same benefits as the tribesmen who had signed the October 21 treaty. Generally, the Apache treaty-signing was ignored by the press representatives. This tribe's chiefs had made little impression on the correspondents. Those who signed the treaty were Wolf Sleeve, Poor Bear, Bad Back, Brave Man, Iron Shirt, and White Horn.[14]

Before the Apache treaty was signed, the Kansas delegation returned to Topeka; on October 25, the day the Apache document was signed, they were reported in the state capital by the local newspapers.[15] No explanation has been made of their leaving the treaty grounds before the Cheyennes came in to talk peace. Insofar as Governor Crawford and Senator Ross were concerned, the Cheyenne treaty had to be the most important order of business of the Peace Commission—it supposedly would end the Smoky Hill troubles. Neither of the Kansas politicians had taken an active part in the Indian councils held by the Peace Commission, but their interests would seem to have been adequate to keep them there, if only as bystanders. This was not the case.

The most unfortunate part of the Kansans' departure was the loss

[14] Kappler, *Treaties*, 982–84; *Cincinnati Commercial*, Nov. 4, 1867; *Missouri Democrat*, Oct. 31, 1867; *New York Herald*, Oct. 31, 1867.
[15] *New York Herald*, Oct. 28, 1867.

of Milton Reynolds. He left with the Governor's party, and from that point on the over-all newspaper coverage of the negotiations suffered. None of the other newsmen had Reynolds' insight into the Indian problem, and except for occasional instances, none of the others tried to analyze what was going on between the Indians and the Peace Commission.

On his return from Medicine Lodge, Senator Ross sent a letter to a number of Kansas editors, giving his views on the Indian situation. His published letter was picked up by the *Missouri Democrat* on November 1 and eventually was printed in most of the large metropolitan papers in the country. His comments did not peddle fright and sensation, as Governor Crawford's comments often did, but they left little doubt of Ross's sympathies.[16]

Ross said feeding the Indians was cheaper than fighting them. But he went on to say that he did not feel the cheapest course was the best one. He wrote, "The forts on the frontier must be permanently and amply garrisoned and additional posts established." He frankly opposed any system of treaty-making with the wild tribes. When the Indians on the frontier had been the stronger of the two parties, treaties had been necessary to pacify the tribes while the country filled up with white settlers, Ross said. But the situation was now reversed, he added gleefully, and it was foolish to dignify the Indians by negotiating with them. In short, when the enemy was stronger, connive to have him talk peace instead of make war; when the tables were turned, refuse him the chance to do the same. A remarkable concept of political—and human—relations. The only possible defense for such a public statement would have to be that many other people in 1867 felt the same way.

The Ross article went on:

> The idea of a nation of 30 millions of people . . . suffering itself to be constantly harassed by a handful of miserable savages, is even more discreditable than that of continuing the petty, mock sovereignties into which they are divided.

[16] *Missouri Democrat*, Nov. 1, 1867, credited to the Lawrence (Kansas) *Tribune*, Oct. 29, 1867.

Some of Reynolds' comments made early in the Medicine Lodge venture—concerning the scruples of Kansas politicians—take on added authority in the light of this published thesis.

Ross's letter gave no hint of his motives, but there is little question about his desire to maintain and even increase the number of military units in Kansas. It was no secret that the Kansas Senator wanted state troops called into service; when the Peace Commission bill had been before Congress, Ross had said from the Senate floor that additional troops should be raised from his state and placed on the federal roles of active frontier army units.[17]

Reynolds' opinion of Crawford and Ross may have been a matter of partisan politics. The reporter was convinced that the two Kansas politicians would do anything to gain title to Indian land. He accused them of having no human feelings for the tribes. The things Crawford and Ross wrote helped Reynolds' case. Had they been trying, the two men could not have done a better job of showing ignorance, narrow mindedness, and prejudice. All Reynolds had to do was call attention to these qualities. Rather than being malicious, perhaps the Kansans were thinking only of the good of their state as they saw it. Reynolds disagreed.

As the days of waiting passed, the correspondents' tent became the social center of the Peace Commission camp.[18] Fayel said the young Indian boys were the first to lose their timidity. They began a systematic inspection of all the tents and ambulances in the area, and no matter how often they came, they went through the whole procedure each time. Stanley said Indian children were underfoot constantly, but soon some of the older Indians joined the daily search, for it could hardly be described as anything but a search. Fayel said the Indians inspected everything—clothing, folding army cots, chests of paper and ink, blankets, spare shoes and boots, and anything else they could find.

[17] *Cong. Globe,* 1867, 703.
[18] Indian visitors discussed in the *Missouri Democrat,* Oct. 25, 1867; *Missouri Republican,* Oct. 25, 28, 1867; for Indian hospitality, see Mayhall, *Kiowas,* 128f.

The women, too, made themselves at home. They came to the Peace Commission camp riding behind their men—Fayel noticed they rode mares and that they rode astride—and then followed the men through the tents. They seemed to like the discarded envelopes which had brought mail to various members of the press gang. Finding one of these on the tent floor, they would pick it up, stare at it a moment, and hide it somewhere in their clothing. Often, Fayel said, he saw an Indian woman riding back toward the tribal camps with an armful of used envelopes. He had no idea what the attraction might be, but he was impressed with the industry of the women in collecting the used envelopes. He said the reporters had to be watchful to keep more valuable items from disappearing among the folds of clothing as the women marched through the tent.

Often, the older men came with paint on their faces and with weapons hanging from their belts. Fayel said it was not difficult to imagine them in the roles of raiders and murderers. At Medicine Lodge, however, they wanted only to talk—or to ask for a drink of whisky from the keg in the correspondents' tent. The reporters soon discovered the warriors' pride and beggary. No contradition was apparent to the Indians, but the white men could not understand. A frequent visitor was Satanta, who had stayed in camp for the Cheyenne talks. He was sometimes painted and sometimes drunk.

Stanley's continuing study of the human race could go on as he sat on his army cot. "Commissioners, officers, soldiers, bull whackers, mule drivers, Indian chiefs, squaws and papooses pass in and out all day long," Stanley wrote. Many of the small children wore scanty clothing. Some wore none at all. There was no sign of anyone disciplining a child. On the other hand, Stanley never saw an adult Indian consoling a crying child. He drew the conclusion that the Indians were cruel and indifferent to their children. Of course, Stanley was wrong. The children were a major asset to the tribe and were cherished as such. But they were never pampered or petted. They could roam about as they pleased, doing whatever they were big and strong enough to get away with—and both Fayel and

Stanley said the young Indians at Medicine Lodge were always recon-
noitering and ransacking everything in sight.[19]

Each day an official party from the Indian camps would pay their
respects to the Peace Commission. Fayel said these social affairs
were as well ordered and controlled as the Grand Councils, although
the object of business was nothing more than smoking and drinking
coffee. The Indians drank their coffee in army tin cups. When the
coffee was gone, they would run their fingers around the bottom of
the cup, picking up the excess sugar on their finger tips. With a great
deal of dignity, Stanley reported, they would lick the sugar from their
fingers as the Negro orderly refilled their cups.

During this period of inactivity, one incident caught the attention
of the correspondents who were in the Peace Commission camp at
the time. The date is not certain, but Stanley and Budd placed it on
or about October 24, while Brown said it happened the same day
the Apache treaty was signed.[20] In any event, three correspondents
were resting in the press tent shortly after a noon meal—Budd,
Brown, and Stanley. The other newsmen were away visiting Indian
camps. Senator Henderson ran into the tent and said an important
chief was coming to say good-by to the Peace Commission. The three
reporters hurried out to the edge of the ambulance compound where
they found the rest of the official party waiting. Soon they saw a
small cavalcade of horsemen approaching them from the trees downstream. With the horsemen was old Satank, the Kiowa chief, come
to say his farewell before departing with family for winter camps in
the south.

Leaving his retinue standing some distance off, the white-mus-
tached Kiowa dismounted and advanced to the commissioners on foot,
leading his well-groomed pony. Satank was not as large as Satanta,
but he was a tall man, only slightly stooped with age. His face had
a definite Mongolian cast, with almond eyes and high, sharp cheek-

[19] Stanley, *Early Travels*, *x*; Wallace and Hoebels, *Comanches*, 119–26.
[20] Satank's speech verbatim in the *Cincinnati Commercial*, Nov. 22, 1867; *Cincinnati Gazette*, Nov. 5, 1867; *Missouri Democrat*, Nov. 2, 1867.

bones. His nose was long and thin except where it flared at the nostrils, and he was wearing ornaments in his right ear.

Standing before the commissioners, Satank looked at each of them in turn before he spoke: "You have heard much talk by our chiefs and no doubt are tired of it. Many of them have put themselves forward and filled you with sayings. I have kept back and said nothing."

Stanley does not indicate at what point in the old man's speech he started to take shorthand, but he told his readers that he had taken the Kiowa's words verbatim. In addition to Stanley, George Willis, Commissioner stenographer, was there, and possibly he also took the speech in shorthand. At any rate, Stanley, Budd, and Brown dispatched a story with the chief's exact words, and their accounts were identical. The speech is quoted here in detail because the three newsmen there reported it that way—an indication of the impact Satank's words had on them. It is significant that Budd and Brown, so often opposed to the cause of the Indians, should pay such close attention to the Kiowa's words. This speech ranks with the best Indian talks heard anywhere on the Great Plains:

> The white man grows jealous of his red brother. The white man once came to trade; he now comes as a soldier. He once put his trust in our friendship and wanted no shield but our fidelity. But now he builds forts and plants big guns on their walls. He once gave us arms and powder and bade us hunt the game. We then loved him for his confidence . . . He now covers his face with the cloud of jealousy and anger and tells us to be gone, as an offended master speaks to his dog.

The pause for interpretation made the words even more effective. McCusker was there. He could have interpreted from the Kiowa, or Satank may have spoken the Comanche tongue. No one indicated exactly what was done. After McCusker finished the first part of Satank's speech, the old Indian lowered his eyes and touched with the fingers of one hand the silver medal hanging from his neck. The correspondents could see Buchanan's profile on it. Continuing to touch the medal, Satank looked at the commissioners:

156

Look at this medal I wear. By wearing this, I have been made poor. Before, I was rich in horses and lodges. Today I am the poorest of all. When you gave me this silver medal on my neck, you made me poor.

We thank the Great Spirit that all these wrongs are now to cease. You have not tried, as many have done, to make a new bargain merely to get the advantage.

Do for us what is best. Teach us the road to travel. We know you will not forsake us; and tell your people also to act as you have done, to be as you have been.

I am old . . . I shall soon have to go the way of my fathers. But those who come after me will remember this day. . . .

And now the time has come that I must go. You may never see me more, but remember Satank as the white man's friend.

The old man slowly passed along the line of commissioners, shaking each by the hand. He did not speak again. Finally he mounted, turned his pony toward the small band that stood waiting for him, and rode away.

Commissioner and correspondent alike were profoundly moved by the old Kiowa's words, Stanley said. He added that this was the best speaking they had yet heard at Medicine Lodge, and he was to say that nothing followed which could equal it. The other two reporters spoke for themselves. Brown said the little talk would rank with anything ever said by Tecumseh or Logan. Budd—violent Indian-hater, baiter of white man and warrior alike—wrote:

I have heard the re-echoing eloquence of statesmen, as it warbled through the House and Senate of our national capitol. I have heard and felt the influence of ministerial oratory as it came from the rostrum . . . But never have I known true eloquence before this day . . . When the last goodbye fell from his lips, it was not the voice of college culture, of prejudice, of partisan strife; it was the voice of nature and of God.

The road from Medicine Lodge would not be an easy one for

old Satank.[21] His eldest and favorite son was killed while taking part in a Texas raid in 1870. Satank recovered his son's bones, wrapped them in a blanket, and carried them on a led pony wherever he went. In May, 1871, he was arrested with Satanta for the massacre of a number of Texas teamsters. As he was being taken to prison in an army wagon, the old man sang his death song. When the song ended, he tore his hands from the manacles, seized a soldier's carbine and was shot by the accompanying escort of cavalrymen. After falling once into the wagon bed, the old man tried to rise and use the weapon still clutched in his hands. They gave him a second volley. The officer in charge of the detail did not bother to count the bullet wounds in Satank's body before the chief was returned to his people. On that day, the silver medal that had made him poor was not hanging from his neck.

[21] Marriott, *Grandmothers*, 112–25; Nye, *Bad Medicine*, xvii; Nye, *Carbine*, 113, 114f.

ELEVEN

"WE HAVE WAITED
A LONG TIME"

—Comanche

All the tribal leaders who were in camp on October 26 met with the Peace Commission to decide whether they should continue waiting for the Cheyennes. The Cimarron warriors were already one day late, but Black Kettle said the Cheyenne medicine-making ceremonies would require two additional days. It was Saturday, and the Commission agreed to stay on the Medicine Lodge until the following Monday. Most of the Indians grumbled, but they said they would remain also if the Peace Commission wanted them. If the Cheyennes were not in by the following Monday, Commissioner Taylor told Black Kettle, the Peace Commission would return to the North Platte to negotiate with the tribes there. The Comanches and Kiowas said they would leave when the Peace Commission did.[1]

A great deal of speculation went on among the newsmen about what the Cheyennes would do when they came in, if they came at all. Brown, who incorrectly located the Cheyenne camp on a fork of the Red River, held out little hope for peace. He warned that the Cheyennes were the bloodiest, wildest Indians on the Great Plains, feared by everyone. This may or may not have been true, but there were no indications that the Comanches or Kiowas were particularly concerned about whether the Cheyennes came talking or shooting. Stanley reported a growing restlessness in the Arapaho camp. On the evening of October 26, Little Raven came to the Peace Commission

---

[1] *Peace Commission*, 20; *Missouri Democrat*, Oct. 28, 1867; *New York World*, Nov. 1, 1867.

camp to warn that Cheyennes might attack the Commission at any time. According to both Stanley and Hall, General Harney expressed confidence in the Cheyennes' peaceful intentions, but Hall said a good many men in the camp were making a joke of Harney's good attitude toward the Cimarron warriors.[2]

Little Raven had hardly finished his warning of Cheyenne trickery when the Commission camp received a visitor from the Cimarron. It was Little Robe, who had come for a short talk. He told the commissioners that his people would come in the next day, and that they would fire pistols into the air. There was no cause for alarm, he said; the shooting would just be an expression of joy at having the opportunity to speak with the representatives of the United States. This comment was not particularly welcome. Everyone understood that it would be foolish to ask the Cheyennes to come in without their weapons, but for the Cimarron braves to ride up with guns in their hands was also displeasing. Hall said that Little Robe realized the tension in the Peace camp might trigger serious trouble. The tall Cheyenne spent a good deal of time in the ambulance enclosure speaking to various commissioners, assuring them that the Cheyenne's intentions were peaceful. Bulkley wrote that Little Robe was concerned that excited soldiers might open fire on the Cheyenne tribesmen, thinking the celebration shooting was hostile. Bulkley said there was a good chance that Little Robe was right.[3] After a while, Little Robe went into Wynkoop's tent and talked privately with the agent. Apparently the discussion was unpleasant, for when the Indian left Wynkoop's tent, he was very angry. Fayel said the Cheyenne refused to shake Wynkoop's hand as he left, and he also refused to take tobacco offered him by the agent. His display of temper could have done little to encourage hopes for a happy meeting the following day. The correspondents drank the last of their whisky that night.

Sunday morning, October 27. A sight-seeing expedition was organized in the Peace Commission camp to travel downstream where the

[2] Stanley, *Early Travels*, 260 f.; *Cincinnati Commercial*, Nov. 4, 1867; *Missouri Democrat*, Nov. 2, 1867.

[3] *Missouri Republican*, Nov. 2, 1867; *New York Herald*, Oct. 31, 1867.

Kiowa Sun Dance of 1866, had been held, and where the Sun Dance Medicine Lodge still stood. After nearly two weeks on the scene, everyone probably knew a Sun Dance lodge was near, and McCusker knew the location. Although Brown gave a detailed account of the trip, and other correspondents mentioned it, no one indicated who organized it or why the party left the Peace Commission camp on the day the Cheyennes said they would come.[4] Many of them probably did not believe the Cimarron warriors would come on that day; the Cheyennes had promised to come before but had failed to do so. For whatever reasons, the little group of tourists was anxious to see the site of a traditional religious ceremony of one of the Great Plains tribes.

With the exception of the Comanches—who had no Sun Dance of their own but often visited the Kiowas to watch the ceremony—all the Plains tribes conducted an annual religious and social celebration that was the high point of the year.[5] Sun Dances were held in an atmosphere of carnival excitement on the one hand, fasting and self-denial on the other. This was a time for the young men of the tribe to prove their fortitude and stamina in various systems of self-torture, all organized, operated, and policed by select organizations of men who were recognized leaders in the tribe. The Kiowas erected a central structure of poles and branches, where the major activities of the affair took place, and this was the building that the white men from the peace camp intended seeing.

According to their own accounts, the correspondents who rode downstream to the Sun Dance Lodge had only a vague notion of what the Sun Dance meant to the Indians. Brown, Howland, and James Taylor, of *Leslie's*, were among the sight-seers. The remainder of the party was Samuel S. Smoot, United States surveyor of the Peace Commission; D. A. Butterfield, Murphy's assistant at the

[4] The sightseeing trip taken from Taylor, "The Medicine Lodge Peace Council," *Chronicles of Oklahoma*, Vol. II (June, 1924), 106; *Cincinnati Commercial*, Nov. 4, 1867; *Missouri Democrat*, Nov. 2, 1867; *Missouri Republican*, Nov. 2, 1867; *Leslie's Illustrated Newspaper*, Nov. 23, 1867.

[5] Mooney, "Calendar History," 227–32; Mayhall, *Kiowas*, 165–67; Nye, *Bad Medicine*, 45, 57, 76; Wallace and Hoebels, *Comanches*, 22.

treaty grounds; A. A. Taylor, the young son of Commissioner Taylor; and McCusker. Early in the morning the party left the Peace
Commission camp and rode a number of miles down the north bank
of Medicine Lodge Creek, crossing to the south side near the Comanche camp. Passing along the edge of first the Comanche and then
the Kiowa villages, they finally came to the clearing where the Sun
Dance Lodge stood, about twelve miles from the Commission camp.

The Sun Dance Lodge was a huge, circular structure, with a rude
framework of poles and a roof of loose timber and branches. Taylor
said as they moved closer they could see the brightly colored ornaments hanging from the walls. The party dismounted and went inside, where they found other talismans on walls and ceiling. Feathers,
arrows, beads, and brightly painted gourds hung there, and a decorated buffalo skull was tied high on the center pole. The temptation
to take away a few souvenirs was too great to resist, and most members of the party took decorations from the walls. The buffalo skull
must have been either too large or too high to reach—there were
no reports, at least, of anyone trying to take it.

Starting back to their own camp, the party rode near the stream,
passing once more along the edge of both Kiowa and Comanche
camps. Everyone seemed nervous over the prospect of meeting some
passing Kiowa who later would discover the pilfering of the sacred
Medicine Lodge. However, Brown said they passed along the south
side of the stream unnoticed by anyone.

The men were still some distance from the Peace camp, still traveling on the south bank of the stream, when McCusker, who was
leading the group at that point, drew rein and listened. From the
direction of the Peace Commission camp could be heard bursts of
gunfire. Someone in the group shouted "Cheyennes," and Brown related that McCusker turned to the others and shouted, "We are
in a God damned bad box, boys." With that, the Comanche interpreter spurred his horse into the stream, closely followed by the
others. Whipping their mounts across the creek, the members of
the party unloaded their pockets, throwing all the Sun Dance souvenirs into the water. McCusker reached the north bank first, with

Howland close behind. Brown wrote that Howland looked back and shouted, "Damn it Brown, throw away that gourd and hurry up your horse."

They were no sooner out of the water than they started meeting Arapahoes, running from their nearby camp and shouting that Cheyennes were coming. Brown said there was still firing from the Commission camp, and they could hear Indians yelling and ponies running. The sight-seers ran their horses through the trees near Little Raven's village, trying to avoid Arapahoes who were streaming out of their lodges, away from the sounds of shooting. Once, with McCusker still leading, the Peace group saw a band of Indian warriors riding to head them off. The men turned back toward the stream but stopped on discovering that the riders were Arapahoes who were also trying to escape.

Brown recorded that McCusker yelled, "We must be damned quick about getting out of the way," and once more the Comanche interpreter led them toward the Peace Commission camp. In the confusion, no one questioned the fact that McCusker was leading them directly toward the sounds of firing. If they were heading directly toward trouble, at least troops were in the area. The important thing seemed to be getting clear of the Indian encampments. Within a few more minutes of hard riding, they broke from the trees and saw the Commission camp. The Cheyennes were there, along the edge of Medicine Lodge Creek, many of them dismounted and shaking hands with the Peace Commissioners. The sight-seers' horses had run into camp before they could be checked, and with the shooting stopped, the noise the horses made caused some of the men along the stream to turn and watch as the party members tried to quiet their mounts. Fayel—in the group beside the stream—remarked that the sight-seers were extremely frightened men, but more than that, they were embarrassed at having charged into camp just as the Cheyenne peace delegation arrived.

Brown told his readers that there had been an Arapaho mock attack on horse thieves during the morning, staged for the commissioners. It had been this, he said, which had frightened the sight-seeing party as it returned from the Kiowa Medicine Lodge. No one else mentioned such a show on October 27, however, and both Fayel and Stanley said the sight-seers had been panicked by the arrival of the warriors from the Cimarron. Fayel reported that the episode became the subject of much humorous conversation in the press tent throughout the remainder of the correspondents' stay at Medicine Lodge. The press members who had been in the party were heckled unmercifully by their companions for the fine show of bravery they had presented to the newly arrived Cheyenne delegation.

While the souvenir hunters were absent from camp, the men remaining were enjoying a pleasant Sunday morning. Hall said the night before had been very cold, but with the coming of the sun, the temperature had gone up, and they sat outside their tent reading, playing cards, and betting on what the Cheyennes would do.[6]

Just before noon, an Indian messenger rode into camp with the news that a great column of Cheyennes was a short distance away, riding toward the Commission headquarters. The Indians would be coming in shortly from south of the Medicine Lodge. Budd, Bulkley, Fayel, Hall, and Stanley found the commissioners discussing arrangements for receiving the Cheyennes. Some argument arose about whether the group should go down to the stream to meet the Indians. General Harney wanted to leave the compound and welcome the Cheyennes at the north bank of the stream, but others among the Peace Commissioners had little stomach for such a meeting. Finally, Harney convinced them that some show of confidence should be made. The entire group, correspondents among them, walked down to the edge of the creek. As they waited, Harney removed his hat, and the others followed suit.

News of the Cheyennes' coming had spread through the Indian camps. Arapahoes were running toward their village. In that direction, the correspondents could see a great deal of activity and evidence that some of the Arapahoes were preparing to leave the peace

[6] The Cheyenne coming described in the *Chicago Tribune*, Nov. 2, 1867; *Cincinnati Gazette*, Nov. 5, 1867; *Missouri Democrat*, Nov. 2, 1867; *Missouri Republican*, Nov. 2, 1867.

grounds in a hurry. Hall reported that a small group of Comanches had ridden up, and they remained seated on their horses near the campsite, watching. The Comanche braves were armed with lances. A few Kiowas had been in the Peace Commission camp all morning and had offered to help fight the Cheyennes in case of trouble. The Kiowa braves said it would be nice if they could have a little whisky first. Men die much better after having a little whisky, they explained to the reporters. The keg in the press tent was empty, and none of the commissioners offered the Kiowas a drink. When the white men walked down to the stream, the Kiowas got their ponies and joined the watching band of Comanches, forming a compact and menacing looking little war party.

Other Indian messengers arrived to remind the commissioners that the Cheyennes would do some shooting as they came in. The messengers also said that all the other Indians should be moved out of camp. By this time, the only other Indians in the area were the band of Comanches and Kiowas standing a short distance off. They were watching the southern ridges across Medicine Lodge Creek, and no effort was made to have them move farther away.

The soldiers on sentry duty at the Commission camp were still at their posts. They had not been moved down to the edge of the stream, but they, like the Indians, were looking south. Upstream, the escort was still in camp. In his report, Major Elliot did not detail his preparations for the arrival of the Cheyennes, but his troopers were undoubtedly ready to move, and if he was doing his job properly, the Gatling guns were sighted to fire on the stream-crossing at the Commission camp.

At noon the commissioners saw the Cheyennes. The Indians, riding at a trot, crested the ridge on the south side of the Medicine Lodge in a long column. Riding four abreast, they moved parallel to the stream. Fayel said a cavalry officer standing with him remarked on the Cheyenne movements. Soon, about three hundred warriors were in sight. As they came directly opposite the Peace Commission camp, the column wheeled into line, facing the stream and the group of white men on the far side.

With loud shouts, the Indians kicked their ponies, and the line of warriors moved toward the commissioners at a gallop. A bugle was blown somewhere in the Cheyenne formation, and as the shouting grew louder, pistols were fired. Fayel said the sounds were like platoon volleys. The leading horsemen struck the far side of Medicine Lodge, throwing up a white spray of water, and pushed their horses straight across the stream toward the commissioners. The second, third, and fourth ranks followed the first into the water, every brave, apparently, firing a pistol into the air as he moved forward. All were shouting, and the bugle continued to blare meaningless notes. As the first Indians whipped their ponies out of the water near the white men, it looked for an instant as though they would leap, driving ahead, riding over the bare-headed commissioners. Then, within a few feet of General Harney—who had not moved— the warriors pulled hard on their reins, squatting their ponies as the riders slid to the ground. With the Indians behind still yelling and firing, the first group of Cheyennes, on foot now, surrounded the commissioners and started shaking hands with everyone. Many of the warriors were painted; all wore weapons hanging from their backs and belts.

Within a few seconds, all the Cheyennes were on the near side of the stream. The shooting stopped as suddenly as it had begun, and then the chiefs pushed through the crowd of braves to take the commissioners by their hands. Most of the Cheyennes in the rear ranks remained mounted while the chiefs and the white men started back toward the ambulance compound. A sudden distraction occurred as the Kiowa Medicine Lodge sight-seers charged out of the trees and rode into the Commission camp. Only a momentary pause in the handshaking, resulted, however, and soon the commissioners were leading the Cheyenne chiefs up the slope, leaving most of the warriors at the edge of the water. The group of Comanches and Kiowas were still standing quietly nearby, watching the main body of Cheyennes.

Little Robe, Gray Head, Tall Bull, and Lean Bear were there, along with a number of others. Both Bent Brothers were also present, as was John Smith, the Cheyenne interpreter. When the group arrived at the Commission tents, the Indians were offered tobacco and coffee. This time, Little Robe accepted the offer of hospitality, and for a short while he and the other chiefs sat smoking and drinking coffee with the commissioners. Little Robe said there had been a number of Kaws following the Cheyenne horse herd on the trip from the Cimarron. The Cheyennes were anxious to protect their ponies, he said, and could not stay to talk, so another meeting was arranged later in the day. The chiefs expressed their gratitude for the coffee, then quickly moved back to their waiting braves. With a few more shouts—and waving lances and pistols—the Cheyennes dashed back through the Medicine Lodge and up the slope on the far side.

If the Cheyennes had been trying to impress the whites with their grand entry to the peace grounds, they had succeeded. Brown said the other Indians had come before the Peace Commission "cringing and submissive," while the Cheyennes entered haughtily and proudly. Brown must have been slightly overwhelmed by the sight of the Cheyenne charge. It would be difficult to reconcile the words "cringing and submissive" with the speeches of Satanta, Satank, or Ten Bears. Brown apparently had forgotten that the Kiowas and Comanches had obstinately fought the provisions of their treaty until they were promised hunting rights outside the reservation. Hall wrote that the Cheyennes were in a position to concede peace but not to beg for it. He and Fayel agreed that the Cheyennes were a splendid looking body of men, and that from what they had seen, settlers had good reason to dread these tall warriors when they were hostile. As a matter of fact, the Cheyennes were regarded by most authorities to have been the most handsome of all the wild tribes of Indians. They were usually taller than Arapahoes or Kiowas, and Comanches were runty in comparison. Most authorities who have studied them agree that they were a high-spirited, sensitive, generous people, as well as handsome. Generally, they were considered

167

more reliable than the Kiowas, but they lacked the practical business sense of the Comanches.[7]

As had been planned, later in the day a number of the Cheyenne chiefs returned to the Peace Commission camp.[8] More coffee was served, and after an hour of genial conversation with the commissioners, the Cheyennes agreed to hold their Grand Council on the following day, October 28, at ten o'clock. Once more, the chiefs thanked the commissioners for the hospitality extended them, and then rode back across the stream to the camp they had established near Black Kettle's village.

Late in the evening, one of the sentries came to the Peace Commission to say that a group of Cheyennes was approaching. Investigation revealed that the group wanted to see General Harney. When he went out to the group, a Cheyenne woman told the General that she had just given birth to a son, and as was the custom, she was giving gifts in celebration of the event. When she led an Indian pony up to General Harney and presented it to him, he accepted the gift with expressions of the deepest gratitude. The gathering had attracted the attention of the press gang, and a number of them gathered around. According to Fayel, the old General was a favorite of the Cheyennes, many of whose leaders he had known for thirty years. Obviously, the Cheyennes were favorites of General Harney, too.

Back in their tent, the correspondents talked about the occurrences of the day.[9] The tension had finally eased with the peaceful—though boisterous—coming of the Cimarron Cheyennes. No one was any longer concerned that there might be bloodshed at the treaty grounds; it was a time for joking and storytelling. Howland and Taylor described the Kiowa Medicine Lodge as well as some of the relics they had taken and had thrown in the creek at signs of trouble. They ob-

[7] Mooney, "Calendar History," 233f.; Wallace and Hoebels, *Comanches*, 22; Campbell, "The Cheyenne Dog Soldier," *Chronicles of Oklahoma*, Vol. XI (January, 1921), 90 ff.

[8] *Chicago Tribune*, Nov. 2, 1867; *Missouri Republican*, Nov. 2, 1867.

[9] *Cincinnati Commercial*, Nov. 4, 1867; *Missouri Democrat*, Nov. 2, 1867; *Missouri Republican*, Nov. 2, 1867.

viously had had no desire to be caught by hostile Indians with evidence of theft in their pockets. The other reporters made fun of the sight-seeing group for their wild dash into the Peace Commission camp. As the evening wore on, visitors from the official party dropped in to join the chat. They talked about the Cheyennes and of how impressive they had been riding across the creek; they talked about the small party of Comanches and Kiowas who had stood silently by while the Cheyennes came in. The evening was relaxed and pleasant. The correspondents were happy that the treaty meetings were nearly over. As Stanley had said, they were eager to get back to the cities.

TWELVE

"WE WILL
TAKE OUR CHANCES"
—Cheyenne

The Cheyenne chiefs seemed in no hurry to talk peace on October 28. They reached the council grove promptly at ten o'clock but stood for a long time talking among themselves while the commissioners waited.[1] Warriors and women were in the grove, and nearby, seated on logs apart from the Cheyennes, were the Comanche and Kiowa leaders. Finally, the Cheyenne chiefs leisurely moved to their places. They sat in a semicircle, facing the commissioners. As soon as the crowd was quiet, Senator Henderson spoke to them.

Henderson explained, as he had to the Comanches and Kiowas, that the Great Father had sent the Commission to make a lasting peace with the Indian. He reminded them of the treaty of the Little Arkansas and said that since then, young men among the Cheyennes "who had more blood than brains" had broken the peace. But he added that the Peace Commission had discovered wrongs committed against the Cheyennes as well. Hancock had heard lies from other white men, Henderson said, which led to his actions on the Pawnee Fork of the Arkansas, where the Cheyenne village had been burned. "We have wicked men who like to profit from the evil doings on both sides," the Senator said, "but the world is large enough for both of us." He said the buffalo would soon be gone, but so long as game was plentiful, the Cheyennes would be allowed to hunt ac-

[1] Cheyenne Grand Council covered in the *Chicago Tribune*, Nov. 2, 1867; *Cincinnati Commercial*, Nov. 4, 1867; *Cincinnati Gazette*, Nov. 5, 1867; *Missouri Democrat*, Nov. 2, 1867; *Missouri Republican*, Nov. 2, 1867.

cording to the provisions of the Little Arkansas treaty—this meant south of the Arkansas River. The plans Henderson outlined for the Cheyennes were identical to the terms of the Comanche-Kiowa treaty. In return for a reservation of their own, the Cheyennes were to be provided with livestock and farm implements, and the Cheyennes and Arapahoes must agree to stop raiding the railroads and white settlers.

This was the first indication to the correspondents that a treaty had already been readied for the Cheyennes. They had not seen a copy of it prior to the meeting, as they had the Comanche-Kiowa document. It was from Henderson's word alone that they concluded that the provisions of the two treaties were essentially the same.

No one has given an explanation of why the correspondents were denied access to the Cheyenne-Arapaho treaty. Although the reporters had been warned not to take verbatim notes from the Comanche-Kiowa document, they had been granted access to the treaty. Some of the correspondents had sent dispatches covering the Comanche-Kiowa treaty in the exact wording of the ratified treaty, despite being told not to do so; one might speculate that the Cheyenne-Arapaho document was withheld by the Commission for this reason. Such an assumption becomes invalid, however, on consideration that the earliest stories from correspondents on the Comanche-Kiowa treaty appeared on the day of the Cheyenne meeting—October 28. These reports had all been in letter form, and by the time they arrived in the east for publication, the Cheyenne-Arapaho Grand Council had already begun at Medicine Lodge. In short, the commissioners could not have been aware as the Cheyenne council began that the reporters had violated their trust on the earlier document.[2]

There may have been another reason the press gang did not see the Cheyenne document. Milton Reynolds was not present, and at the time of the Comanche-Kiowa treaty he had been. He had spent more time with the official party than he had with the press group and possibly had known of the Comanche-Kiowa treaty draft and had asked that it be shown the press people. With Reynolds absent—

[2] See Chapter V.

and no other reporter enjoying his respect and confidence among the commissioners—the document may not have been volunteered simply because no one bothered to ask for it, and no one else may have been on close enough terms with the commissioners to know of its existence. Whatever the reasons, the correspondents expressed no concern or disapproval that they had not been informed of the contents of the paper presented to the Cheyennes.

In contrast to the Comanches' and Kiowas' stonily silent reaction to Henderson's words, the Cheyennes and Arapahoes expressed their approval and satisfaction when the Senator concluded his remarks. After Henderson took his seat, Little Robe said that his Arapaho friend Little Raven should have the honor of speaking first. The Arapahoes had been waiting at Medicine Lodge a long time, and they should be allowed first voice, the Cheyenne chief said. The correspondents reported Little Raven was somewhat taken aback and that he was reluctant to rise. The Cheyennes all prompted him, and finally the fat Arapaho stood up and turned to the Cheyennes.

Little Raven said the Cheyennes were like his own flesh, that he had always loved them, and that the Arapahoes and Cheyennes would be friends forever. None of the correspondents mentioned that two nights earlier Little Raven had been warning the Peace Commission of Cheyenne treachery and asking that he and his people not be considered in the same negotiations with the Cheyennes.

Once Little Raven had paid his respects to his powerful allies, he turned to the commissioners. For a man reluctant to speak, he had a great deal to say once started. "There are General Harney and General Sanborn and Mister Smith," he said, "who were at the treaty of the Little Arkansas. We have always held that treaty." Little Raven went on to say that he was a peaceful man and would welcome the benefits of reservation life. "As for myself, and men aged like me, we will be gone before the farms get to be productive, but those who come after us will enjoy them." He said the white man should send guns and ammunition to peaceful Indians, to show good faith, adding that he doubted such supplies would be received. He told the commissioners that his home had always been near Fort Lyon, in Colorado, and he wanted a reservation there. No place else would do as well, he said. When the Arapaho chief had finished—at last and to the obvious satisfaction of Senator Henderson—the Cheyennes shouted their approval.

Of all the correspondents, only Budd seemed favorably impressed with the fat Arapaho's talk. He wrote that all men should be as frank as this "untutored savage" if the country ever expected to be free of "convulsions and bloodshed." The Cincinnati correspondent appeared to mellow with the extension of his visit to the open plains.

The first Cheyenne chief rose. He was Buffalo Chief, a man the correspondents did not know; he had not been among the many visitors to the Peace Commission camp for the preliminary Cheyenne meetings. He was a tall, handsome man, the reporters noted, with hair well greased and hanging in two braids on either side of his face. Like many of the other Cheyennes—and unlike most Comanches—he wore feathers at the back of his head.

Buffalo Chief asked if it was really true that the Peace Commission had come from the Great Father in Washington, and whether the white man really wanted peace. He paused, obviously expecting an answer, and Senator Henderson assured him that it was all true. The Cheyenne seemed pleased, the correspondents reported, and after looking about him at the other chiefs, he made his speech, much the same kind of speech Satanta and Ten Bears had made one week earlier. The Cheyennes wanted no houses, nor did they expect to be treated as orphans by the white man. They wanted to depend on themselves, Buffalo Chief said, and when the time came that the Cheyennes needed help, they would be ready to talk about it. "We are willing, when we desire to live as you do," he said, "to take your advice about settling down; but until then, we will take our chances."

Buffalo Chief said the Cheyennes were happy to allow railroads to be built, and to let the white travelers pass across the prairies unmolested. All the Cheyennes wanted was to hunt where they had always hunted. "We never claimed any land south of the Arkansas," he said. "But that country between the Arkansas and the South Platte is ours."

This land claim was the raw nerve that everyone had been afraid would be touched, and Buffalo Chief touched it very hard. The Cheyenne war with the Comanches and Kiowas had been brought on when the Cheyennes had started moving south of the Arkansas. Their peace of 1840 more or less established the Arkansas as the boundary between the two tribes. Although the Cheyennes sometimes traveled south of the river, and the Southern allies traveled north, none of the tribes claimed areas on both sides of the Arkansas as exclusively their own.[3] Unfortunately for the Cheyennes, their country included an area of rapidly growing white settlement and road building. When he referred to "that country between the Arkansas and the South Platte," Buffalo Chief was talking about the vast range drained by the Smoky Hill, Republican, Saline, and Solomon rivers. He was talking, in short, about the whole of western Kansas plus a great expanse of country in eastern Colorado.

Before the end of the meeting, it became obvious that Cheyenne removal from Kansas was completely unacceptable to the Indians. Stanley said the Cheyennes would not budge from their claim to hunting rights between the Arkansas and the South Platte. Hall wrote that denial of the Smoky Hill range to Cheyenne hunting parties would wreck the peace meeting and cause a continuation of the war on the Smoky Hill.

When Buffalo Chief finished, the commissioners waited for another Cheyenne to speak. After a moment, they realized that there would be no more speakers. Buffalo Chief had said everything the Cheyennes wanted said.

The commissioners started whispering among themselves, and seeing a chance to add to his original remarks, Little Raven stood up again. With Margaret Adams interpreting for him, the Arapaho said he wanted Mrs. Adams assigned as the regular interpreter for his tribe, with appropriate pay and a buggy for traveling. After Buffalo Chief's message, it is not difficult to imagine how little attention the

[3] Mooney, "Calendar History," 165–68; Grinnell, *Fighting Cheyennes*, 5–7; Mayhall, *Kiowas*, 74.

Peace Commission gave to Little Raven. Fortunately, the reporters were listening and recording what the fat chief said.

Little Raven wanted a good trader; some he had seen in the past had been dishonest. He said he would like to have C. A. Butterfield, Murphy's assistant at Medicine Lodge, or if this was not possible, Butterfield's brother Isaac would be acceptable. Or, he said, John Tappan, a cousin of Commissioner Tappan might make a good trader to the Arapahoes. Little Raven rambled on for a long time, listing things he wanted on his Colorado reservation. He appeared to be the only person present unaware that he had no chance whatsoever of getting a reservation in Colorado.[4]

No one else was prepared to speak, so the commission began to discuss the situation among themselves once more. The treaty, as Henderson had drawn it up, was unacceptable to the Cheyennes, they all agreed. There was some talk of adjourning the meeting to revise the document, and as they talked, the commissioners became aware of the correspondents' taking notes on their discussions. They made no objection, nor had they ever during the course of the treaty councils. Apparently, it was taken for granted that if reporters were going to be present, it was only right that they hear what was being said.

While the Commission was thus engaged on discussion of the Cheyenne treaty, an Indian arose whom the correspondents identified as Little Man, a Cheyenne war chief. He began a tirade against the Southern tribes, accusing the Kiowas and Comanches of saying bad things about the Cheyennes and spreading rumors that the Cheyennes might attack the peace camp. According to Hall, Little Man became extremely excited as he spoke, waving his arms and shouting. He said nothing against the Arapahoes, even though all the warnings against the Cheyennes had come from Little Raven, and all the camp alarms concerning Cheyennes had been generated in the Arapaho camp. Actually, throughout the treaty meeting the Comanches and Kiowas had maintained an attitude of calm indifference to the

[4] "Journal," Aug. 13, 1867.

Cheyenne situation, and luckily for the peace of the camp, after Little Man was finished with his verbal attack, they continued to be undisturbed and apparently untroubled by the Cheyenne's accusations.

Ignoring the interruption, the commissioners went back to their discussion, with Henderson objecting strenuously to the adjournment discussions. The correspondents reported that Henderson said he could get the treaty signed that day. The interpreters were called forward, and after a short discussion, they walked with Henderson away from the rest of the commissioners. Some of the Cheyenne chiefs were asked to join Henderson and the interpreters where they stood some distance from the brush arbor. None of the newsmen joined the group, but they watched as Buffalo Chief and other Cheyenne leaders walked over to join Senator Henderson. The group was too far away for any of the correspondents to hear what was being said. As they watched, the reporters saw Buffalo Chief reach out and take Henderson's hand and hold it as he spoke, and in a moment John Smith and George Bent, the Cheyenne interpreters, were speaking emphatically with the Indians.

It was some time before the group returned to the brush arbor. It had become apparent to the reporters that the outcome of that small meeting would determine the fate of the Cheyenne treaty. The Indians seemed pleased, and Senator Henderson was relieved as the group returned to join the others. Henderson quickly told the other members of the Commission and the correspondents what had been said.

According to his own account, Henderson had told the Cheyenne leaders that they need not enter reservations right away. He promised them hunting rights between the Arkansas and the South Fork of the Platte, so long as there were buffalo, but only under the terms of the treaty of the Little Arkansas. He explained specifically for the correspondents that this meant Indian hunters could go no nearer than ten miles to routes of travel or white settlements. Henderson was offering less than at first appeared. Routes of travel and white settlements were expanding rapidly across Kansas at the time, and to stay ten miles from either rather severely limited Cheyenne hunting. In return for all this, the Cheyennes were expected to take permanent homes in Indian Territory as soon as the buffalo were gone —which would be shortly, Henderson said curtly.

The Henderson promises had convinced the Cheyennes that they should sign the treaty. There was no effort to change the wording of the document at that time, and the chiefs were called forward to make their mark—to "touch the feather." When there was talk among the commissioners of making necessary changes to the treaty before the signing, Fayel said Henderson commented, "It's no time for bickering." The document was presented to the chiefs as it was, and they began to mark it.

An atmosphere of geniality prevailed in the council grove as the Cheyennes and Arapahoes came up to the table to put their marks on the treaty.[5] The Indians laughed and talked among themselves as they waited their turn. Many of them shook hands with the commissioners before entering their mark. Arapahoes who signed the treaty were Little Raven, Yellow Bear, Storm, White Rabbit, Spotted Wolf, Little Big Mouth, Young Colt, and Tall Bear. For the Cheyennes there was Black Kettle, Little Bear, Spotted Elk, Buffalo Chief, Slim Face, Gray Head, Curly Hair, Tall Bull, Whirlwind, and Heap of Birds.[6]

A tense moment followed when Bull Bear, White Horse, and Little Robe refused to sign. Little Robe explained through the interpreter, John Smith, that the treaty had enough marks already. For a time, the commissioners were satisfied with this explanation, but Superintendent Murphy was much disturbed. He told a number of the correspondents that these three were powerful and influential men. The treaty without their blessing would not be worth "a cent."

The commissioners told the three chiefs that the Great Father

---

[5] The treaty signing was covered in the *Chicago Tribune*, Nov. 4, 1867; *Cincinnati Commercial*, Nov. 4, 1867; *Missouri Democrat*, Nov. 2, 1867; *Missouri Republican*, Nov. 4, 1867; *New York Herald*, Nov. 1, 1867; *New York Tribune*, Nov. 6, 1867; *Harper's Magazine*, Nov. 16, 1867; *Leslie's Illustrated Newspaper*, Nov. 16, 23, 1867.

[6] Kappler, 989.

would be disappointed if their names were not on the treaty. It made no difference to Little Robe and the others about the Great Father's disappointment; there were already too many marks on the paper, and they refused to mark it further. Henderson and Taylor asked Smith and George Bent to see what they could do to convince the three Indians. A short, heated discussion followed. The correspondents were very attentive to this argument, but they could not understand a word being said. Finally, the three chiefs agreed to sign, and they reluctantly walked to the table and marked the treaty. The press gang was highly impressed with Smith and Bent in this episode, but no one has ever determined what the two men said that made the Cheyennes change their minds and sign.

Hall and the St. Louis reporters listed a number of the Indians who signed the treaty on October 28, but they did not bother listing them all. Everyone seemed disappointed that Roman Nose had not appeared at the council. The commissioners had asked about the famous warrior and had been told that he was still on the Cimarron, suffering from a slight sickness. Fayel called this a lame excuse, concluding that the Cheyenne brave was still angry with Wynkoop and white men in general, a valid assumption.

After the signing, the meeting broke up, with small groups of Indians and whites standing about talking. The reporters were with Senator Henderson as he spoke with Bull Bear and other Cheyennes. Henderson asked if Bull Bear would be willing to come to Washington and see the Great Father. Bull Bear considered for a while, then said he might, but only after the United States had concluded a satisfactory treaty with the Cheyennes north of the Platte. Tall Bull, standing in the same group, said he had signed the treaty of the Little Arkansas, and had tried to keep it. But when Hancock came, he was ashamed that he had made an agreement for peace. He told Henderson that he and his people were willing for a railroad to be built across the Great Plains, but he could not allow armed soldiers to come into his camp, as Hancock had allowed them to do on the Pawnee Fork of the Arkansas. He said that after Hancock burned the Cheyenne village, the Indians had conducted many raids. "I am not ashamed of anything I did," Fayel reported the Cheyenne chief as saying.

Commissioner Taylor interrupted the various conversations that were going on around the peace table, announcing that the time had come for issuing treaty presents and annuities. Although the Cheyennes had said they were not interested in gifts, they appeared well pleased with Taylor's words. They laughed and shouted, Hall said, shaking hands and slapping each other on the shoulders. Taylor led the group upstream through the grove of trees. Everyone walked to the Commission headquarters, and the crowd of warriors, women, children, horses, and dogs stretched out for half a mile through the woods.

At the wagon park, Cheyenne and Arapaho presents were stacked, ready for issue.[7] There had been no dallying, once the Cheyennes came in; compared to the pace of the Comanche-Kiowa negotiations, the Cheyenne-Arapaho dealings were conducted with breakneck speed. Once again, the reporters all commented on the great number and variety of gifts, but none of them were so detailed as they had been when presents were given the Comanches and Kiowas. Fayel said the Indians gathered around the wagon park, looking at the piles of treaty goods, with "an acre of ponies in the rear to carry away the portion that fell to the owners."

Tribal leaders placed themselves before the crowd—which had formed in a half-circle—and as gifts were pointed out by Murphy or Sanborn, the two men shouted out the names of members of the tribe. When an Indian's name was called, he moved forward, generally followed by women and children leading horses. The presents were loaded on the ponies, and the Indian family would move away, making room for the next group. Fayel reported that the Cheyennes were in such high spirits that even the issue of defective pistols did not seem to disturb them. The St. Louis correspondent said weapons made of cast iron were given the Indians, and that the faulty pistols would not snap a cap. Although the Comanches and Kiowas received

[7] The discussion of the distribution of gifts is taken from the *Chicago Tribune*, Nov. 2, 1867; and *Missouri Republican*, Nov. 2, 1867.

a few Colt revolvers, none of the reporters saw any of these excellent weapons issued to the Cheyennes and Arapahoes.

Shortly after the Cheyennes and Arapahoes carried away the last of their presents, Senator Henderson gave the correspondents a written summary of the treaty.[8] Included was a history of the Cheyenne-Arapaho negotiations with the United States, considerable detail being given to the terms of the treaty of the Little Arkansas specifying that hunting parties would not go closer than ten miles to routes of travel or white settlements. In most instances, Henderson's summary as reported by the newsmen was identical to the treaty ratified in the Senate one year later. It is interesting to note here that the Senator from Missouri used what is currently called a press handout to tell his story. As Stanley pointed out, Henderson's reputation for credibility was good among the correspondents, and as a result, they did not question his reports of the treaty which they had not seen.

Provisions for buildings, farm implements, allocation of land titles, and the distribution of annuities were the same as in the Comanche-Kiowa treaty. The same restrictions were placed on the Cheyennes and Arapahoes as well; they were to allow railroads to pass through the country, and they were not to molest white travelers or settlers. Hall reported that the annual money to be spent on the tribes—in addition to annuity clothing—would be $20,000, the amount specified in the ratified treaty. Making the same mistake he had made on the earlier document, Howland said the sum was $30,000.

All the newspaper reports of reservation boundaries that came from the press gang at Medicine Lodge were correct. The reservation lay in the Indian Territory, taken from lands originally given the Civilized Tribes, but reclaimed after the Civil War—the majority of these Indians had fought on the wrong side. The area was bounded on the north by the southern boundary of Kansas, on the west and south by the Cimarron River, and on the east by the Arkansas River. Howland said the reservation was larger than the one specified in the treaty of the Little Arkansas. This was incorrect, but Senate re-

[8] Treaty provisions cited by newsmen taken from all newspapers indicated in fn. 5 above.

vision of the treaty of the Little Arkansas made specified boundaries meaningless. The 1865 treaty had authorized the Cheyennes and Arapahoes to live in the country they had originally claimed, but they would have no reservation of their own until title could be gained from other Indian tribes for such an area.[9] In short, the Cheyennes and Arapahoes were left to wander about the prairie until the United States could find a way to reclaim lands which had been promised to other Indians in the Indian Territory. Not that it mattered too much to the Cheyennes and Arapahoes—Great Plains wild tribes did not think in terms of "permanent homes." To a Cheyenne, his "permanent home" was most of Kansas, Nebraska, South Dakota, and large chunks of Colorado and Wyoming. At any rate, this provision of the Little Arkansas treaty was in Henderson's summary, and Fayel covered it in detail in his dispatches.

The one major difference between Henderson's abstract and the Cheyenne-Arapaho document as it was ratified concerned hunting rights. As the Senator had told the correspondents at the treaty council, in order to obtain Cheyenne agreement to the treaty, the Indians were promised the right to continue hunting north of the Arkansas River. A provision permitting this was included in Henderson's summary, and all the Medicine Lodge correspondents reported the clause. Commission Secretary A. S. H. White mentioned the same provision when he wrote General Sherman that a Cheyennne-Arapaho treaty had been signed.[10] He said that Cheyenne and Arapaho hunting parties were authorized to range throughout the unsettled portion of country south of the South Platte, ". . . with the permission of the agent, and not coming within ten miles of a military post or public road." Both Hall and Fayel reported this provision in essentially the same language that White used. Sherman published a general order for all units of his Division of the Missouri to this effect, and the order was recorded in the minutes of the Commission meetings after the board returned to St. Louis. Bulkley re-

[9] Kappler, *Treaties*, 989f.
[10] *Ibid.*, 984–89; "Journal," Nov. 3, 1867; White, Letter; *New York Herald,* Nov. 5, 1867.

ported Sherman's general order on November 3. However, no such provision was in the treaty ratified by the Senate on July 25, 1868. The hunting rights of Cheyennes and Arapahoes were identical to those specified for Comanches and Kiowas: ". . . to hunt on the lands south of the Arkansas."

Fayel specifically pointed out that none of the Medicine Lodge press gang ever saw the document the Indians signed. They reported solely on the basis of Henderson's abstract and the verbal promises the Senator said he made to the Indians at the treaty meeting. Certainly, Henderson promised something in that private talk with a few of the chiefs; they came back to the brush arbor and signed the document. But if that change ever appeared in written form, the correspondents did not record it, nor was it recorded in the Peace Commission minutes. The Senate ratified the treaty as it was presented to them, and the funds necessary to fulfill the terms were appropriated by the House without modification of the document.[11] Sherman informed his subordinates that the Arapahoes and Cheyennes had the right to hunt between the Arkansas and the South Platte, but such right was granted by the treaty as ratified.

This was another example of promising the Indians one thing on the scene and giving them something else at Washington. If there ever was a Smoky Hill hunting clause in the document and it was later deleted, no further consultation was held with the Cheyennes or Arapahoes—October 28, 1867, was the last time the representatives of the United States ever sat at a treaty table with any of the Southern Plains tribes. The next time red and white diplomats met, terms were not offered, they were dictated.

The promised but missing hunting clause could have caused considerable misunderstanding. But the weaknesses of the Treaty of Medicine Lodge never had time to materialize. The rapid march of events overtook the frontier before treaty mistakes could have any effect. Other forces which were at work led to war.

General Sherman blamed Congressional inaction for the violent outbreaks in 1868. He said also, in his annual report for that year:

[11] *Cong. Globe*, 1868, 3279, 4450.

Our people continue as heretofore to settle on exposed points of the frontier, to travel without the precaution which a well-known danger would suggest, and to run after every wild report of gold or other precious metal, thus coming into daily and necessary conflict with discontented and hostile Indians.[12]

What made the Indians discontented and hostile was explained in some measure by the lack of funds to start improvements on the reservations. Silver Brooch had repeated his plea for quick action on the building program. The Comanche had not speculated on what would happen; he said point-blank that he would return to his wild brothers.

On the reservations yet another point of friction existed immediately after the talks at Medicine Lodge. The treaty did not specifically say that the Indians would be fed, but the tribes certainly assumed they would be. Henderson had said food and clothing would be provided by the reservations. But the only food available on the reservations during the winter of 1867–68 was what little the army could afford to issue. The Comanches provided their own, in part, by raiding the nearby Wichita Indian agency.[13]

Just as bad as discontented Indians on the reservations were those who had made no agreement to settle down and felt no obligation to do so. Leaders of every tribe represented at Medicine Lodge remained hostile throughout the time of the meetings, with the possible exception of the Arapahoes and Plains Apaches. Most of the tribes had stopped raiding to see what would happen on the Timbered Hill River. When the proceedings were finished, they went back on the war trail. Besides being a hazard in themselves, they provided the frontiersman with an excuse for shooting at any Indian on sight.[14]

There was a great variety of reasons for the resumption of war in Kansas in 1868, with increased bitterness and fury on both sides. Too much friction was being generated by both sides to avoid an

[12] *Sec. of War 68*, 1 f.

[13] Commissioner *Report 68*, 3f.; Nye, *Carbine and Lance*, 47; Wirth, *Soldier and Brave*, 36f.

[14] Commissioner *Report 68*, 64f.

outbreak. A simple peace treaty was not adequate to the need. On the one hand existed Congressional inaction, white disregard of Indian rights, an increasing pressure of settlement along routes of travel, and a growing demand for buffalo hides; on the other hand were disgruntled Indians drifting off reservations, a sharp increase in fighting among the Indians themselves, and a hard core of hostiles from each tribe who had never talked peace and had no intention of doing so. In view of these factors—and there were others as well— it would probably be wrong to claim that omission of hunting rights from the Treaty of Medicine Lodge was a cause, or even a factor, in continuing war.[15]

An awareness of conditions existing at the time the treaty was signed—that is, exclusive of hunting rights—may have prompted Bulkley and Hall to say the treaty made at Medicine Lodge meant little more than temporary peace. Neither reporter claimed that treaty faults might cause war; but neither felt the treaty could cause peace, either.

The correspondents did not find fault with the Peace Commission for failing to allow them access to the Cheyenne-Arapaho treaty. Their modern counterparts, it is suspected, would not have accepted the concealment in as good grace. Nor did they criticize Henderson's abstract of the treaty, or complain about this method of informing them of the treaty contents. They were not suspicious of press handouts, as modern reporters have become because of abuses of the technique. As Stanley pointed out, Henderson was the major source of information, and in the case of the Cheyenne-Arapaho treaty, he was the only source. Fayel made no claim that the Henderson abstract was true; he only said he assumed it was what the public needed to know about the Peace Commission's work, and what the Commission wanted the public to know.

With the last treaty signed and the last gift distributed, the correspondents hurried to get out a dispatch on the last mail run from Medicine Lodge. The courier on horseback left Medicine Lodge for Larned and Harker the same night the Cheyenne-Arapaho treaty

[15] *Ibid.*, 266f.

was signed. All the reporters wrote hurried dispatches, obviously caught up in the activities of a camp preparing to move. As a result, the wrap-up stories on the Cheyenne-Arapaho treaty making were not as complete as they had been on the Comanche-Kiowa councils.

It had been work well done, Fayel reported. To him, the treaty meant an end of profits for army contractors who made their living from strong frontier garrisons and Indian wars. Others among the press gang agreed with Fayel that money followed Indian-fighting troops, and there was strong support from outside the press circle, too. General Sherman had discussed his opinions on that subject in a letter to the Secretary of the Interior in 1866. Investigating claims that Indians around Denver, Colorado, were hostile, Sherman said he could find no evidence of such a thing, but that local merchants who would profit from the influx of troop units imagined dangers for the benefit of their pocketbooks.[16]

Stanley was optimistic about the prospects for peace. After the Cheyenne-Arapaho treaty was signed, he wrote: "Peace has been concluded with all the Southern tribes. Civilization is now on the move, and westward the Star of Empire will again resume its march, unimpeded in the great work of Progress."

The *Democrat* correspondent singled out Harney, Sanborn, Henderson and Taylor for special praise; he felt the nation owed these men a debt of gratitude. He added that Governor Crawford and Senator Ross of Kansas had accomplished their purpose, for Kansas was at last free of Comanches and Kiowas.[17] Stanley did not elaborate on this statement, but the Kansas problem centered on the Cheyennes, not the Comanches and Kiowas. All the tribes were authorized to hunt in the Big Bend country of the Arkansas—a part of Kansas— and insofar as vocal promises were concerned, the Cheyennes were still allowed to hunt the Smoky Hill range if they stayed clear of white men. Stanley may also have been unaware of Crawford and

[16] *Special Report 13, 3; Cincinnati Commercial,* Nov. 4, 1867; *Missouri Democrat,* Nov. 2, 1867; *Missouri Republican,* Nov. 2, 1867; *New York Herald,* Nov. 21, 1867; *New York Tribune,* Nov. 6, 1867.

[17] *Missouri Democrat,* Nov. 2, 1867.

Ross's stated purposes of vacating Osage land titles and maintaining strong military garrisons in Kansas.[18] Neither of these purposes was served by the treaty. Just the same, Stanley was optimistic.

Brown was as confident as Stanley that the Treaty of Medicine Lodge would bring peace on the frontier. He was the only reporter at the councils who suggested that the army might be disappointed when peace came:

> The violent men of the border who have so long said that their lives and property were no longer safe on the Plains, must now sheath their swords. The Army, so anxious for opportunities for distinguishment seeking a quarrel with the red men, will be disappointed, for this day peace with the Cheyennes has been concluded.

Brown's inexperience on the frontier was showing. In 1867, Lieutenant Colonel George A. Custer had as yet to find those "opportunities for distinguishment" which he later sought and found on the Washita and Little Big Horn. With Custer's frontier reputation for belligerency not yet well started, it is not readily apparent whom Brown was accusing of wanting an Indian war. Such Indian-fighting soldiers as Harney, Earl Van Dorn, and Christopher "Kit" Carson had found nothing in Indian wars but hard campaigning from Texas to Wyoming. Sherman, top-ranking military man on the frontier at the time of Brown's observations, did not agree that the army could distinguish itself in Indian wars. Sherman said Indians were extremely hard to catch and, once caught, equally hard to defeat. He pointed out that fifty hostile warriors could checkmate three thousand troops required to stand guard on railroads, stage stations, and settlers. In short, Indian war involved guard duty—and trying to guess where the war parties would strike next.[19] Perhaps Brown was thinking of Colonel J. M. Chivington's massacre of Cheyennes at Sand Creek, in 1864. If he was, Brown's choice of words was unfortunate, and he did the active army a great disservice; the army had not been

[18] *Cong. Globe,* 1867, 703; Crawford, *Kansas,* 255f.
[19] *Sec. of War 68,* 34; *Special Report* 13, 4.

186

involved in the Sand Creek massacre. Chivington had been a militia officer, commanding state troops and operating under the orders of the governor of Colorado.[20]

Of all the correspondents at Medicine Lodge, only Hall and Bulkley were pessimistic about the treaty, and they only vaguely so. In reporting the Cheyenne-Arapaho treaty, Hall said peace—even though temporary—had come to the Great Plains. Bulkley reported that the Cheyenne treaty had brought a truce instead of peace. The *Herald* correspondent did not specify if he was reporting someone's opinion rather than his own. No one noted that although Medicine Lodge was supposed to have been the beginning of the reservation system, not one of the wild tribes had agreed to be confined until such time as they themselves decided to take "permanent homes." Such a comment probably would have been made had Milton Reynolds have been there.

[20] Wirth, *Soldier and Brave*, 10–34.

THIRTEEN

"WE GAVE YOU OUR HEARTS— YOU NOW HAVE THEM"
—Kiowa

It was finished. The next day—October 29, there would be an early start for everyone still left in camp. Already, with the Cheyenne and Arapaho gifts distributed, many empty wagons had started back toward Fort Larned. With evening, the sounds of the camp were different. So few mules were left in the wagon park that the racket of their braying was less irritating than it had been since the Peace Commission first arrived. The orderlies were packing much of the housekeeping gear and getting it into the ambulances. Well-rested horses were rubbed down and harness checked; grease buckets hanging under the ambulances were brought out and wheel bearings packed. When the sun came up, the few remaining wagons would start for Larned, one ambulance-borne infantry company with them. The rest of the party would strike directly across the prairie for Fort Harker, 110 miles away, passing far to the east of Larned. While the correspondents ate or wrote their last dispatches, all the camps were tightening gear and getting ready for the trip. General Harney and Senator Henderson—now that the councils were completed—were of one mind. They wanted to get back home as soon as possible.[1]

Down the valley, the pony herds had been driven in close to the Indian camps. Indian women were making bundles of hides, blankets, and treaty gifts for pack horses and travois. Many of the tipis were already gone. Along the edge of the creek, the correspondents could

[1] The final two days described in the *Chicago Tribune,* Nov. 4, 1867; *Missouri Republican,* Nov. 3, 1867.

see small groups of Indian men talking, discussing which trails to take and where to look for winter range.

In the early evening, General Terry went to the press tent and called the reporters' attention to a brilliant meteor, streaking across the southern sky. Although the sky was still light, the meteor cast a yellow sheen on the hills south of the Medicine Lodge. The bright glow lasted for a few minutes and was gone, but the press gang stayed outside, commenting to one another about the odd coloring in the sky. Purple clouds were scudding along, their undersides brightened by the sun below the horizon. At first, the winds were high above the ground, but soon they had settled, and the reporters had to hold their hats as they went back into the tent. Flashes of lightning lit the sky, and Fayel said it was an uncommon sight for October.

Above the sounds of the coming storm, they heard Indians singing and shouting, and when they opened their tent flap they saw a large group of men and women riding toward the Peace Commission camp. The Indians were Arapahoes, and they were dressed in ceremonial regalia. Most of them were painted, and feathered headdresses and beaded shirts could be seen. When the horses stopped near the Commission camp and the Indians dismounted, they began to shake bone rattles and blow on buffalo horn whistles. Forming a great circle, the Arapahoes started to dance. The sky overhead was black, and the wind was blowing so hard most of the sounds of singing were carried away from the watching white men. Members of the Peace Commission had come out to see the dance, and they stood holding their hats in the wind as the Arapaho dancers moved before them.

William Fayel stood with John Smith, the Cheyenne interpreter. The *Republican* correspondent called his companion "Old Smith." Throughout the treaty conferences, Fayel had shown great respect for the interpreter. Shouting to make himself heard above the noise of the wind and the dancers, Old Smith explained to Fayel the various forms of Indian dancing.

As the correspondents watched the dance, the weather grew worse.

Rain began falling, and the wind ripped a number of tent ropes loose from their pegs. All the whites ran to secure their tents, but the Arapahoes continued to dance. Fayel wrote that the wind had reached tornado force and there was danger of the Peace Commission being blown away. The sky was still discolored, and south of the Medicine Lodge lightning had set fire to the prairie. As yet it was not raining enough to put it out. The men lashed down their tents as orderlies drove more tent pegs into the ground. Before the job was finished, the grass fires across the creek were so close they cast a red glare on the camp.

Although the Arapahoes were still dancing, the whites stayed under the cover of their tents. Hall reported that the press party tried to sleep, wrapped tightly in their blankets. Time after time, he said, they had to dash out again to refasten ropes loosened in the gale. Toward midnight the rain increased, but the correspondents could still hear the Indians singing above the sounds of the wind. It was nearly dawn before the Indians stopped dancing. By then, the storm was gone.

It was a muddy camp when the sun finally came up. The only sign of the previous night's storm were the pools of water and a few trees across the stream that had blown down. Soldiers helped the orderlies stow the gear and strike the tents. General Harney conferred with Major Elliot, and upstream the troopers were saddling their mounts and policing their camp. Little ceremony was observed as the camp broke and the vehicles pulled into line. A few blanket-wrapped Indians stood nearby to wave good-by, and farther back a group of mounted Arapahoes watched. None of the other tribes were represented.

The Peace Commission took "K" Company, Fifth Infantry as their escort, while the two cavalry companies under Elliot lagged behind to accompany the small number of Commission supply wagons that would head for Fort Harker, following the tracks of the Commission.[2] It was not a leisurely march. General Harney continued to press the ambulance drivers, and they moved quickly in their light

[2] Elliot, "Report."

190

vehicles. Eating a cold lunch, they spent only a few moments to stretch their legs and check the horses before pushing on again. For a while on the first day, the soldiers could see the cavalry companies and the heavy wagons with supplies, but soon these were out of sight. They had loaded all the equipment they needed for the trail in the ambulances, although this meant they would not sleep in tents. They crossed the Arkansas somewhere upstream from the present city of Hutchinson. Bulkley, who may have been the only one not too tired to write a telegram, reported the party reached Fort Harker on the morning of October 31. It had taken fifty-two hours.[3]

Although the press gang seemed to fall away from the official party at Harker, the Peace Commission itself wasted no time getting on with their final order of business. Two days after arriving at Fort Harker, they were in St. Louis conducting a meeting. General Sherman, just returned from his Washington trip, greeted the others, and they all looked over the treaties signed at Medicine Lodge. The officials discussed the planned northern trip, but Senator Henderson suggested that such a trip should come at a later date, perhaps in the spring. All agreed. The meeting promised with the tribes along the Platte was postponed until after the first of the year, and Taylor sent dispatches to his agency people to so inform the Indians.[4]

When the meeting closed, Sherman said he would like to study the treaties in the privacy of his own headquarters. He said he would be back in a few days. On the following morning, A. S. H. White expressed some surprise to see General Sherman back, with his approval of the treaties. Obviously, the Peace Commission had been anxious about Sherman's reaction. Unquestionably, he was still considered the military head of the board even though he had not been to Medicine Lodge.

During this second meeting, Senator Ross of Kansas visited the Commission and asked once more that they consider a meeting with the Osages in order to vacate title to Indian lands still held in

[3] *New York Herald*, Nov. 1, 1867.
[4] Commission activities taken from "Journal," Nov. 2, 3, 15, Dec. 11, 1867 and Jan. 3, 7, 1868.

Kansas. Henderson was willing, from all reports, but the rest of the Commission refused to consider it.

Plans were made for the Commission to travel to Washington, where the final report would be made to the President and subsequently to the Congress. With these details arranged, Sherman said he would publish an order to his division, and he read the document to the other commissioners. It was a short summary of what had happened at the Peace Commission meetings with the Southern Plains tribes.[5]

In the newspapers represented at Medicine Lodge, there were no further reports of Peace Commission activities under dateline of "Special Correspondent" after the board returned to St. Louis. Apparently, once the Commission left Indian country, the reporters stopped covering the story, and the remainder of it was told through local reporters and press associations. There was one exception, however. A story in the *New York Herald*, with the dateline "Special Telegraph, November 3," announced Sherman's publication of General Order Number 10. It was a typical Bulkley dispatch, short and to the point:

> A General Order will be made by General Sherman tomorrow, announcing to the troops of his division that treaties of peace have been made. Although the right to hunt north of the Arkansas, but south of the South Platte, was given the Cheyennes and Arapahoes only, the order makes no distinction in this respect. Commanding Generals may use force to compel mischievous citizens to keep the peace.[6]

Sherman was taking no chance of error in not saying who could hunt north of the Arkansas. He obviously felt that allowing Comanches or Kiowas to hunt in Kansas would cause less trouble than shooting a Cheyenne through mistaken identity. Here was a striking example of an officer doing all he could to prevent an army violation of Indian rights.

[5] *Peace Commission,* 14f.
[6] *New York Herald,* Nov. 5, 1867.

Bulkley had been in the meeting of the Peace Commission of November 3. This was the date that Sherman read his general order to the other members of the group. This was Bulkley's last dispatch on Medicine Lodge, and it was sent from a train in Alton, Illinois. He was going home.

The last St. Louis meeting was on November 15, but a number of the commissioners were already on their way to Washington. The next full membership meeting was held in the capital on December 11. There was a long discussion of the report to be prepared. Henderson, Sherman, and Taylor were selected to write the document, and they worked on it through the holidays. On January 3, 1868, the first draft was read to the full membership of the board, and a few changes made. The final copy was prepared, and on January 7, in the last meeting of the Commission concerning the Southern Plains tribes, the report was adopted and then forwarded to the President.

FOURTEEN

"DO FOR US WHAT IS BEST"
—Kiowa

The Peace Commission *Official Report* reflected the thinking of a number of men who were directly involved in Indian affairs and with the making of the treaties at Medicine Lodge. The correspondents who covered the Medicine Lodge councils did not remain with the Commission until the findings were compiled and published, on January 14, 1868. Coverage on the *Report* came out of Washington long after the Timbered Hill River press gang had broken up, each man going his own way. However, much of what the document contained had been discussed in the news dispatches from the Plains. In fact, a remarkable similarity existed between many of the newspaper accounts filed by the reporters on the scene and what later appeared as a part of the official *Report*.

No one can ever be sure what was said or left unsaid at Medicine Lodge—whether opinions were expressed openly or only with a frown, a smile or a nod of the head. But many of the opinions expressed in the *Report* were unquestionably put forth at the treaty grounds in language loud and understandable to the correspondents, for they wrote about those opinions months before the report was published. Some of the commissioners did not agree with the report in certain respects, but it is quite probable that disagreements not reported by the press gang from Medicine Lodge were made known only in private conversations and personal letters. For the Peace Commission was being monitored by a group that fed on controversy —the correspondents—and had there been argument, they would

194

have delighted in telling of it. Indeed, many differences of opinions that came into the open were reported, and the assumption appears valid that any not reported were not made openly.

According to Commission records, the *Official Report* was not begun until the commissioners arrived in Washington, but it should be no mystery that the report so often echoed the words which had first appeared in news columns. The Medicine Lodge official party, which included the reporters, lived close together for three weeks, under conditions that were bound to create an intimate relationship among some of the members. A number of times, correspondents were there when important discussions were being held separate and apart from the councils. Fayel, Stanley, and Reynolds in particular indicated many instances of commissioners' discussing hearings, the treaties, or the general situation on the Great Plains, all within hearing of the reporters. Much of what was said found its way into the newspaper accounts—and obviously into the final report of the Commission.[1]

The *Report* was divided into four distinct parts, although the document was not specifically broken down in this way by the authors. The first concern of the Commission was a survey of conditions which were found on the Plains prior to the wars of 1867—and which to a great extent had brought on the fighting. The second part was a summary of what had been wrong with the Indian policy in the past— actually, a continuation of the causes of war. The third portion was a series of recommendations, and the last a financial report.[2]

The report started with a short history of the frontier beginning in 1849. The Sand Creek Massacre was chosen for the position of dishonor which more than any other single incident had brought on continuous and festering hostility. Additionally, the treaty of the Little Arkansas was pointed out as a failure, and General Hancock was accused of acting too hastily in his spring campaign in Kansas.

[1] "Journal," Dec. 14, 1867; *Chicago Times*, Oct. 28, 1867; *Missouri Democrat*, Oct. 28, 1867; *Missouri Republican*, Oct. 28, 1867.

[2] For all references to the official Peace Commission Report, see *Peace Commission*, 1–24.

The Commission said the Indians were not paragons of virtue, but major incidents plus minor irritations gave them cause to be belligerent.

Concerning what was wrong with U.S. Indian policy, the understatement of the entire document was the claim that there was a wide diversity of opinion in this area. Primarily, however, the Commission felt that public and government apathy, uncertainty, and lack of co-operation lay at the base of a poor attitude that was not helped by rumors, false reports, and scare stories from the frontier. The Commission was concerned with the morality of the Indian question, too, and said that the United States had been universally and consistently unjust in dealings with the tribes of the Great Plains.

The Commission recommended that state governors be relieved of their responsibilities for Indian affairs, and that there be a distinct separation of the duties of federal agencies in regard to handling Indians. The recommendation gave no specific instructions about how these duties should be divided. They recommended also that white settlers be removed from Indian lands and not allowed to return to those areas promised the tribes. Further, they recommended that Indian traders be regulated, that a Presidential commission make periodic inspections of Indian problems, and that Indian officials come under the strict control of a Civil Service System.

Each of these major subjects, as well as a number of others, were discussed at one time or another by members of the press corps at Medicine Lodge. In every major point detailed in the *Report* the majority of correspondents who wrote of the same point were in agreement with the Commission. The opinions causing the Peace Commission to conclude as it did were overwhelmingly apparent among the newsmen who told the story. Considering that the news reports were published first, the Peace Commission paper to the President served to validate the news stories. Whether the Commission's conclusions were right—judged with the valuable assistance of hindsight—is not the important thing here; the important thing is that two groups of men, one official the other completely unofficial, generally agreed on what was causing the problem and some of the ways it might be solved peaceably, if that were possible at all.

Clearly, the Commission *Report* provided few answers to existing problems; it suggested ways of setting in motion the machinery that would eventually find solutions. The misunderstandings that had plagued the government were pointed out but not remedied. Some recommendations were impractical, others impossible. Certainly the task of restricting white settlement on Indian lands would have required a vast army, one much larger than the one stationed on the frontier in 1867.[3] But if the document which the Peace Commission submitted to the President was impractical in part, it was at least tempered by the opinions of men whom none of the reporters—nor anyone else—had ever called visionary or unrealistic: Harney, Henderson, and Sherman.

The widest disagreement among the Medicine Lodge press corps members concerned the money spent on the treaty councils. Less real than apparent in most instances, the discrepancies resulted from failure of the reporters to clearly define their terms. It was often extremely difficult to tell exactly which expenses they were reporting. This, of course, was in keeping with their concept of news writing— they outlined the general theme of things; they did not consider themselves bookkeepers, as becomes obvious from a study of their financial reporting.

It appears that the correspondents were given no clear picture of Peace Commission expenses. At the time the Medicine Lodge councils were being held, the commissioners themselves may not have known what the operation was costing. An expenditure of $150,000 had been authorized by Congress.[4] If the Commission had financial records at Medicine Lodge, there were no indications from newspaper dispatches that the correspondents ever saw them.. Sanborn's "Accounts" were not submitted to the rest of the board until January 3, 1868, but he surely maintained working papers throughout the

[3] *Sec. of War 67*, 44.
[4] "Accounts"; *Cong. Globe*, 1867, 667.

trip. These figures may have been discussed between Sanborn, Henderson, and Commissioner Taylor during the course of the treaty meetings, but none of the reporters were involved. It appears that their stories of expenses came from casually mentioned figures by various members of the Commission.

In the final *Report*, the balance sheet showed these transactions:

Presents to the Indians	$ 44,706.69
Subsistence for the Indians	1,939.67
Transportation	4,508.13
Commission expenses	39,857.80
Outstanding debts:	
Presents to the Indians	$ 10,490.16
Transportation	8,202.37
Expenses	12,000.00
Total disbursements	$121,704.82

There were other expenses not listed by Sanborn. The Army provided 50,000 rations, and the Little Arkansas annuity goods had been purchased from appropriated funds prior to the Commission's arrival on the Plains.[5]

There were two sources for gifts and presents: the Commission appropriation and the Little Arkansas treaty. Sanborn spent $55,196.85 on gifts for the Indians. The treaty of the Little Arkansas specified that for Comanches and Kiowas, ten dollars a head would be appropriated each year; for the Cheyennes and Arapahoes, the amount was twenty dollars a head.[6] In 1867, there was a total annuity appropriation of $40,000 for Comanche and Kiowas, $56,000 for the Cheyennes and Arapahoes. One-third of this had been issued in the spring. In August, the time the Peace Commission ordered all annuities held, a total of $63,998 worth of treaty items were still to be issued. These, with the Commission presents purchased specifically for the Medicine Lodge councils, totaled $119,194.85 in value.

[5] "Journal," Aug. 16, 1867.
[6] Commissioner *Report 67*, Statistics Annex; Kappler, *Treaties*, 890, 894.

With the three sources of supply—the Army, the annuity contract of the Little Arkansas treaty, and the Peace Commission itself—it was difficult for the correspondents to come up with valid figures. Any one of the correspondents' estimates could be fitted to some portion of the financial transactions and be close to correct. With circumstances as they were, the real cost of the treaty will probably never be known, but it certainly fell below a quarter of a million dollars, discounting salaries.

If the *Official Report* was the published majority opinion of the Peace Commission, there was another official document that came out of Medicine Lodge which bears examination as an example of individual opposition—generally opposed, in fact, to both the *Official Report* and press corps opinion.

Although a study of the report and newspaper accounts written at the treaty grounds would indicate that everyone who went to Medicine Lodge came away with a consensus of opinion, this was not the case. Major Joel Elliot, commander of the military escort, filed his own account of what happened, and the document provided adequate proof that the frictions and disagreements in the conduct of Indian affairs had not been eliminated.[7] Elliot submitted his account to his superiors at the Department of the Missouri, and it was forwarded to Sherman on November 30, well in advance of Sherman's going to Washington and helping to write the *Official Report*.

The Elliot report was much shorter than the *Official Report*, and it was written without a trace of optimism about the Indian situation. Elliot said:

> The proceedings throughout were conducted in such a manner that anyone unacquainted with the relative strengths of the two contracting parties would have imagined the Indians to have been the stronger and we the suppliants.

Moving to specific incidents, Elliot claimed the commissioners had tried to induce the Indians into charging Hancock with responsibility for the war in Kansas. But if any of the Cheyennes blamed Hancock

[7] Elliot, "Report," "Journal," Dec. 9, 1867; *Peace Commission*, 1–24.

199

for hostilities, Elliot said, they did it in private conversations and not in the treaty councils. With the exception of Brown and Budd, the correspondents disagreed. Not only had the Cheyennes blamed Hancock at their Grand Council, they had done so in the Hancock hearings as well. Elliot was either ignoring the facts, or he was absent from the Hancock hearings. At the Grand Councils, the Indian accusations against Hancock had not come during one of the speeches; the charges were made in a conversation between Henderson, Taylor, and a number of Cheyenne chiefs within hearing of the correspondents.[8]

The Seventh Cavalry officer accused one commissioner, whom he did not name, of telling the Cheyennes they had acted properly in striking back at the white man. The commissioner told the Indians it was too bad they had not killed more whites, Elliot claimed. It is difficult to imagine such a statement being ignored if it was made within hearing of any of the reporters, yet no account of the comment came from the Medicine Lodge press gang. Stanley and Fayel recognized that General Harney seemed pleased when he heard of the Indians' killing Kaws, Pawnees, or other "tame" Indians, but no one ever hinted that Harney or anyone else on the Peace Commission encouraged or applauded the slaughter of white men.[9]

Elliot's most serious charge was that the treaties were never interpreted to the Indians and that the chiefs had no idea what they were signing. Stanley agreed that the Indian leaders had signed without realizing the significance of their act, but he and all the other correspondents gave verbatim accounts of Henderson's outlining the treaty terms. Elliot, after complaining that the Indians did not know what was contained in the treaties, said the tribesmen insisted on having hunting rights in the country which they had always considered their own; for the Comanches and Kiowas, south of the Arkansas, for the Cheyennes, the Smoky Hill area. The contradiction

---

[8] *Chicago Times*, Oct. 12, 1867; *Chicago Tribune*, Oct. 17, 1867; *Cincinnati Commercial*, Oct. 17, 1867; *Cincinnati Gazette*, Aug. 22, 27, 1867; *Missouri Democrat*, Oct. 23, 1867.

[9] *Missouri Democrat*, Oct. 28, 1867; *Missouri Republican*, Oct. 28, 1867.

was not an obvious one, but it was a contribution nonetheless. Had the Indians not known what the other provisions were, it is difficult to understand why they would object to them and insist on changes.[10]

Finally, Elliot reported that General Augur protested when the Cheyennes were promised the right to hunt north of the Arkansas River, but the other commissioners paid no attention to these remonstrances. According to the press corps members, the Cheyenne hunting rights were promised at the Grand Council, in a private talk between Henderson and the chiefs, as noted earlier. If this was the case, no one reported that Augur objected during the course of the discussion heard by the correspondents. The addition to the treaty could have been discussed beforehand, in private, but if so, no change to the treaty was actually made until the group had assembled in the council grove.[11]

In those instances in which Elliot was not in accord with the Commission *Report* or the correspondents, the weight of evidence given by eyewitnesses to the treaty councils was overwhelmingly against the escort commander. The fact that he was living apart from the official party throughout the peace meetings may or may not have been an advantage to Elliot. On the one hand, separated as he was, he was not in a position to see and hear as much as were the reporters; on the other, he was not so closely associated with the members of the Commission that he could as easily have been prejudiced by friendship and camaraderie.

Comparing Elliot's report with the correspondents' story of Medicine Lodge, the greatest contrast was in temperament, not in cases of disagreement on specific incidents. Even if Bulkley and Hall wrote pessimistically about the prospects of a lasting peace, and Brown and Budd made no effort in their dispatches to be kind to the commissioners, at least all of the correspondents at one time or another indicated that the Peace Commission had accomplished something. Elliot, in his report, was not ready to admit that anything had been done which would help the Indian situation on the frontier. Of

[10] *Ibid.*, all newspaper sources cited in fn. 8 and 9.
[11] *Ibid.*

course, at that point, nothing could be done to avert more trouble, for too many forces had been at work too long. But at least the newsmen gave the Peace Commission credit for sincerely trying, and this Elliot was not willing to do.

FIFTEEN

"I SHALL WAIT TILL NEXT SPRING —AND JOIN MY WILD BROTHERS"

—Comanche

Because they were not hampered with the objective reporting that would come later, the men in the Medicine Lodge press party could write as they saw fit—and they saw fit to be personal. The word pictures they drew were full of opinion, bias, and emotion, but in writing as they did they created an intimacy unknown in modern news reporting. This characteristic was most pronounced when they described other people, and a great deal of their material was about the people they saw and heard. They were frank and candid and as often as not, unflattering. There was nothing cold or detached about what they said; frequently their words were charged with heat and passion. And before the great councils were over, they surely felt that they knew their subjects well, and hence, particularly toward the end, their words had understanding and compassion. They appeared to develop —in most cases—an unusual empathy with the commissioners and the Indians as well. This was perhaps their major contribution to the history of Medicine Lodge.

In telling the human side of the story of Medicine Lodge, the correspondents often agreed with one another in their evaluation of the men around them. Their descriptions were based on personal observations, and the descriptions coincided quite closely. Of course, the fact that two reporters, or three, or eight represented a man's personality in identical terms was not proof that the representation was factual. On the other hand, when more than one correspondent saw the same qualities in another man, there was at least some basis for a claim of validity.

There is no question about which of the Indian chiefs made the strongest impression on the press party; he was Satank, the old Kiowa who had come to Peace Commission headquarters to say good-by. He only made one speech at the meeting, but it affected the correspondents deeply—their praise of his eloquence, grace, and intelligence was given in the most elaborate terms, even by those reporters who, until then, had found little good to tell about Indians. One of the most vivid images produced by the pens of the Medicine Lodge correspondents was that of Satank, standing alone before the Peace Commission camp, his hair blowing, his long fingers clasping the silver medal at his chest, his slanted eyes peering intently at the commissioners as he told them that the white man's friendship had made him poor.

Whereas Satank said little at the councils, Satanta talked constantly. The big Kiowa presented a commanding figure, and his words were well chosen, but he became somewhat of a bore after having been on his feet throughout most of the first day of speech making; many of the reporters, tongue in cheek, called him the "Orator of the Plains." There were implications in the descriptions of Satanta that he was insincere. His words, when he said he knew of no Kiowa hostilities, may have struck a sour note to those who knew that only a short time before he had been at Fort Dodge selling white captives. Satanta was respected, but he was also feared. The correspondents enjoyed his clowning, strutting, boasting, and bugle blowing, but they appeared to realize that this Indian was a great deal more than court jester. He was mentioned often as a linguist, and his influence among all the Southern Plains tribes was a recognized factor in the negotiations. He was regarded by the reporters as a competent, dynamic, defiant, and physically powerful warrior, and in the face of his professed friendship for the whites, most of the correspondents saw in him the embodiment of savage treachery.

No such distrust of Ten Bears or Silver Brooch was ever indicated by the members of the press group. Ten Bears, older even than Sa-

tank, who was sixty-seven, was lively and quick witted. The correspondents seemed to enjoy watching the startled expressions on the
commissioners' faces when the old Comanche made sarcastic remarks
from his seat in front of the brush arbor. There had been particular
appreciation of the old man's cutting tongue on the second day of the
Comanche-Kiowa meetings, when his verbal barbs sent Satanta away
from the council grove in a rage. Throughout the councils, Ten Bears
was the only man ever successful in making Satanta stop talking. Ten
Bears was a skinny old warrior with thinning gray hair and a lined face
that smiled easily. From many of the accounts, one may almost see
him making a curt comment, then turning to grin at the reporters,
who obviously appreciated his remarks.

Silver Brooch was a gloomy man who lacked the eloquence frequently associated with Plains Indian leaders. But the newsmen were
impressed with his bluntness. He did not have the high spirit the
other speakers displayed and appeared emaciated in mind and body,
the reporters claimed, as a result of his long exposure to the white
man's whisky and disease.

Little Raven, the Arapaho chief, was the happy fat man on the
Indian side of the council table. He was constantly loitering about
the Peace Commission camp, extending invitations to visit his camp.
Some of the reporters went to Little Raven's village early in the proceedings, but later they all appeared to grow a little tired of him.
He seemed to get on everyone's nerves with his constant harping
about Cheyenne intentions or his sulky attitude after some of his
horses were stolen. Still, he remained socially popular with the reporters, even though it was apparent to everyone that his words in
the council meetings carried little weight. At least he never caused
very much trouble, which may explain his popularity around Denver
in earlier times.

The only Cheyenne chief at the treaty grounds from the beginning
was Black Kettle. He slipped in and out of the Commission camp
every night, conferring with various members of the official party,
for he was constantly worried about what his cousins on the Cimarron
might do. Black Kettle, though admired by the correspondents for

advocating peace among his people, in the face of much opposition, began to irritate people after a few days of slipping through the camp as though he expected to be shot and scalped at any moment. When the other Cheyennes arrived, he dropped into the background, though it was clear to the reporters that he was still insisting on negotiations. The newsmen agreed that Black Kettle placed himself in grave personal danger from his own people by speaking so consistently for a treaty.

Little Robe, Gray Head, Buffalo Chief, and the other Cheyennes who came in from the Cimarron camp seemed cast from the same mold. Perhaps the newsmen's descriptions suffered because these particular leaders were in camp for so short a time, but the correspondents were impressed with them: They conformed more closely to the white man's concept of what an Indian chief should be than anyone else at Medicine Lodge. They presented a well-planned and united front, and the newsmen assumed that the rank and file of the tribe stood just as firmly on issues and intentions as did their leaders. Once the Cheyennes came to Medicine Lodge Creek, they let Buffalo Chief do the talking, and once he was finished, nothing more was to be said. In addition to being well organized, the Cheyennes showed defiance, according to some reporters, even more so than had Satanta. Like Satanta and Ten Bears, these Cheyenne leaders appeared sincere in wanting peace, but they made clear what they expected from peace, and if these expectations were not realized, they were fully prepared to start war again. They were not overbearing or arrogant in the view of most press corps members; they showed great courtesy and respect for the commissioners. But the Cheyennes had not come to beg.

Facing these men across the treaty table were the two most forceful white men the reporters encountered during the Medicine Lodge venture—Harney and Henderson. Even in the few instances when the reporters disagreed among themselves about the activities of these two men, no one ever accused either of being weak. Strong wills and differing opinions on the customs and motives of Plains Indians often brought Harney and Henderson into conflict, and the reporters commented with some relish on these sometimes heated clashes.

Harney knew more about Indians than anyone else on the Commission, the correspondents felt. A practical, down-to-earth man, he was more concerned with supplying food and clothing than about the more illusive problems of Indian souls and morality. Possibly, this common-sense characteristic of Harney's made him attractive to the reporters. He did not have to be figured out; his intentions and motives seemed apparent. A good soldier, Harney was accustomed to command, and he ran the Peace Commission column and camp as though it were a regiment of infantry, to the particular delight of many reporters. The news reporters enjoyed seeing well-regimented subordinates, as long as they could maintain their status as on-lookers. General Harney was highly complimented by very nearly everyone in the press party for his conduct of the march, the organization of the camp, his handling of the escort through Major Elliot, and the feeding of the press and official party. Sanborn had purchased the food, but Harney distributed it.

Terry and Augur, the two soldiers still on active duty during their service on the Peace Commission, received little attention from the correspondents. Both were quiet men, and the Commission minutes reveal that they generally supported Harney's views. The minutes also show that both were active in Commission discussions, but they apparently did not carry this over to the councils. The press gang respected them and made various comments about their gentlemanly deportment and well-tailored uniforms—especially Terry's—but the newsmen seem to have been out of touch with the officers themselves.

General Sherman, of course, was the highest ranking military man on the Peace Commission. He did not make the trip to Medicine Lodge, however, and it is possible that the correspondents were unaware that Sherman was still a member of the board and that he would take an important hand in the final discussions and preparation of the *Official Report*. After the initial dispatches from Harker, when the reporters had learned Sherman would not be along, General Sherman was seldom mentioned.

Sanborn was the Commission expert on the treaty of the Little Arkansas, having been at the negotiation site; he was also Commission procurement and disbursement officer, as has been seen. In an energetic group, he stood out as most active. The correspondents admired the quantity of his work. Commissioner Sanborn was at Taylor's elbow most of the time, and when something needed doing, Sanborn was off to handle it. Although he was not universally admired by the reporters, none of them accused him of being unfriendly. On the contrary, he was a great storyteller, and he laughed a great deal. A few of the newsmen thought he drank to excess.

The reporters were less kind to Tappan. The dispatches from Medicine Lodge gave the impression that all Tappan ever did was to sit and contemplate the ground between his feet, or on more active days, whittle on a stick.

Commissioner Taylor was a quiet man, too, without the driving energy of either Henderson or Sanborn; he was too large of girth to be capable of rapid movement. But Taylor emerges from the correspondents' reports as a powerful man in the councils. Significantly, each time Harney and Henderson had a dispute, Taylor made the decision that settled the argument. Although Henderson was selected as Commission spokesman for the meetings, all looked to Taylor when decisions had to be made. The correspondents noted that when Henderson promised the Cheyennes hunting rights north of the Arkansas, he came to Taylor and discussed the issue before he made a general announcement. Like Sanborn, Taylor was not universally admired by the press party. A few times he was characterized as being visionary in outlook. Most such comments in the 1867 press came from newspapers not represented at Medicine Lodge, however. Taylor was at least practical enough to supervise Murphy in the touchy job of collecting the Indians at Medicine Lodge. Although some of the reporters disliked him, none despised him for laziness or indecision.

For Henderson, the press corps had only good words. He was very nearly established among them as the official voice of the Peace Commission. In many instances, he was exactly that insofar as the correspondents were concerned, for as the press secretary he was the first source of news on those activities they could not see at first-hand. Henderson was not a press secretary—a modern term—but he had the same power that any press secretary has; he was the tuning board of the Commission to the public, through the press. His most important task was preparing Peace Commission statements addressed to the Indians. But he was generally regarded by the reporters as the business manager of the official party, just as Harney managed the details of travel and defense.

The press corps was unanimous in its appraisal of Murphy, one of the lesser lights. He had been invaluable when the Indians were being gathered for the treaty talks and in his work as the councils continued—supervising the storing and distribution of Indian rations, constructing the treaty council site, and seeing to the needs of tribesman and white man alike. His two subordinates, Leavenworth and Wynkoop, were less in the limelight once the Hancock hearings were completed. Both men were called brave, but reservations existed about Leavenworth's ability as an agent. The reporters saw him at a time when his troubles were beginning to mount faster than he could cope with them. Wynkoop generally had a good press, and as mentioned above, Stanley, who had not been impressed with the Cheyenne-Arapaho agent earlier that year, wrote that he was a capable Indian administrator. Both agents were said to be extremely loyal to their Indian charges, a condition that might sometimes have stood in the way of clear judgment; yet none of the correspondents ever accused either of the men of being fraudulent or dishonest.

There were still others mentioned. The Bents—brothers George and Charlie and sister Julia—were great curiosities. Their father, William, who had helped Murphy talk the Cheyennes into coming to Medicine Lodge, apparently was not present. William Bent was one of the frontier's most famous traders. He and his brother Charles —later the first governor of territorial New Mexico, afterward killed in a Taos massacre—had established a number of trading posts throughout the Great Plains. As late as 1867, old William was still at his Colorado trading post on the Arkansas River; this was the post called Bent's Fort. It is unfortunate that such a fine frontier character was not present for the reporters to see and write about; but it was his fame which made his children objects of interest to some of the correspondents. The two Bent brothers were in the Peace Commission camp often, and some of the reporters spoke at length with them about the Cheyenne situation. The newsmen were surprised, apparently, that these half-blood Cheyennes could express themselves so well. The press dispatches gave little indication that Charlie had a streak of wildness.

The Bents' half-sister stayed in the Indian camps, and the correspondents saw her only at the councils. Sharing the stage with Julia Bent as the only other woman of note at the councils was Margaret Adams. She, too, stayed near the Indian camps, and no reports came of her visiting the Peace Commission except in the role of Arapaho interpreter.

While writing of women, one cannot help but note how interesting it would be to know more details of the wagon park fight that ended in a shooting and was said to have been caused by a women. Had the reporters been more sensation seeking than they were, perhaps the identity of the lady in question would now be known, along with other circumstances.

There were other men attached to the Peace Commission who were never mentioned by the correspondents. A. S. H. White, Department of the Interior Secretary, was often identified, but no picture of him emerges. Government officials were there as observers—a land surveyor, for example. Some people at the site were "hangers-on," as Stanley called them, among whom was Commissioner Taylor's son. A great many interpreters were employed, but only McCusker's name appears repeatedly. Like everyone else, the correspondents regarded the Comanche interpreter as a most valuable and trusted individual. A number of men made up Butterfield's work party, including Butterfield himself, but apparently he and his employees stayed clear of the official party, and hence the correspondents.

Taken as a whole, the correspondents portrayed the Peace Commission as a hard-working, conscientious body of men. The two Cincinnati reporters were often prompted, for unspecified reasons, to attack the group as pompous mollycoddlers, or to hint at the dishonesty of certain members, but once the treaties were signed, even Brown and Budd were ready with praise for the work that had been done.

Of the men who provided these impressions, Howland and James Taylor were the least productive. But their work as artists cannot be compared with the production of the writers in the group; they can only be compared with each other. Five times as many Medicine Lodge illustrations appeared in *Leslie's* as in *Harper's*. Taylor's eleven published drawings, appearing in two consecutive issues of *Leslie's*, showed great attention to detail and composition. He had the ability to construct his sketches in such a way that the eye was drawn to the point of the illustration providing the main theme. In his drawings of the Comanche-Kiowa Grand Council, all the Indians and commissioners were done in low tone shades, but Margaret Adams, the Arapaho interpreter, was shown in a patch of sunlight, making her figure the outstanding one in the illustration. Taylor's grasp of the dramatic was obvious; in the midst of savage, soldier, commissioner, and a great crowd of other men, the lone figure of a woman appeared in full-length gown.

Taylor was not the extrovert that Howland appeared, despite his joining the Sun Dance lodge sight-seeing tour. While on the tour, he produced an illustration of the lodge, which, short of photographs, still stands as the best illustration ever made of a medicine lodge. Taylor was never mentioned by other correspondents in connection with visits to the Indian camps, nor was he ever included in the existing accounts of after-supper jokes and conversation in the press tent.

Howland, Taylor's counterpart for *Harper's*, was listed by the Peace Commission as a clerk. It is difficult to imagine when he found time to perform any official duties other than taking notes during the meetings; perhaps it was only at the councils that he was expected to work. At any rate, when a formal meeting was not in progress, he seemed to be one of the most restless members of the press party, riding on the prairie and visiting Indian camps. The

Harper's artist, lively, gregarious, and well-traveled, was well liked by his press tent companions. If he produced little work, he was still a great asset to the newsmen, for he, more than any other, seemed to keep their spirits high and their sense of humor awakened. Howland was generally not far away from the center of any unusual activity. Although Brown criticized him mildly for killing buffalo, a note of jealousy may have crept into what Brown wrote. On the Medicine Lodge sight-seeing tour—when the tourists had become frightened—Howland had stayed abreast of Phil McCusker in the wild dash back upstream toward the Commission camp, which speaks well of his horsemanship, for McCusker was as expert on his pony as were his Comanche in-laws.

Only two of Howland's Medicine Lodge drawings were published, and those resembled a great many of the less rewarding illustrations in the mid-nineteenth-century weeklies, with a minimum of line and a great deal of white space in between. Although his sketches of persons indicate his professionalism, the background of his drawings leave the uneasy feeling that he drew them to fit his taste rather than reality. In one sketch from Medicine Lodge, he drew in a tall peak, when no such peak existed nearer than Colorado. Indeed, although Howland contributed much to the well-being of his fellows at Medicine Lodge, it is Taylor who after a century emerges as the only artist who went to the Timbered Hill.

Of the writers at the councils, George Brown was probably most prolific. Such a statement can only be speculative, however, for many of the reporters were sending free-lance material to a great many newspapers. But judging by the amount of copy that he had published in the paper he represented, Brown must certainly be considered a newspaperman of great energy.

The *Commercial* reporter consistently attacked the Peace Commission members and had very little good to say about the Indians. He occasionally wrote in positive terms, but his work is filled with degrading descriptions of Indian women, tribal customs, and the personal habits of Indian men. He admired Little Raven and Satank, but his attitude toward Plains culture and its people as a whole was rather bluntly negative. He strongly supported the use of force as an answer to the Indian problem; on the other hand he condemned what he called the frontier proclivity for indiscriminately killing Indians. This and other contradictions in his comments on Indians are often confusing. But if he was inconsistent in his writing about the Indians, he remained steadfast in his distaste for the members of the Peace Commission. He never explained why he felt as he obviously did, and his copy brands him a cynic. Apparently the only white men Brown admired at Medicine Lodge were two other newspapermen, Budd and Howland.

In one instance, Brown broke away from his usual style. The story he told of the Medicine Lodge sight-seeing trip was one of the reportorial highlights of the entire adventuue. He wrote with wit and charm, adding the spice of danger that was undoubtedly felt by everyone in the group. Brown was disappointing, but not because he was unable to write, for he wrote quite well. Apparently his prejudices made the bulk of his material somewhat sour, for no dictating editor could have completely changed the tone of his dispatches.

H. J. Budd, the other half of the Cincinnati team, was possibly more anti-Indian than Brown. His treatment of the tribes was as bitter as Brown's, but he did not return to the subject as often. His writing was flowery and ornate, often so heavy with embellishment that it was difficult to follow his line of thought. Gaps occurred in the chronology of his report, but they may have been the result of editorial cuts made by the *Gazette* newsroom. Budd tended more toward sensationalism than any other correspondent at Medicine Lodge, going into bloody detail in his reports of Indian habits and hostilities. Like Brown, Budd attacked the integrity of some of the Peace Commission members, but also like Brown, he was extremely vague in giving his reasons.

The *Chicago Tribune*'s S. F. Hall apparently was the most studious member of the press gang, for his background writing on the Indians indicates that he had tried to learn as much as he could about the Kansas situation before going to the Plains. His reports indicate an empathy for the Indians' position, and he commented that the red man was simply trying to retain his ancient homeland. Like Stanley and Reynolds, he stayed close beside the commissioners. Hall was interested in the politics of the frontier, and with the exception of Reynolds, he gave more attention to the Kansas delegation meeting than any other reporter. Some editorial direction may have come from Chicago concerning this aspect of Hall's dispatches. Railroad interests in that city wanted information on the political goings on, and undoubtedly many Chicago people were interested in the overall Kansas situation and how it would influence the construction of a railroad to the Southwest. Hall managed to keep his own opinions fairly well concealed in his political comments. Unlike Reynolds, he was not trying to embarrass Governor Crawford's administration.

Hall's writing flowed easily, and he was both interesting and informative. He often left gaps in his story—once more perhaps the result of an editor's scissors—but he was a polished writer. Tending strictly to business during the day, at night he was one of the Howland-Brown group of socializers. Comparatively humorless in all his writing, he reported the theft of Howland's Navy Colt without a trace of wit.

Milton Reynolds was less concerned with the events of the treaty councils than with their implications—although his straightforward account of the Comanche-Kiowa treaty was the most comprehensive to come from Medicine Lodge. Reynolds had been in the newspaper business for a number of years by 1867, and he had developed a sharp and cutting style of prose. He used wit, sarcasm, understatement, and innuendo to make his point, and in most cases he directed his comments to the Kansas political situation and how it was involved with the Indian problem. He stabbed Governor Crawford with the sharpest words at his command, and for Reynolds this included a considerable range of language. He probably understood the Indian question as well as anyone at Medicine Lodge, including those in the official party, and it was this knowledge that made possible his meaningful comments on the futility of trying to civilize Plains tribes to white standards.

Reynolds saw interpretation as his major function. In modern terms, he would have been called a news analyst. His views, obviously, were respected by the Peace Commission, for throughout the Medicine Lodge venture he was constantly with the official party—more associated with the commissioners, really, than with the press gang. He did not visit the village, for unlike many other members of the news party, he had seen Indians before. His function seemed to be that of shadowing Governor Crawford and Senator Ross and listening to what they and the commissioners had to say. Unfortunately, when the Kansas delegation left, Reynolds followed.

The Kansas editor did not make an effort to join the other press personnel either during the day or at night. If he found himself among them, it was because they had come to him at his post with the commissioners. The correspondents called him "Mister Reynolds" in their dispatches, and although few of the other newsmen had ever heard of him before the Medicine Lodge trip, each indicated their respect for the Lawrence editor. Although Reynolds included many fine descriptive passages in his dispatches, his most important contribution was the insight he provided. His report of the buffalo hunt, his account of the Kansas delegation meeting, and his description of the council grove during the Comanche-Kiowa Grand Councils were brilliantly done. But his penetrating analysis of the Plains Indian tragedy is what made him unique of all the newspapermen who went to Medicine Lodge.

Next to Reynolds, Stanley was apparently more closely involved with Commission discussions than anyone else in the press group. Perhaps his extensive use of verbatim copy is what gave this impression. He quoted members of the Commission throughout the trip, in the small meetings as well as during the Grand Councils. Like most reporters of that day, he wrote his dispatches in the form of letters to his editor, but there was something more personal in his material than there was in many of the stories that came from Medicine Lodge. He tried to establish a close relationship directly with his readers. He used the device of addressing them as though he stood face to face with them, assuring them repeatedly that he was on the job, that he had been telling them the frontier story for some time and that he would do all he could to insure that nothing of consequence passed his attention.

The Welshman may have been as biased as any reporter at Medicine Lodge, but he showed an admirable flexibility in the Hancock controversy. He changed his mind and admitted it. One suspects that others changed their opinions also; but rather than admit it, they simply made no mention of the subject in subsequent dispatches. Stanley's writing was somewhere between the ornate sentimentality of Budd and the straightforward, factual reporting of Fayel. His writing was a great deal like that of Reynolds except that he tended to wander away from his subject. He produced a great mass of material during that three-week period, often giving the impression that he was constantly cutting other activities short so that he could rush to the press tent and dash off a dispatch.

Stanley's style made easy, enjoyable reading, but often his humor fell rather heavily. However, his treatment of the Arapaho dance— and the pistol-stealing sequence—was done with taste and wit, and of course, with the typical Stanley flamboyance. His stories always bounced along with gaiety and charm, but with a good deal of conceit as well. From his own material as well as from the dispatches of other reporters, Stanley appeared somewhat pompous. Generally an optimist, the veteran newsman but occasionally allowed his own good spirits to lag.

Reporting the social life and the jokes and antics of the other newsmen seemed to give Stanley great plasure. In the evenings he was always nearby when jokes began and whisky was passed around. He was there more as an onlooker, however, than as a participant. He showed a real affection for most of the press party, and only twice did he have anything to say about any of them that was not completely complimentary. There were good indications that many of the reporters did not return Stanley's affection.

William Fayel, the other St. Louis reporter, was as different from Stanley as another man could possibly be. He wrote in short, loaded paragraphs, covering in half a column the same story which Stanley needed half a page to tell. Like Hall, he included very few of his personal opinions, although he gave detailed accounts of the opinions of other people. He was, in short, reporter of the news. Unlike Hall, he was not concerned with background material for his stories; if he knew little of the frontier situation prior to Medicine Lodge, he obviously felt that that had been someone else's job—his job was reporting the Medicine Lodge treaties, and that is what he did. His account of the Cheyenne-Arapaho treaty and the Cheyenne-Arapaho Grand Councils were the most complete of all the dispatches covering those events. One of the most outstanding stories of the entire treaty meeting period was his description of the Cheyennes coming to the council grounds. His treatment was modern; it struck straight at the events themselves, yet it had enough of the emotion and passion of the moment to make it exciting. Because he crammed sentences with facts, Fayel did not write as much as many correspondents. Despite his lack of verbosity, Fayel would have been a good selection if but a single reporter had been chosen to tell the entire story of Medicine Lodge.

To Fayel, Stanley ranked very low indeed as a newspaperman, and there is no indication from his writing that Fayel regarded the Welshman in any higher esteem as a person. Fayel appeared to take some pleasure in telling of Stanley's riding about the treaty grounds on a mule with one of the Negro orderlies. There was no humor in his description of the *Democrat* correspondent clutching the Negro about the waist, bouncing up and down, legs protruding awkwardly on either side as the mule trotted along.

Fayel spent his evenings with the other reporters, especially with Howland, Brown, and Hall, but his days were generally taken up with walking through the Indian camps. Generally he stayed clear of the Peace Commission unless it was meeting formally. He had a consuming curiosity about the Indians apparently, and he stayed among them a considerable part of the time. He went to all the camps along the Medicine Lodge excepting the Kiowa, which was farthest downstream from the Commission headquarters.

Discounting Reynolds, whom the other correspondents regarded as an editor, not a reporter, Solomon Bulkley stood highest in the esteem of the press party. Those mentioning him did so in terms of respect, not camaraderie. He held himself aloof from the other reporters, taking no part in their horseplay or excursions. At night, he sat in the press tent, smoking a pipe and listening, but never taking part in the arguments or jokes. Of all the correspondents, Bulkley's copy most nearly resembled modern news writing. Part of this was due to his reliance upon the telegraph rather than letters to tell the story. Brevity was not the only mark of Bulkley's writing; in the two letters he sent from Medicine Lodge, less opinion, value judgment, and speculation was present than generally could be found in the other reporters' accounts. Among newspapermen of that time the *New York Herald* of 1867 enjoyed the reputation of being a great newspaper, and as far as the other correspondents were concerned, Bulkley lived up to his paper's reputation. Although he had published fewer lines than any other writing member of the Medicine Lodge press gang, he apparently considered the story important— he stayed with it longer than anyone else.

These, then, were the men who told the story of Medicine Lodge. They told it as no one else did, as no one else who was there could have told it. Very quickly, these men showed themselves professionals, and despite their individual weaknesses, the product of their combined talents was an indication of professionalism. They gave a comprehensive, clear report of what happened, as they saw it. Exaggeration, sensation, rumor, and distortion were not the marks of their dispatches. More significantly, the journalists showed no decided taste for the kind of newspaper copy that had previously characterized frontier reporting, which frequently had been bloody and exciting, but often untrue. They were not legend makers. These newsmen appeared to have a keen sense of responsibility to their readers, a responsibility demanding attention to facts—a quality so lacking in journalism only a few short years before. This is not to say that the reporters who went to Medicine Lodge to tell what happened there began the trend toward objectivity, or indeed that they were instrumental in it. But they were obviously a part of that movement in American journalism. They were unique only because they

came together at Medicine Lodge to tell of one more painful episode in the final destruction of the Plains Indians. For although the
official records contained the major elements of the story, no one
but they would have told of the chilling sight of those first fires Hall
saw on the prairie, the pistol shot Reynolds heard in the wagon park,
the sweating, near-naked Arapahoes Stanley described in the Sibley
tent dance, the two white captive women Fayel interviewed in the
Kiowa camp, and the mad dash back from the Kiowa Sun Dance
grounds with Howland, Brown, and Taylor throwing their stolen
trophies into the Medicine Lodge; the Comanche horse show Budd
witnessed, and the last report sent by Bulkley from a train in Southern
Illinois. There were few instances in frontier history when so many
writers descended upon such a small plot of ground and within such
a short space of time told the story of only one major episode. As
a result, the story was well told. And in the telling of it they became
a part of it.

They never came together again as a group. Mostly, they have
been forgotten. Perhaps this is appropriate, for the events which
transpired in the small natural basin where Elm Creek joins the
Medicine Lodge have been forgotten, too. The treaties that were
made there did not stop Plains Indian wars. The grounds where the
great councils occurred did not become yet another monument to
man's efforts for peace. Even as the last reporter was returning to
his newsroom, even as the Peace Commission was preparing the final
report to the President, even as the soldiers of the escort were settling down to new duties at scattered frontier posts, evidence that
a meeting had been held was fast disappearing from that small valley.

On Timbered Hill River, winter had set in. The leaves still cling-
ing to the branches of the cottonwoods and elms would be brown and
crisp, and the persimmons would be rust red and sweet from heavy
frosts. One of the Kaws or Osages who had been watching the
Peace Councils from a safe distance could ride the entire length of
the valley and fail to see any of his old tribal enemies. Traces of
the meeting would still be there: the beaten-down circles in the
buffalo grass where lodges had stood, with darkened patches of earth

marking the locations of fires. Here and there, over some of the blackened spots, perhaps long sticks were still in the ground, bent at an angle over the place where the fire had been, glazed with the grease of meat hung there to broil. In the winter-withered under-brush, there might remain the peeled-pole racks that Cheyennes and Arapahoes had used to sun blankets or dry their saddle gear. The banks of Medicine Lodge Creek, hard with frost, were no longer visited each morning by the pony herds. Beaten paths through the brown grass would show for a little longer where the horses had come down to drink.

In the council grove, the brush arbor already would be falling apart, limbs from the roof hanging down where the Peace Commission had sat. Among the log benches, perhaps there was the short stub of a Comanche cigarette, sodden and flat from rain and snow; under the arbor, partially protected from the elements, bits of crumpled paper, some likely marked by a correspondent's pencil.

Farther up the valley were the circles of pounded earth where Indians had been dancing, the broken parts of an iron pistol, the heavy ruts of loaded wagons, and the hard-packed floor of the Peace Commission compound. There may have been scatterings of cans and bottles, an empty whisky keg, coffee grounds, and in the wagon park perhaps the dark stain of a teamster's blood. Father, still, up-stream, might have been seen the neat rows of matted grass where the soldiers pitched their tents, the lost picket pins of the horse line, and a scattering of grain from feeding the animals, left to lie until spring birds would find it.

Men had come to the valley of the Medicine Lodge from many places and for many reasons. But now—with people waiting to the south in deep Indian country for promises to be fulfilled, waiting to be fed, to be housed—the basin was empty. Only a few marks of a great meeting remained, and soon these too would be gone forever from the valley of the Timbered Hill River.

BIBLIOGRAPHY

BOOKS

Alter, J. Cecil. *Jim Bridger.* Norman, University of Oklahoma Press, 1962.

Andrews, J. Cutler. *The North Reports the Civil War.* Pittsburgh, University of Pittsburgh Press, 1955.

Berthrong, Donald J. *The Southern Cheyennes.* Norman, University of Oklahoma Press, 1963.

Billington, Ray A. *Westward Expansion: A History of the American Frontier.* New York, Macmillan Co., 1960.

Bowles, Samuel. *Our New West: Records of Travel.* Hartford, Hartford Publishing Co., 1869.

Brill, Charles J. *Conquest of the Southern Plains.* Oklahoma City, Golden Saga Publishers, 1938.

Britt, Albert. *Toward the Western Ocean.* Barre, Mass., Barre Publishing Co., 1963.

Carlson, Oliver. *The Man Who Made News: James Gordon Bennett.* New York, Duell, Sloan and Pearce, 1942.

Carter, Thomas D. *On the Border with MacKenzie.* Washington, Eynon Printing Co., 1935.

Commager, Henry Steele (ed.). *Documents of American History.* New York, Appleton-Century-Crofts, Inc., 1949.

Corwin, H.D. *The Kiowa Indians: Their History and Life Stories.* Lawton, Okla., 1958.

Crawford, Samuel J. *Kansas in the Sixties*. Chicago, McClurg and Co., 1911.

Crozier, Emmet. *Yankee Reporters*. New York, Oxford University Press, 1956.

Custer, George Armstrong. *My Life on the Plains*. Lakeside Classics. Chicago, R. R. Donnelley & Sons, 1952.

Custer, Elizabeth B. *Tenting on the Plains*. New York, 1887.

Diehl, Charles S. *The Staff Correspondent*. San Antonio, Clegg Co., 1931.

Dodge, Colonel Richard I. *The Plains and the Great West and Their Inhabitants*. New York, Archer House, 1959.

Drago, Harry Sinclair. *Red River Valley*. New York, Clarkson N. Potter, Inc., 1962.

Dunn, J. P. *Massacres of the Mountains*. New York, Archer House, 1958.

Emery, Edwin. *The Press and America*. Englewood Cliffs, Prentice Hall, 1962.

Estergreen, M. Morgan. *Kit Carson: A Portrait in Courage*. Norman, University of Oklahoma Press, 1962.

Fey, H. D., and D'Arcy McNickle. *Indians and Other Americans*. New York, Harper and Brothers, 1959.

Foreman, Grant. *The Last Trek of the Indians*. Chicago, University of Chicago Press, 1946.

Gilmore, Frances, and Louisa Wade Weatherill. *Traders to the Navahos*. Cambridge, Riverside Press, 1934.

Graves, John. *Goodbye to a River*. New York, Alfred Knopf, 1960.

Gregg, Josiah. *Commerce of the Prairies*. Max L. Morehead (ed.). Norman, University of Oklahoma Press, 1954.

Grinnell, George Bird. *The Fighting Cheyennes*. New York, Charles Scribners' Sons, 1915.

Hafen, LeRoy, and Ann W. Hafen (eds.). *Reports from Colorado: The Wildman Letters*. Glendale, Arthur H. Clark, 1961.

———, and W. H. Ghent. *Broken Hand: The Story of Thomas Fitzpatrick, Chief of the Mountain Men*. Denver, Old West Publishing Co., 1931.

Hicks, John D. *The American Nation*. Cambridge, Riverside Press, 1946.

Hoig, Stanley. *The Sand Creek Massacre*. Norman, University of Oklahoma Press, 1961.

Hollon, W. Eugene. *The Southwest Old and New*. New York, Alfred A. Knopf, 1961.

Hyde, George E. *Indians of the High Plains*. Norman, University of Oklahoma Press, 1959.

Jackson, Clyde, and Grace Jackson. *Quanah Parker*. New York, Exposition Press, 1963.

Jackson, Helen Hunt. *A Century of Dishonor*. New York, Harper & Brothers, 1881.

Josephy, Alvin M., Jr. (ed.). *The American Heritage Book of Indians*. New York, American Heritage, 1961.

Knight, Oliver. *Following the Indian Wars: The Story of the Newspaper Correspondents Among the Indian Campaigners*. Norman, University of Oklahoma Press, 1960.

Lavender, David. *Bent's Fort*. Garden City, Doubleday & Company, Inc., 1954.

McReynolds, Edwin C. *Missouri: A History of the Crossroads State*. Norman, University of Oklahoma Press, 1962.

———. *Oklahoma: A History of the Sooner State*. Norman, University of Oklahoma Press, 1954.

Marriott, Alice. *The Ten Grandmothers*. Norman, University of Oklahoma Press, 1945.

Mathews, John Joseph. *The Osages: Children of the Middle Waters*. Norman, University of Oklahoma Press, 1961.

Mayhall, Mildred P. *The Kiowas*. Norman, University of Oklahoma Press, 1962.

Merrington, Marguerite (ed.). *The Custer Story*. New York, Devin-Adair Company, 1950.

Morse, Frank P. *Cavalcade of the Rails*. New York, E. P. Dutton, 1940.

Myers, John M. *The Deaths of the Bravos*. Boston, Little, Brown & Co., 1962.

Nunn, William C. *Texas under the Carpetbaggers*. Austin, University of Texas Press, 1962.

Nye, Wilbur Sturtevant. *Bad Medicine and Good: Tales of the Kiowas*. Norman, University of Oklahoma Press, 1962.

———. *Carbine and Lance: The Story of Old Fort Sill*. Norman, University of Oklahoma Press, 1937.

Olson, James C. *A History of Nebraska*. Lincoln, University of Nebraska Press, 1955.

Pearce, Roy H. *The Savages of America*. Baltimore, Johns Hopkins Press, 1953.

Priest, Loring Benson. *Uncle Sam's Stepchildren*. New Brunswick, Rutgers University Press, 1942.

Richardson, Rupert N. *The Comanche Barrier to South Plains Settlement*. Glendale, Arthur H. Clark Co., 1933.

Rich, Everett (ed.). *The Heritage of Kansas*. Lawrence, University of Kansas Press, 1960.

Riegel, Robert E. *America Moves West*. New York, Henry Holt & Co., 1956.

Rister, Carl Coke. *Border Captives*. Norman, University of Oklahoma Press, 1940.

Sandoz, Mari. *The Buffalo Hunters*. New York, Hastings House, 1954.

Seitz, Don. *The James Gordon Bennetts*. Indianapolis, Bobbs-Merrill Co., 1928.

Seymour, Flora Warren. *Indian Agents of the Old Frontier*. New York, D. Appleton-Century, 1941.

Simpson, Lesley Byrd (ed.). *The San Saba Papers*. San Francisco, John Howell Books, 1959.

Spicer, Edward H. *Cycles of Conquest*. Tucson, University of Arizona Press, 1962.

Stanley, Henry M. *My Early Travels and Adventures in America and Asia*. New York, Charles Scribners' Sons, 1895.

Starr, Louis M. *Bohemian Brigade*. New York, Alfred Knopf, 1954.

Utley, Robert M. *Custer and the Great Controversy*. Los Angeles, Westernlore Books, 1962.

Verrill, Hyatt. *The Real Americans*. New York, G. P. Putnam's, 1954.

Vestal, Stanley (Walter S. Campbell). *Warpath and Council Fires*. New York, Random House, 1948.

Wallace, Ernest, and E. Adamson Hoebel. *The Comanche: Lords of the South Plains*. Norman, University of Oklahoma Press, 1952.

Watson, Elmo Scott. *A History of Newspaper Syndicates*. Chicago, 1936.

Weisberger, Bernard A. *Reporters for the Union*. Boston, Little, Brown & Co., 1953.

Wellman, Paul I. *Death on the Prairie*. New York, Macmillan Co., 1934.

Wheeler, Colonel Homer W. *Buffalo Days*. New York, A. L. Bart Company, 1925.

Wirth, Conrad L. *Soldier and Brave*. New York, Harper & Row, 1963.

Government Documents

Augur, Maj. Gen. C. C. Letter to the Peace Commission, October 12, 1867. Letters Sent, Department of the Platte. Document File 364, Indian Treaties, National Archives, Washington, D. C.

Commissioner of Indian Affairs, Department of the Interior. *Annual Report for the Year 1867*. Washington, Government Printing Office, 1867.

———. *Annual Report for the Year 1868*. Washington, Government Printing Office, 1868.

———. *Special Report, 1867*. Washington, Government Printing Office, 1868.

Department of the Army. *The Army Lineage Book*. Washington, Government Printing Office, 1953.

———. "Troop Returns, 7th Cavalry Regiment, 1867." Office of the Chief of Military History. Washington, D.C.

Department of War. *The Official Army Register for 1867*. Washington, Government Printing Office, 1867.

Elliot, Maj. Joel H. "Official Report, November 2, 1867." Letters Received, Department of the Missouri. Army-Navy Branch, National Archives, Washington, D.C.

Hancock, Maj. Gen. W. S. *Reports of Maj. Gen. W. S. Hancock upon Indian Affairs with Accompanying Exhibits*. Washington, McGill & Witherow, 1867.

Indian Peace Commission. "Accounts Current." John Sanborn, Purchasing Agent, 1867–68. Microfilm File, Legislative Branch, National Archives. Washington, D.C.

———. "Journal of Proceedings." August 7, 1867–January 7, 1868. Microfilm File, Legislative Branch, National Archives. Washington, D.C.

Kappler, Charles. *Laws and Treaties*, 58 Cong., 2 sess., 1904, *Sen. Doc. 319*, Indian Affairs. Washington, Government Printing Office, 1904.

Mooney, James. "Calendar History of the Kiowa Indians," *17th Annual Report, Bureau of American Ethnology*, 1895–96. Washington, Government Printing Office, 1898.

Secretary of the Interior. Letter to the Peace Commission, August 8, 1867. Document File 364, Indian Treaties, National Archives, Washington, D.C.

U. S. Congress. *The Congressional Globe, Volume 38, March to December, 1867*. 40 Cong., 1 sess., 1867. Washington, Government Printing Office, 1867.

U. S. Congress. (H.R.). *Report of the Indian Peace Commission*. 40 Cong., 2 sess., *Exec. Doc. 97*, 1867–68. Washington, Government Printing Office, 1868.

———. *Report of the Quartermaster General, 1867*. 40 Cong., 2 sess., *Exec Doc. 148*, 1867–68. Washington, Government Printing Office, 1868.

———. *Report of the Secretary of War, 1867*. 40 Cong., 1 sess., *Exec. Doc. 1*, 1867. Washington, Government Printing Office, 1867.

――――. *Report of the Secretary of War, 1868,* 40 Cong., 3 sess., *Exec. Doc. 1,* 1868. Washington, Government Printing Office, 1868.

U. S. Congress (Sen.). *Special Report, Secretary of the Interior.* 40 Cong., 1 sess., *Exec. Doc. 13,* 1867. Washington, Government Printing Office, 1867.

――――. *Special Report, Secretary of the Interior.* 40 Cong., 2 sess., *Exec. Doc. 60,* 1868. Washington, Government Printing Office, 1868.

White, A. S. H. Letter to Lt. Gen. W. T. Sherman, Nov. 2, 1867. Letters Received, Records of the Adjutant General, 1867. Microfilm File, Army-Air Corps Branch, National Archives, Washington, D.C.

PERIODICALS

Bryan, Frank. "The Llano Estacado," *Panhandle and Plains Historical Review,* Vol. XIII (1940), 21–37.

Buntin, Martha. "Difficulties Encountered in Issuing Cheyenne and Arapaho Subsistence, 1861–70," *Chronicles of Oklahoma,* Vol. XIV (March, 1936), 37–45.

Byers, O. P. "Railroading in the Wild West," *Kansas Historical Collections,* Vol. XVII (Winter, 1926–27), 339–48.

Campbell, W. S. "The Cheyenne Dog Soldier," *Chronicles of Oklahoma,* Vol. XI (January, 1921), 90–97.

Chapman, Berlin B. "The Claim of Texas to Greer County, Oklahoma," *Southwest Historical Review,* Vol. XVIII (July, 1949), 19–34.

――――. "The Pottawatomie and Absentee Shawnee Reservations," *Chronicles of Oklahoma,* Vol. XXIV (July, 1949).

Connelley, William E. "The Treaty Held at Medicine Lodge," *Kansas Historical Collections,* Vol. XVII (Winter, 1926–27), 26–27.

Downey, Fairfax. "Frontier Army," *Army,* Vol. XIII (February, 1963), 48–52.

Dunham, Harold H. "Governor Charles Bent," *Denver Western-ers Brand Book*, Vol. VII (1951), 222–36.

Dunn, William E. "Spanish Reaction against French Advances toward New Mexico," *Mississippi Valley Historical Review*, Vol. XI (December, 1915), 350–51.

Foreman, Carolyn Thomas. "Colonel Jesse Henry Leavenworth," *Chronicles of Oklahoma*, Vol. XIV (March, 1936), 14–29.

Garfield, Marvin H. "Defense of the Kansas Frontier," *Kansas Historical Quarterly*, Vol. I (February, 1932), 326–44.

Guback, Thomas H. "General Sherman's War on the Press," *Journalism Quarterly*, Vol. XXXVI (Spring, 1959), 171–76.

Haley, J. Evetts. "The Great Comanche War Trail," *Panhandle and Plains Historical Review*, Vol. XXIII (1950), 11–21.

Kansas Historical Society, "Indian Treaties and Councils Affecting Kansas," *Kansas Historical Collections*, Vol. XVI (1923–25), 746–72.

Jacobs, Captain R. T. "Military Reminiscences," *Chronicles of Oklahoma*, Vol. II (March, 1924), 9–36.

Lindquist, General E. E. "Indian Treaty Making," *Chronicles of Oklahoma*, Vol. XXIV (Winter, 1948–49), 416–48.

McClure, C. B. "The Battle of Adobe Walls, 1864," *Panhandle and Plains Historical Review*, Vol. XXI (1948), 18–65.

McNeal, T. A. "The Indians Agree to Abandon Kansas," *Kansas Historical Collections*, Vol. VI (1897–1900), 344–46.

Montgomery, Mrs. Frank C. "Fort Wallace and Its Relationship to the Frontier," *Kansas Historical Collections*, Vol. XVII (1926–28), 189–283.

Neighbours, Kenneth F. "The Assassination of Robert S. Neighbors," *West Texas Historical Association Yearbook*, Vol. XXXIV (October, 1958), 38–49.

Perry, Dan W. "The Honorable Milton W. Reynolds," *Chronicles of Oklahoma*, Vol. XXIV (March, 1936), 46–62.

———. "Oklahoma, A Foreordained Commonwealth," *Chronicles of Oklahoma*, Vol. XXIV (March, 1936), 37–46.

————. "The Kiowas' Defiance," *Chronicles of Oklahoma,* Vol. XXIV (March, 1936), 30–36.

Richardson, Rupert N. "The Comanche Reservation in Texas," *West Texas Historical Association Yearbook,* Vol. V (June, 1929), 46–47.

Swett, Morris. "Sergeant I-See-O: Kiowa Scout," *Chronicles of Oklahoma,* Vol. XIII (September, 1935), 339–54.

Taylor, A. A. "The Medicine Lodge Peace Council," *Chronicles of Oklahoma,* Vol. II (June, 1924), 98–118.

Thoburn, J. B. "Horace P. Jones, Scout and Interpreter," *Chronicles of Oklahoma,* Vol. II (December, 1924), 380–91.

Watson, Elmo Scott. "A Checklist of Indian War Correspondents," *Journalism Quarterly,* Vol. XVII (December, 1940), 310–12.

————. "The Indian Wars and the Press," *Journalism Quarterly,* Vol. XVII (December, 1940), 301–10.

ENCYCLOPEDIA

"The Indian Wars," *The American Annual Cyclopedia & Register of Important Events, 1867, 1868,* Vol. VII : 399–400; Vol. VIII : 383–84. New York, D. Appleton & Company, 1867–68.

Dictionary of American Biography, Vol. I : 427–28; Vol. VIII : 280–81; Vol. XVIII : 378–79. New York, Scribners' Sons.

NEWSPAPERS

Atchison Daily Champion, August–October, 1867.

Chicago Times, July–November, 1867.

Chicago Tribune, August–November, 1867; January, 1868.

Cincinnati Commercial, June–November, 1867; January, 1868.

Cincinnati Semi-Weekly Gazette, July–November, 1867.

Missouri Democrat (St. Louis), October–December, 1867; January, 1868.

Missouri Republican (St. Louis), October–November, 1867.

New York Herald, July–December, 1867; January, 1868.

New York Tribune, October–November, 1867.

New York World, July–December, 1867; January, 1868.

CONTEMPORARY PERIODICALS

The Army-Navy Journal, August–December, 1867.
Frank Leslie's Illustrated Newspaper, September–December, 1867.
Harper's Weekly, July–December, 1867; January, 1868.

INDEX

Adams, Mrs. Margaret: 107–108, 111,
149, 174, 210 f.
Annuities and treaty gifts: 124 f., 133,
135, 136–37, 142, 143–44, 146,
179–80, 188, 198–99
Antelope Hills, Oklahoma: 144
Apache Indians: 28, 75–76, 80, 82, 108,
141, 151; conference with Peace
Commission, 144–45; *see also names
of specific tribes*
Apache treaty: *see under* Comanche-
Kiowa Treaty of Medicine Lodge
Arapaho Indians: 26, 50, 57, 65, 72 f.,
75 f., 78, 80 f., 94, 102, 107, 110 f.,
143, 146, 151, 159, 163, 164–65,
167, 180, 183, 198, 220; hunting
grounds of, 6, 8, 26, 38, 181–82,
192; trouble with whites, 9 f., 27;
dance attended by correspondents,
91–92, 93, 216, 219; language of,
108; conference with Peace Commission, 144 f.; visit to Peace Commission camp, 147; farewell dance
of, 189–90; *see also* Cheyenne-
Arapaho Grand Council *and* Cheyenne-Arapaho Treaty of Medicine
Lodge
Arapaho treaty: *see* Cheyenne-Arapaho
Treaty of Medicine Lodge
Arkansas: 4, 120
Arkansas River: 6, 8, 10, 25 ff., 37,
44, 48, 60, 67, 69, 75, 120, 135, 171,
173 f., 176, 180 ff., 191 f., 200 f.,
208 f.; Pawnee Fork of, 12, 87, 95,
170, 178; Big Bend of, 41, 43, 55,
118, 128, 134, 185; description of,
54
Augur, Major General Christopher
Colon: 19, 69, 81, 100, 138–39, 140,
201, 207

Bad Back (Apache chief): 151
Beecher's Island, Battle of: 77
Bennett, James Gordon: 15, 32, 34, 97
Bent, Governor Charles, of New Mexico
Territory: 209
Bent, Charlie: 77, 106 f., 111, 149, 167,
209 f.
Bent, George: 77, 106 f., 111, 149, 167,
176, 178, 209 f.
Bent, Julia: 106, 111–12, 149, 209 f.
Bent, William: 76 f., 209–10
Bent's Fort, Colorado: 210
Black Kettle (Cheyenne chief): 10 f.,
70–71, 72 f., 81 f., 85, 98, 110, 137 ff.,
140 f., 147, 159, 168, 205–206; at
Comanche-Kiowa Grand Councils,
111 f., 177
Box, James: Comanche-Kiowa raid on
ranch of, 97–98
Bozeman Trail: 8, 26
Brave Man (Apache chief): 151

The text for *The Treaty of Medicine Lodge* has been set on the Linotype in 11½-point Caslon Old Face, an exact and faithful reproduction of the original letter designed by William Caslon, one of the great English type designers of the eighteenth century. The paper on which the book is printed bears the watermark of the University of Oklahoma Press and has an effective life of at least three hundred years.